that as many as 40,000 are created every year, most of which rely on volunteers to further their cause. Leading this surge in American volunteerism is our youth, undeniably this country's greatest resource. Volunteerism among college students has increased significantly over the past few years, perhaps heralding America's first glimpse of a new civic-minded generation that some suggest is doing more to serve others than any generation has in a long time. The environmental crisis has also been credited as the tipping point, with small tasks leaving everyday citizens with a gratifying sense of empowerment. The notion of community has experienced a much-needed resurgence, and community leaders are taking their own initiative and seeking to instill the values of leadership and responsibility. The benefits to the community and society as a whole are profound. Not surprisingly, our cities with higher volunteer rates are also the cities that have lower crime, higher employment, better education, and an overall better quality of life.

The individuals in this book are living examples of some of our most impassioned and motivating change agents. We can all learn from their life's example, from their selflessness, and their commitment to helping others. As you read this book, I hope you will make an effort to better understand the issues, to go to their websites, read about their causes, and learn from their examples. In an effort to further support and encourage acts of volunteerism, I have created the Awearness Fund, a not-for-profit entity, to be funded by various initiatives, including this book. The funds from this will be dedicated to promote volunteerism culturally, as well as in regard to some of the organizations discussed in the book.

As you read the inspiring stories that follow and think about what you can do, consider what you have to offer, what special skills you possess, what unique resources are at your disposal. Also, what resources do you have that are not so unique? It is important to remember that it is most often ordinary resources that have initiated and/or inspired some of the most extraordinary change.

So whatever you do—should you choose to join a movement or start your own, help your neighbor two doors away or your world neighbor two continents away—you won't likely regret it. In the end, although it should not be what inspires the journey, and even if you never reach your intended destination, the person who will most likely benefit the most is yourself.

In the words of an inspired New York designer, a businessman, an activist of twenty-five years, and a self-proclaimed social entrepreneur: Life is not a dress rehearsal and you can change your outfit, you can outfit change, or both.

THE FOUNDATION FOR AIDS RESEARCH

My first AIDS initiative was an ad I did on behalf of amfAR, the Foundation for AIDS Research, in 1985. There was no known cure for AIDS back then, nor today, but we did know how to contain it. I thought, "If people just knew this then we could stop the spread of AIDS," and created an ad I believed would help do so. Clearly, it wasn't that simple. Soon after I joined amfAR's board of directors, a post I expected to be short-lived. Since then I have continued to spread awareness about AIDS and today, some 20 years later, I have agreed to serve as the chairman of amfAR's board of directors... again, a post I expect to be very short-lived.

POLITICAL ACTIVISM
TAKE A STAND OR STEP ASIDE

When we first started our company we set out to establish a different kind of relationship with our clients, seeking a deeper bond than your typical fashion company. We wanted to address what we believed was important to a person on the inside, as well as on the outside. Truthfully, we have always believed that being aware is more important than what you wear. One topic we have often addressed in our advertising is the role guns (usually automatic weapons) play in a civilized society. In return we have gotten many responses, some of praise from gun control advocates, others of outrage from gun enthusiasts. We have received countless letters and e-mails (often sprinkled with expletives) from the latter telling us to "mind our own business," to stick to what we know—fashion—and to respect their Second Amendment right to bear arms. Our response has been consistent and genuine, stating something to the effect of "the Second Amendment may protect your right to bear arms, but the First Amendment protects our right to tell you how we feel about it." Then we go on to praise this great country we live in. ➜ **After all, if we don't stand up for our rights, what's likely to be left? —Kenneth Cole**

ROBERT REDFORD

On Keeping Speech Free

Robert Redford

*Actor and director Robert Redford has been a passionate environmentalist and political activist since the early 1970s. As founder of the **Sundance Institute**, he supports thought-provoking, independent voices in film and theater. He has served for more than thirty years as a trustee of the **Natural Resources Defense Council**, and is a board member of the **Smithsonian Institution**, **Environmental Policy Center**, the **Navajo Education Scholarship Foundation**, and **Yosemite Institute**, among others.*

➡ *sundance.org; nrdc.org*

The first time I became aware of the power of speaking up was at the end of World War II. I was in the third grade, and suddenly there was a wave of anti-Semitism. I didn't know what was going on, but felt the backlash against Jews. A friend of mine, Lois Levenson, who had been well liked, was now being ostracized. One day she stood up and announced, "My name is Lois Levenson." And I thought, "Well, this is weird—we all know who Lois is." She continued, "I am a Jew." A shudder went through the entire classroom. She then began to make a speech about why she was proud of being Jewish. I was so taken I proceeded to make sure I walked with her, talked with her, and remained her friend. That was the beginning of what became a fairly radical point of view about freedom of speech and equal rights.

When I initially decided to speak out based on my politics, principally on Native American rights and the environment, I was warned, "You better watch out, because you're going to get a counterforce against you that will be overwhelming and could get real serious."

About five years later, in 1974, I helped build a campaign against five energy companies in California, Utah, and Arizona that had formed a consortium to build eleven coal-fired power plants throughout the West. They had been promising an economic boom to the locals in the impoverished communities. The people believed it and they needed to believe it, but it was not the truth. Instead, it would have absolutely decimated the air, the land, and the water. So, I put together an underground movement to fight the energy companies, because they weren't holding public hearings. As a last resort, I went to the news program *60 Minutes*, suggesting they look into it. The producer, Don Hewitt, said he would do it if I would be a spokesperson. I agreed, as long as they gave equal time to the people on the other side so we could have an honest debate. If there was going to be a battle, I wanted it to be fair. I took *60 Minutes* into the area, walking and boating and climbing through the ruins to show what was at stake. The show was a huge success. There were so many letters against the plant that they pulled the plug on it. However, I was burned in effigy in several counties, counties that

Change is going to come from the ground up, not from the top down.

FILMS

Since the 1970s, producer, director, and actor Robert Redford has made films that challenge the social and political status quo:

The Candidate (1972)
An idealist loses his moral compass on the Senate campaign trail.

All the President's Men (1976)
How reporters Bob Woodward and Carl Bernstein broke the Watergate story and helped bring down a president.

Brubaker (1980)
A prison warden fights against a deeply corrupt prison system.

The Milagro Beanfield War (1988) Activists and local Hispanic farmers fight a real estate developer in New Mexico.

A Civil Action (1998)
A lawyer represents the families of Massachusetts children who died of leukemia after being exposed to toxic chemicals.

Lions for Lambs (2007)
A professor encourages a passive student toward activism.

The Unforeseen (2007)
A documentary examining the opposition of local residents to development in Austin, Texas.

ROBERT REDFORD'S ADVICE ON SPEAKING OUT

➡ Make certain you know what you're talking about by carefully researching the matter as deeply as you can.

➡ Understand both sides of the issue.

➡ Work with a local group rather than going in as the Lone Ranger without any connection or support.

➡ If you're going to get up and speak, keep it simple and give examples to create pictures people can relate to. Explain why you support your side, what it means to you, and why you're willing to commit your civic time to it.

➡ Whenever possible, use a sense of humor and be self-effacing. Those are important things.

had been sold a bill of goods about economic benefits. That was the point when I realized exactly the consequences when you step out on a very controversial issue. I was getting threats against my family and myself. But I'd been in countries where people were thwarted from speaking freely, and the value of freedom of speech was a cherished freedom I was committed to.

Around the same time, the press was probably enjoying the highest position that it had ever had. If the reporters hadn't been really aggressive during Watergate and the Nixon administration had gotten away with its illegal activities, who knows what we would have lost over the course of time. I think it spared us from the loss of our First Amendment rights. So, in 1976 I made *All the President's Men*—not just because it was a great story from an entertainment perspective but also because it was a story that most people didn't know. You just looked at that moment in history and thought, "God, we came so close."

Much to my dismay, we've been struggling for our First Amendment rights again. A lot of press members don't want to admit that they haven't been as uniform as they had been in the past in challenging and questioning the Bush administration. It's also unhealthy that so much of the press is now controlled in a very few corporate hands. And on top of that, they're struggling to find out if they're going to survive as an industry. I don't think we're going to know anything until the dust settles. We can't go back to where we were, but in the new climate, I think hope's going to rest on the imprimatur of quality and trust that might be attached to a news-gathering source like National Public Radio.

Change is going to come from the ground up, not from the top down. We'll have a better movement from the grass roots—where the public is, where the voices of America are. Of course, as an artist, I first and foremost believe in using art to exercise freedom of expression. It should be supported more and treated as a driving force for peace and truth. Just start putting out what you can when you can with whatever new venue comes your way, and give audiences a chance to decide for themselves how they feel about it.

A GREAT AMERICAN TRADITION:
PROTEST MARCHES ON WASHINGTON

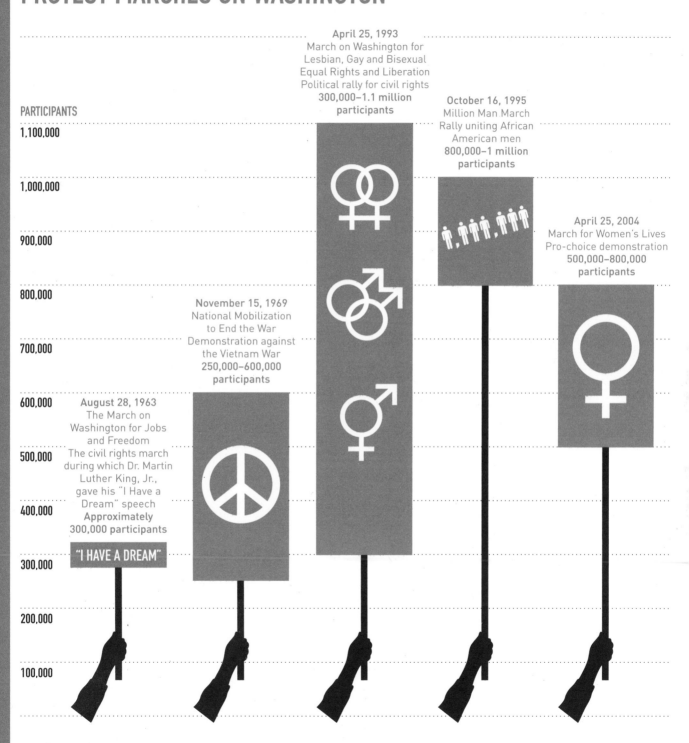

April 25, 1993
March on Washington for
Lesbian, Gay and Bisexual
Equal Rights and Liberation
Political rally for civil rights
300,000–1.1 million
participants

October 16, 1995
Million Man March
Rally uniting African
American men
800,000–1 million
participants

PARTICIPANTS

1,100,000

1,000,000

900,000

April 25, 2004
March for Women's Lives
Pro-choice demonstration
500,000–800,000
participants

800,000

November 15, 1969
National Mobilization
to End the War
Demonstration against
the Vietnam War
250,000–600,000
participants

700,000

600,000

August 28, 1963
The March on
Washington for Jobs
and Freedom
The civil rights march
during which Dr. Martin
Luther King, Jr.,
gave his "I Have a
Dream" speech
**Approximately
300,000 participants**

500,000

400,000

"I HAVE A DREAM"

300,000

200,000

100,000

MELISSA ETHERIDGE

On Making Politics Personal

Melissa Etheridge

Known for being politically outspoken, Melissa Etheridge writes songs that reflect her stance on issues from gay rights to the environment. Accepting an Academy Award® for her global warming anthem "I Need to Wake Up" from An Inconvenient Truth, *Etheridge reminded the audience, "We can become the greatest generation, the generation that changed, the generation that woke up and did something." She is on the board of **Love Our Children USA**, and supports **The Dream Foundation**, **Live Earth**, and **The Human Rights Campaign**, among others.*

➡ *loveourchildrenusa.org; dreamfoundation.org; liveearth.org; hrc.org*

All I really ever wanted to be was a little ol' rock star. That was my total dream. Nevertheless, my involvement with politics started in the '80s, when I first got to Southern California and became part of the thriving gay and lesbian community. I knew Ronald Reagan had been elected president, but I didn't know why. I was in my early twenties and had a job in a Long Beach bar called the Que Sera, where I would play during my breaks. One time, this woman from the local gay and lesbian chapter came up to me and asked, "Are you registered to vote?" And I said, "No, I don't know how to do that." She signed me up and explained it all. It was the first time I understood there might be somebody interested in my rights.

At the time, those of us in the gay community were just trying not to get fired from our jobs and to get police protection—gay marriage wasn't even a thought. We saw we had to get involved politically or we would die. There's a clip of President George Bush, Sr., giving a speech, and somebody stands up all of a sudden and says, "You have to talk about AIDS." We got leaders that way, and through that I started to understand local politics. Then I got down to the lesbians who are involved in gay rights, and, of course, they're hugely involved in women's rights.

The political opportunities have presented themselves to me. I don't say, "What mountain can I climb now?" My political side has always been there out of necessity. I fight for gay rights because I'm gay; I fight for women's rights because I'm a woman. I remember after I released my first couple of albums, NARAL, the pro-choice gals, contacted me and asked if I would do some benefit concerts for them. So I got to know what they're fighting for. It was weird—I was like, "Didn't we win *Roe v. Wade*?" And I learned that no, we have to go back every time there's opposition.

But once you open up to the idea that politics is actually about people, then it becomes really fun and exciting. One of the most surprising things I've learned is how much I enjoy politics and trying to enlighten people.

Also, what I went through with cancer really empowered me. I had to make a change in my life not to get cancer again. When my body was so knocked out on the chemotherapy, I started thinking about being connected to the earth and how we're poisoning the planet. And I see that in the world around me, not a lot of people want to change. That's when Al Gore called me. "I Need to Wake Up" means a lot to me, because it's not just about the climate crisis. That song is about everyone waking up to our oneness on earth, and if you can call that politics, then that's what politics is.

I used to think, "Nobody wants to hear from me—I'm not a professional politician." We've totally forgotten that it takes people getting inspired to make change. Change comes with your thinking, "I want peace in my day. I need more love in my day, and I want to give more love. I want to be happier." It's like we're afraid to ask for that. And it's up to us every day to decide which we're going to choose: love or fear. It's how I act with the stranger on the street, how I treat my children. It's about service—normal, everyday people serving their city, state, country, their government. Whatever you're looking at—equal rights, environmental protection, new systems of capitalism—you can look at all of them and ask, "Is this coming from love or fear?" If we were fearless, there would be no war.

SINGING FOR CHANGE

➡ A breast cancer survivor, Melissa Etheridge wrote the song "I Run for Life" to help raise awareness and funds for the Susan G. Komen Breast Cancer Foundation and Dr. Susan Love Research Foundation. Royalties and proceeds from download sales of the song during Breast Cancer Awareness Month were donated to breast cancer charities.

➡ Proceeds from the sale of the 2007 *Live Earth* CD/DVD package, which includes Melissa Etheridge's performance of her song "I Need to Wake Up," benefits the Alliance for Climate Protection.

NORMAN LEAR

On Civic Activism

Norman Lear

*Television and film producer Norman Lear is a longtime political activist and the founder of several nonprofit organizations, including **People for the American Way**. In 2000 he started the **Declaration of Independence Road Trip**, a cross-country tour to promote civic activism. **Declare Yourself**, a spin-off of the Road Trip, reached out to young and first-time voters.*

➜ *pfaw.org; declareyourself.com; remixamerica.org*

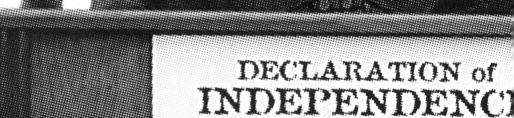

DECLARATION of INDEPENDENC

Road Trip

When I first saw the Declaration of Independence, I was drawn in. There are only twenty-five original copies that exist in the world, and looking at one of the documents sent around the thirteen colonies by horseback on the night of July 4, 1776, I thought, "This is our nation's birth certificate—it belongs to all of us." After my wife, Lyn, and I purchased that copy, we launched the Declaration of Independence Road Trip—right before the 2004 presidential election, a time when the percentage of people voting was low; it's still too low. We moved the document around the country so people could spend a moment with it, as a reminder of the freedoms we all cherish, and to inspire Americans, especially young people, to participate in civic activism. As part of the Road Trip, we created the Declare Yourself campaign to encourage young Americans to exercise their right to vote.

It pays to know a little bit about history. Know what other people have done in the past and follow the patterns of those who you admire. We've all had relatives, uncles and aunts who have been citizens in ways that we can seek to emulate. Look back at your parents' or grandparents' lifetime and you'll see these massive changes. I've lived through a depression, civil rights legislation, and the women's movement in postwar America. And though the changes seem to happen so glacially, the results make a retreat impossible.

Between the ages of ten and thirteen, I lived with my grandfather, who wrote letters to the president. I was the kid who ran down three flights of stairs to pick the mail up, and every once in a while there would be a little envelope that said "White House." I couldn't get over it. Later, in high school, my classmates and I would send a ten-word Western Union telegram that would blanket Congress. It was an experiment in democracy. We didn't always get a letter from the president, but it's amazing how responsive some parts of the government would be. During the

Know what other people have done in the past and follow the patterns of those who you admire.

DECLARE YOURSELF

Declare Yourself was launched in 2003 as a culmination of the Declaration of Independence Road Trip and registered more than 1.2 million people in the 2004 and 2006 elections, and more than 300,000 people in the 2008 primary season.

➡ Nationally 18–25-year-olds make up 14% of the population of eligible voters in the United States.

➡ 4 million 18-year-olds will be eligible to vote in 2008.

➡ Generation Y voters will be one third of the electorate by 2015.

➡ People for the American Way Foundation is a non-profit organization that promotes civil rights and constitutional liberties.

➡ RemixAmerica.org is a multipartisan, nonprofit website that offers free historical texts, video, and music in digital form, inviting users to create their own mash-up videos using clips from the site's "American Playlist" as well as their own elements.

summer before the 1940 presidential election, my friend Sidney and I were either going to get jobs or do something more entrepreneurial. We wound up loading our Model T with FDR and Wendell Willkie pennants and pins, selling them door-to-door throughout New England. Of course, communication being what it is today as opposed to what it was then, the volume of passion and effort expressed by youth is technologically enhanced.

The collective voice is the voice of every person. I believe this because of an ancient piece of philosophy: A man should have a garment with two pockets. In the first pocket should be a piece of paper on which is written "I am but dust and ashes"—the proverbial grain of sand on the beach of life. And in the second pocket should be a piece of paper on which is written "For me the world was created." If you look at the earth, or our universe, as being part of maybe a million or more universes, and you appreciate the vastness of the enterprise, we all matter to the same extent.

If you can't reach the place where you think your single vote matters for the reasons I've offered, then think about it this way. You will always feel better for having done something, even if you question how much it may matter. What can you do? I think one can waste a lot of time asking that question when there are solicitations every day on your computer, in the mail, in the newspaper, and from friend to friend to help in this cause and that cause. Open up conversations about situations in your local community, in the larger community, and in the nation that have an impact on you at this moment and will have an impact on you tomorrow. Edit your own digital videos at RemixAmerica.org to share your hopes, dreams, and frustrations about our country.

I am a person in a culture and a country that blessedly tell me I matter. They treat me sometimes like I don't, but the laws are there to assure me that I do. Therefore, I believe that I do. I will never stop talking about what matters to me, and I will never stop acting on what I think I can do. And I will never stop looking for older heroes, following their patterns and understanding that I matter.

You will always feel better for having done something, even if you question how much it may matter.

CRISTI HEGRANES

On Empowerment Through Journalism

Cristi Hegranes

*Cristi Hegranes is an award-winning journalist and the founder of the **Press Institute for Women in the Developing World**. The Institute is an international nonprofit organization that creates change by training women in Nepal, Mexico, and Rwanda to produce fair journalism on issues vital to them. These stories, disseminated locally and internationally, provide necessary income and attention for the women and their communities.*

➡ *piwdw.org*

The concept for the Press Institute was born out of my passion for and frustration with the field of journalism. In 2005 I had just gotten back to the United States after working as a foreign correspondent abroad. I had landed a great job as a feature writer in San Francisco, but it wasn't long before I became disillusioned by the questionable ethics that pervade our media markets. For several months I had been fixated on an experience I'd had the year before, while I was reporting a story about the civil war in Nepal.

Her name was Pratima. She was the matriarch of a small village. I was there trying to paint a picture of the realities of the war. I speak Nepali; I had been in the country for some time. In many ways I was the ideal foreign correspondent. Yet my stories lacked something. Finally, I realized that I might not be the person best suited to tell these stories. One morning I handed Pratima a pen and a notebook. I told her to write about what it was to watch your sons join a rebel army and your country in a constant state of tumult. She had only rudimentary literacy skills and it took her several days to return the notebook to me. As I read her words I realized what Pratima had produced was a piece of journalism. Her story had what my work and the work of other foreign correspondents lacked: a first-hand social, historical, cultural, and political context. Many months later, I decided to create an organization that would allow me to empower women like her all over the world to tell the true stories of their communities. The most amazing experience of my life has been to watch these women choose the profession of journalism to elevate themselves.

FACT

The Press Institute for Women in the Developing World diverts 90% of all funds raised to the global training sites. Local applicants to the Institute's six-month training programs in Nepal, Rwanda, and Mexico are only required to have very basic literacy skills. Eventually the female reporters earn an hourly salary and are paid for each article, including royalties if the articles are reprinted elsewhere.

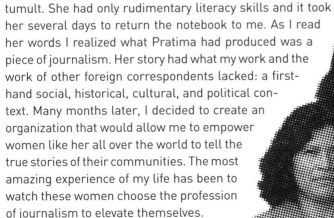

ROSARIO DAWSON

On Mobilizing the Latino Community

Rosario Dawson

*In 2004 actress Rosario Dawson co-founded **Voto Latino**, which works to empower young Latinos to vote and promote positive change in the United States. She has participated in "The Vagina Monologues," and supports the **ONE Campaign, Oxfam**, and **Amnesty International**.*

➜ *votolatino.org; one.org; oxfam.org; amnesty.org*

Ever since I participated in a save-the-trees march when I was ten, I've worked with many groups to support numerous causes, from women's issues and workers' rights, to HIV/AIDS awareness and poverty. But I spend most of my time working with Voto Latino, a nonpartisan organization I co-founded a few years ago, because it covers all the issues.

Voto Latino basically provides people with the resources to register to vote; we ran the first national text-messaging voter-registration project back in 2006, for example. We have no agenda other than representing Latinos in an effort to collapse walls and create a stronger, more unified voice for the community. As their numbers grow, Latinos may become a swing vote in several states: 50,000 Latinos turn eighteen every month, with eighty-seven percent of them eligible to vote. But despite many of them wanting to be proactive, they're not all getting the information they need to fully understand their opportunities. Many don't believe our government is supposed to work for us. They're not raised to think, "One day I could be president." But that's the thing that's been most incredible about this project—the people who come in and say, "Thank you for looking at me this way and giving me the encouragement to do it myself."

A lot of it comes down to giving people that power, even if it's only starting a dialogue and letting them carry the conversation. Now when I see thousands of Latinos mobilizing with no apparent leader, communicating over the Internet and text-messaging about issues they care about, I'm truly inspired. The truth is, Voto Latino operates with very little money and very few resources, and with only one full-time staffer. It continues today as an incredible movement of people, mostly volunteers, who are inspired by the idea of reaching out to a community, or better yet, building a new community.

You don't have to start your own organization. Simple things can make a tremendous difference. You can make a couple of phone calls or send a couple of e-mails. When

FACT

➜ The Census Bureau estimates that Latinos will comprise nearly 25% of the U.S. population by 2050.

➜ Latinos are the nation's largest minority group, making up 13% of the U.S. population. But they currently account for only 9% of the nation's eligible electorate.

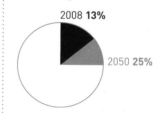

2008 **13%**

2050 **25%**

Black History and Hispanic Awareness months happen, pick up books about them. Let them touch you.
Be creative. You can give rides to the election
booths so everybody has an opportunity to
vote. You can offer translation services,
like my grandmother does for her
church. Maybe you can organize
the people in your building.
Ask questions: Where did your
parents come from? What
lifestyle do you want? Do you
feel strongly about health
care, foreign policy, or education? Is the school you attend
giving the best it can?

It doesn't have to be your life all
the time. It just has to be a part
of your life. Change is going to be
gradual, but if you don't do anything at all, then know for sure
that that's making a statement.

**As their numbers grow, Latinos may
become a swing vote in several states.**

MAYOR CORY A. BOOKER

On Moving Mountains

Cory A. Booker

*The Honorable Cory A. Booker is the mayor of Newark, New Jersey. Elected in May 2006 with a clear mandate for change, Mayor Booker has embarked on ambitious governmental reform with a focus on public safety, economic empowerment, and children and families. He founded **Newark Now** in 2002 to provide residents with the skills and support to transform their neighborhoods.*

➡ *newarknow.org*

In May 1998 I, then the youngest person ever elected to municipal office in Newark, was elected to the Newark Municipal Council as a reformer. I had enormous idealistic enthusiasm and enormous ideas—but found myself, time and again, unable to pull together the necessary votes to support my ideas. In fact, I was regularly outvoted eight to one. I felt incapable of delivering anything for my supporters and began to doubt my reasons for entering public service.

One day, about one year after I had been elected to the Council, I received a call from a tenant leader at a subsidized housing complex in the Central Ward, which I represented. The security company for the complex was threatening to quit after a violent incident with some alleged drug dealers. The tenant leader was desperately seeking my help as she sought to maintain safety for the residents. I tried to explain to her that I was a legislator—that I didn't run city departments and couldn't tell the police what to do. By the end of the conversation, we were both deeply frustrated at our seeming inability to come up with a solution. That evening, as I returned to the public housing complex in which I lived, I was stopped by our tenant president. I told her the whole story and she told me she knew exactly what I should do. She looked at me and said, "You should do something." That was it, just "Do something."

I left her feeling even more frustrated. As was typical, the elevators did not work, so I walked up the sixteen flights of stairs to my apartment. When I got there, I opened my Bible looking for a little inspiration. I found one of my favorite and often quoted passages in Matthew, which says you can move mountains with faith the size of a mustard seed. It was the following passage, however, that really resonated with me: It says that sometimes you just have to fast and pray.

That led me to immediately call one of my aides—I asked him to purchase a tent. We took that tent and set it up in the housing complex where the violence had taken place. I told the alleged drug dealers that I was not there to fight them but would not leave or eat any food until the problems were resolved. I know they thought I was insane.

The first night was long. Word of what I was doing began to spread. The next morning, I was greeted by twelve correctional officers from a nearby facility who took positions around my tent and announced, "We are not going to let you stay out here alone." The media also came to see what I was doing. I had them speak to local residents who were good people and told them, "This is the United States of America, the greatest country on the globe. We should not have American citizens living in terror within their own neighborhoods." People began arriving from all over Newark to stand with me and collectively demand change. There were ministers and college students who fasted with me, hospitals conducted health screenings for children and the elderly, and businesses set up job fairs. The crowds grew by the day. At the end of the two weeks, there were hundreds of people from so many walks of life, from so many different faiths. There were imams, rabbis, priests, and ministers. They were black, white, and Latino. We all held hands in a circle, praying for peace, strength, and our community. They were speaking English, Spanish, Hebrew, and Arabic, yet they were all speaking with one powerful voice. I remembered the old African saying "When spider webs unite, they can tie up a lion," and Golda Meir's saying that Jews together are strong but Jews with other people are invincible. Both speak to the very idea of America: e pluribus unum—out of many comes one.

After two weeks, the drug dealers left and the tent came down, but the momentum in the area continued. The experience was transformative. It taught me that each of us has infinite power for progressive change, but if you want a different tomorrow, you must be willing to do things differently. What was extraordinary about the civil rights movement was that its leaders imagined new ways to accomplish their goals— Freedom Riders engaged in creative forms of activism. Those were solutions of young people finding innovative approaches to a problem.

Social or political change does not simply occur by winning an election. But when people unify under a collective spirit with righteous aims, there is not a single unsolvable or intractable problem. It is all a test of the creative capacity of our community and of our persistence, determination, and willingness to sacrifice.

MENTORING NEWARK

In an effort to curb youth crime in Newark, Mayor Booker challenged city residents to become mentors. In 2008 both he and General Colin L. Powell appeared in public service announcements launching National Mentoring Month. Mayor Booker began mentoring youth as an undergraduate student.

The Mentoring Month ads were created in partnership with the Newark Community Foundation, an umbrella organization formed in 2007 to efficiently direct philanthropic support towards worthy causes. The organization, one of the several philanthropic initiatives created since Mayor Booker took office, has devoted $21 million to Newark nonprofits, arts programs, and scholarships.

AL FRANKEN

On Supporting Our Troops

Al Franken

*Author, comedian, and political commentator Al Franken was the host of **Air America Radio**'s flagship program for three years and has volunteered for seven **USO** tours to date, four in Iraq. He announced his candidacy for U.S. senator in February of 2007.*

➡ *uso.org*

n 1999 I got a call from someone in Secretary of Defense Cohen's office, asking if I wanted to entertain troops in Bosnia and Kosovo with the USO. It seemed like a great opportunity to have an adventure, so I immediately agreed and asked if my family could come too. Up until then, I had had almost zero contact with the military. So, in a sense, by joining the USO I was finally serving.

The tours are sobering, inspiring, wrenching, and incredible fun. And participating in them is the most apolitical thing I do. I don't do anything political in my comedy on

FACT

After reading a Gallup poll that found 21% percent of Americans get most of their news from talk radio, Al Franken got involved with Air America Radio, a progressive radio network. The station, launched in 2004, broadcast *The Al Franken Show* for almost three years.

the tour. Instead, it's really about volunteering to show appreciation to our troops. There's nothing quite as bonding as being on one of these tours. I've gone with a lot of right-wing rednecks (country musicians and stars), but now we love each other because of the shared experience.

Our troops love the shows. It's a piece of home: a country artist, a comedy act, the cheerleaders. I am incredibly impressed by the dedication and professionalism of the people in the military, the sacrifice that they make by being away from their families for so long. Over and over they say, "You don't know how much this means to us, having a USO tour." At first I thought, "That's nice of them to say." Then it became very clear they really meant it. We were at the Baghdad International Airport, the same airport Bush brought the plastic turkey to. There was a guy who was the manager of a girl group from Washington D.C., and this soldier goes up to him and says, "Sir, it's an honor to meet you." And the guy says, "I'm just the manager." Then the soldier says, "I met President Bush here a few weeks ago. He's the commander-in-chief. He has to be here. You, sir, are here because you care."

I'll never forget one performance in Kabul, which at that point was in awful shape (and still is). We were the first USO tour that had ever come through this camp. At the end, the army band comes along—it's about an eight- or ten-piece band—and does a song called "American Soldier" by Toby Keith. All the troops know the song. Seeing them sing along with enormous pride, knowing every word, their arms around each oher, sometimes with tears running down their cheeks—that's an image I'll always remember. It brings tears to my eyes.

I've gone with a lot of right-wing rednecks...but now we love each other because of the shared experience.

Most people think the USO is part of the military or that it's paid for by Congress, but it isn't. It's privately funded. Civilian groups founded it during World War II as a morale booster for the troops. Money is always an issue. That's why volunteerism is so important and why the organization relies on its 25,000 volunteers so much. Not everyone can join the celebrity entertainment tours, but people can help the USO in many ways. I donate to the USO every year, and a lot of airports have USO welcoming centers. You can go down and welcome troops home and give them some home-cooked food or distribute care packages. It's a great way for people who want to show their support of the troops, but not necessarily of the war.

USO

The USO relies on donations to support programs and services for 1.4 million active-duty service members and 1.2 million National Guardsman and Reserves. In 2006 USO volunteers spent 488,798 hours putting together care packages, welcoming troops home, and helping soldiers at the 130 USO centers around the world.

PERIEL ASCHENBRAND

On Fashioning a Statement

Periel Aschenbrand

*Outspoken feminist, activist, and author Periel Aschenbrand wears her politics on her chest. As the founder of **Body as Billboard**, she merges fashion with social commentary to raise awareness of issues ranging from domestic violence to gay rights and AIDS.*

➡ *bodyasbillboard.com*

The truth is I love fashion, and I'm always asked to reconcile my feminism with that. But I don't think the two are mutually exclusive. In fact, I think that fashion is an incredibly powerful means of expressing your political views. As women, our bodies are objectified. If we use our bodies to flip the power dynamic by placing our political views across our tits, we can be damn sure people will pay attention.

The first T-shirt I made was for me. It boasted, "The Only Bush I Trust Is My Own," the title of a book I was working on, and people went totally wild for it. People kept asking me to make them shirts. It was pretty amazing to see people galvanized by this idea. Of course, it's not enough just to wear them, you have to walk the walk, you know? But wearing them is a great first step.

I'm a writer, so all my work is really rooted in words. I was teaching philosophy and cultural criticism to high school students in a summer arts program, and I was appalled by the sheer idiocy of the shirts the kids were wearing—"Princess," "Mrs. Timberlake," and so on—so I taught them how to silk-screen and we made political T-shirts instead.

The main way I give back is by using my talent to do something helpful for causes that I believe in—that usually means coming up with a cutting-edge idea. It's important to be true to yourself—everyone has a talent. If you are a webmaster or a graphic designer, you can use those skills and offer your services to help. I have a strong sense of what will make people stop in their tracks and a knack for saying the thing everyone is thinking and wants to say but won't. While I don't believe in shock value for gratuitous purposes, I do believe it can be an effective means to an end.

HOW TO... SOME TIPS ON POLITICAL ACTIVISM

TIME

Register to vote and register others to vote. Work with an organization like Declare Yourself (www.declareyourself.com) or Voto Latino (www.votolatino.org) to see how you can most effectively help sign up new voters.

Write an op-ed piece or letter to the editor for your local or national paper. Publishing well-articulated political opinions in a public forum allows you to influence people on a large scale using a fairly simple method.

Speak fearlessly. The most effective way to fight censorship and violations of the First Amendment is to exercise your right to speak freely. Free speech is at the core of all human rights—without a voice, no human rights abuses can be questioned, analyzed, criticized, publicized, or rectified.

Start a petition. Petitioning the government can be a quick and effective method of enlisting a community to support your cause. Check with the government agency for their petition guidelines or use websites such as thepetitionsite.com or gopetition.com.

Join an Internet freedom organization. For now, because the Web is a global entity, there are few restrictions. If we aren't vigilant, we could lose our current liberties online.

ITEMS

Purchase blank T-shirts and emblazon them with your own slogans. Using fabric-friendly paints, more sophisticated screen-printing processes, or even just a permanent marker, you can express yourself without sending letters, making phone calls, or knocking on anyone's door.

Broadcast your political opinions 24/7. Use novelty string lights to spell out political messages such as "V-O-T-E" during election time and hang them in your balcony, or put a poster for your favorite politician in your window or front yard for passers-bys to read. Seeing that you're politcally aware could inspire your neighors to be, too.

Make protest signs and stand up for your cause. Organized demonstrations can be an effective way of getting concerns answered. Show that activism is alive and well, check protest.net for information on protests and rallies that are happening in your community.

EXPERTISE

Run for office. It doesn't have to be on a national or state level. It doesn't even have to be on a municipal level. It could be as simple as running for your community board, PTA, or housing-association board. And who knows—once you get on the side where you have the power to make change, you may very well be campaigning for a higher seat one day.

Become a convention delegate. Being a delegate is one of the most important components to the electoral process and a great way to be politically active. Each state determines the process by which its delegates are chosen, contact your party's state office to learn more.

Create art. Depict taboo subjects to stir up debate and spread knowledge. Shoot movies, write books, take photographs, compose songs, paint pictures, build sculptures—work in whatever form inspires you and will make people think and discuss.

Become an online citizen journalist. First, educate yourself on how to responsibly report news. Contact organizations like the Committee for Concerned Journalists that have tips on how to start blogs, write effective and honest posts, and become aware of your basic rights and protections as a blogger. The more sources for information there are, the more freedom we have.

DOLLARS

$ Host a political fundraiser. Turn your next concert, happy hour, or barbecue into a chance to raise money for your favorite candidate or political campaign. Check the campaign's website for its guidelines on the types of events and contribution amounts it can accept. Any fundraiser, no matter how small, can bring new donors and votes to your chosen candidate.

$ Shop the Sundance Catalog. Robert Redford started the jewelry/apparel/home decor catalog in 1989 as an extension of the Sundance Institute, which supports independent film and theater artists. Proceeds benefit the artists and craftspeople whose goods are featured inside (www.sundancecatalog.com).

$ Buy a political ad. Purchase space on one of your favorite blogs or community websites. Ads can cost as little as a few dollars. Information about political advertising on Internet websites can be found at the Center for Democracy and Technology's Net Democracy Guide (www.netdemocracyguide.org).

WHERE TO... SOME PLACES ON POLITICAL ACTIVISM

→ ACLU
www.aclu.org
The ACLU's mission is to preserve the principles that form the basis of the American system of government and to extend rights to segments of the population that have been denied them.

→ ACORN
www.acorn.org
ACORN is a network of community organizations that are committed to social and economic change through direct action, legislative advocacy, and voter participation.

→ ACTIVE VOICE
www.activevoice.net
Active Voice consists of a team of strategic communication specialists who put media to work for change in communities, workplaces, and campuses across America.

→ AMERICA SPEAKS
www.americaspeaks.org
America Speaks designs and facilitates large-scale town meetings on public policy issues in order to reinvigorate American democracy.

→ AMERICAN ASSEMBLY
www.americanassembly.org
The American Assembly is a public affairs forum that illuminates issues of public policy by commissioning research and publications, sponsoring meetings, and issuing reports.

→ AMERICAN LIBRARY ASSOCIATION OFFICE FOR INTELLECTUAL FREEDOM
www.ala.org
The Association provides information to libraries and the general public about the nature and importance of intellectual freedom in libraries.

→ APIA VOTE
www.apiavote.org
APIA Vote encourages and promotes civic participation of Asian Pacific Islander Americans in the electoral and public policy processes at the national, state, and local levels.

→ BEACON FOR FREEDOM OF EXPRESSION
www.beaconforfreedom.org
An international database on censorship of books and newspapers, it also provides information on freedom of expression.

→ BIPARTISAN POLICY CENTER
www.bipartisanpolicy.org
The Bipartisan Policy Center was formed to develop policy solutions that make sense for the nation and can be embraced by both parties.

→ BODY AS BILLBOARD
www.bodyasbillboard.com
Body as Billboard is a T-shirt company that merges fashion and social commentary.

→ CENTER FOR CAMPUS FREE SPEECH
www.campusspeech.org
The Center for Campus Free Speech is dedicated to preserving the marketplace of ideas on college campuses by providing specialized support.

→ CENTER FOR SOCIAL MEDIA
www.centerforsocialmedia.org
Part of the School of Communication at American University, the Center offers strategies to use media as creative tools for public knowledge and action.

→ CONGRESS.ORG
www.congress.org
A nonpartisan online resource, Congress.org helps users identify and contact elected leaders in Congress, the White House, and state legislatures.

→ THE CREATIVE COALITION
www.thecreativecoalition.org
The Creative Coalition is a leading nonprofit, nonpartisan social and political advocacy organization, working to mobilize the arts community on issues of First Amendment rights, support for the arts, and public education.

→ DECLARE YOURSELF
www.declareyourself.com
Declare Yourself is a campaign that works to encourage young people to register to vote by combining education, entertainment, and community outreach.

→ DEMOCRACY IN ACTION
www.democracyinaction.org
Democracy in Action provides e-advocacy tools to other nonprofits, and encourages organizations to use technology as a tool for social change.

→ DEMOCRACY LAB
www.democracylab.com
The Democracy Lab provides services, information, and consultation for the purpose of enhancing participatory democracy.

→ THE DEMOCRATIC PARTY
www.democrats.org
The Democratic Party website offers background information on the party, including agendas, forums, and press.

→ ELECTRIC FRONTIER FOUNDATION
www.eff.org
An advocacy and legal organization, the Electric Frontier Foundation works to preserve free-speech rights such as those protected by the First Amendment in the context of the digital age.

→ FAIRVOTE
www.fairvote.org
FairVote works to change the election process by achieving universal access to participation, broader ballot choice, and majority rule with fair representation for all.

→ FIRST AMENDMENT CENTER
www.firstamendmentcenter.org
The Center offers comprehensive research coverage of key First Amendment issues and topics, news, and a First Amendment library.

→ FREE PRESS
www.freepress.net
Through education, organizing, and advocacy, Free Press promotes diverse and independent media ownership, strong public media, and universal access to communication.

→ FREEDOM OF INFORMATION ACT (FOIA)
www.state.gov/m/a/ips/
The Freedom of Information Act allows for the full or partial disclosure of previously unreleased information and documents controlled by the U.S. government.

➔ GLOBAL YOUTH ACTION NETWORK
www.youthlink.org
A collaboration among youth and youth-serving organizations, the Network aims to share information, resources, and solutions to promote greater youth engagement.

➔ INNOVATIONS IN CIVIC PARTICIPATION
www.icicp.org
ICP is a leader in the global movement to promote sustainable development and social change through youth civic engagement.

➔ INTERNATIONAL FREEDOM OF EXPRESSION EXCHANGE
www.ifex.org
The International Freedom of Expression Exchange is comprised of 81 organizations working together as a global community to preserve freedom of expression.

➔ LEAGUE OF WOMEN VOTERS
www.lwv.org
The League of Women Voters encourages participation in government, and works to increase understanding of major public policy issues.

➔ McCORMICK FREEDOM MUSEUM
www.freedommuseum.us
Located in Chicago, the McCormick Freedom Museum is the nation's first museum dedicated to freedom and the First Amendment.

➔ OPENNET INITIATIVE
www.opennet.net
The OpenNet Initiative analyzes Internet filtering and surveillance practices by countries around the world.

➔ PEOPLE FOR THE AMERICAN WAY
www.pfaw.org
As an advocacy group, PFAW has been active on issues such as civil rights, voting rights, and separation of church and state.

➔ PRESS INSTITUTE FOR WOMEN IN THE DEVELOPING WORLD
www.piwdw.org
The Press Institute trains women with no prior journalism experience to report on issues such as HIV/AIDS, violence against women, and community development.

➔ PROJECT VOTE SMART
www.vote-smart.org
Project Vote Smart works to provide detailed background information on political candidates and elected officials, including voting records, campaign contributions, public statements, and biographical data.

➔ PUBLIC FORUM INSTITUTE
www.publicforuminstitute.org
The Institute is committed to developing the most advanced and effective means of fostering public discourse through organizing public policy forums.

➔ REPORTERS WITHOUT BORDERS
www.rsf.org
Reporters Without Borders gives financial aid to journalists or media outlets in difficulty, fights against censorship, and defends journalists and media assistants who have been imprisoned or persecuted.

➔ THE REPUBLICAN PARTY
www.gop.com
The official website of the Republican Party, GOP.com offers visitors the opportunity to register to vote, make a contribution, write to officials, or sign up to volunteer.

➔ ROCK THE VOTE
www.rockthevote.com
Rock the Vote engages youth in the political process by incorporating the entertainment community and youth culture into its activities, with the goal of increasing youth-voter turnout.

➔ ROOSEVELT INSTITUTION
www.rooseveltinstitution.org
The Roosevelt Institution is a nonpartisan network of campus-based student think tanks. Its members conduct research on pressing political issues in an effort to influence policy change.

➔ SUNDANCE INSTITUTE
www.sundance.org
The Sundance Institute is dedicated to the discovery and development of independent artists and audiences.

➔ UNESCO
www.unesco.org
The United Nations Educational, Scientific and Cultural Organization functions as a laboratory of ideas and a standard-setter to forge universal agreements on emerging ethical issues.

➔ USO
www.uso.org
The United Service Organizations serve as the primary bridge between the American people and the U.S. armed forces, delivering morale-building, counseling, and recreational services.

➔ VOTO LATINO
www.votolatino.org
Voto Latino seeks to empower the Latino community by leveraging celebrity voices, the latest technology, and youth to promote positive change and an enfranchised America.

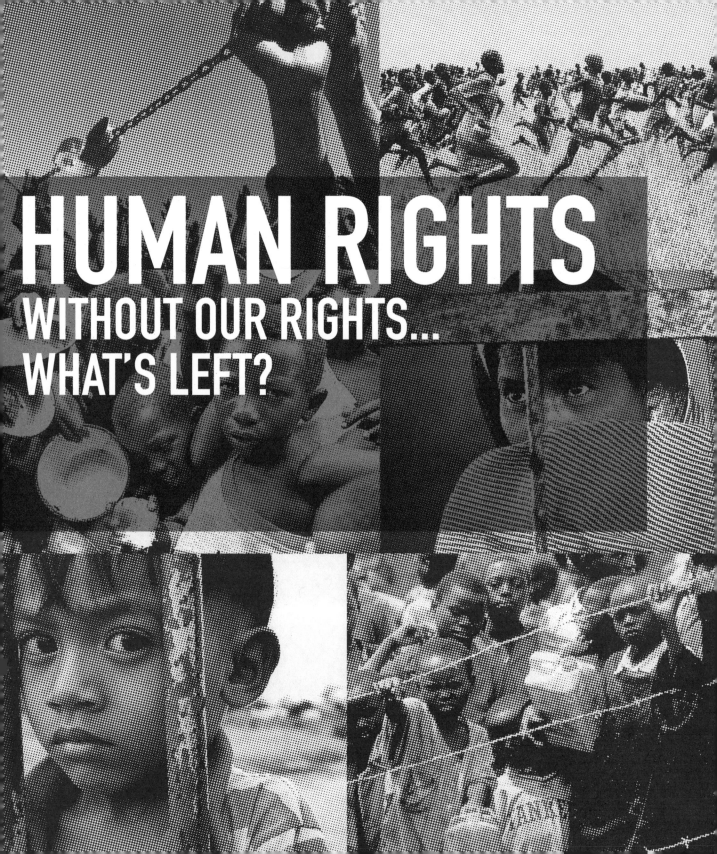

HUMAN RIGHTS
WITHOUT OUR RIGHTS...
WHAT'S LEFT?

Due to a random and fortunate set of circumstances, several years ago I found myself on an airplane seated next to Nelson Mandela. After a few minutes of pleasantries, I asked him the question I knew he had been asked many times before: "How were you able to maintain your drive, determination, and will, let alone your sanity, during your twenty-seven years in prison?" I spent the next two and a half hours listening to one of the most inspiring and uplifting stories I have ever heard. He shared that while incarcerated he was cut off from the world he had known his whole life. Yet he remained patient, knowing that justice would prevail. His fellow political prisoners became a form of family, his guards, his friends. Nelson Mandela taught the world that although you can't always control life's circumstances, you can control how you respond to them. He showed us just what the human spirit is capable of, even in dire circumstances. He had every right to be angry, bitter, and resentful. Instead, he remained hopeful, accepting, and forgiving, which enabled him to eventually lead South Africa out of the darkness of its past. ➜ **After witnessing what Nelson Mandela accomplished under such circumstances, how can we believe that any one person can't make a difference? — Kenneth Cole**

DON CHEADLE
JOHN PRENDERGAST

On the Movement to End Genocide

Don Cheadle

Don Cheadle was nominated for an Academy Award® for his performance in the film Hotel Rwanda, which helped draw attention to the horrors of genocide. Having traveled throughout western Sudan's Darfur region in 2005, he became one of the first celebrities to speak out against the atrocities in Darfur. He is co-founder of Not on Our Watch and co-produced the documentary Darfur Now.
➡ *notonourwatchproject.org; darfurnowtour.com*

John Prendergast

Leading human rights activist John Prendergast is co-founder of the ENOUGH project, an initiative working to end genocide and crimes against humanity. He has worked for the White House during the Clinton administration, members of Congress, the United Nations, human rights organizations, and think tanks, and authored eight books on Africa, including Not on Our Watch, co-authored with Don Cheadle.
➡ *enoughproject.org*

JP: I've been working in war zones and on African conflict resolution now for twenty-five years. A few years ago, we took a journey together to Darfur, and so began our partnership. What were your first impressions?

DC: I had no idea what to expect. I was trying to prepare myself for the very worst, and obviously there was a lot of devastation, but what I didn't expect to see was a lot of resiliency. We have such a preconceived notion about what Africa is. If you don't look at it in depth, you get only these thin slices of "please give" infomercials. It becomes a monolithic idea of what an area like that is, and what the people are. When we got there, we were greeted by tons of kids running up to us and playing with us and laughing. You saw that there was a lot of hope there.

> **For the first time since the word "genocide" was invented, there is a mass movement of people all across the United States trying to stop a genocide while it is happening. —JP**

JP: Africa itself is not a hopeless place. In my years of working, more wars have ended than have begun. Look at Rwanda, where you portrayed a character in the film *Hotel Rwanda*. Fourteen years ago, the genocide took 800,000 lives in 100 days, the fastest recorded rate of killing in human history. Now, fast forward to the present. This is a country at peace, with the highest percentage of female parliamentarians in the entire world. Although there are certainly political problems, as there are everywhere, Rwandans are committed to justice, as well as reconciliation. Places all over Africa, including Liberia, Sierra Leone, Mozambique, Angola—even in southern Sudan, where a war raged for twenty years—have ended their conflicts and come home by the thousands to rebuild their communities. So, to me, Africa is full of extraordinary success stories. There are some conflicts that remain, stubbornly, like the one in Darfur, but it just redoubles my desire to help in any way I can.

The Genocide Intervention Network created the first anti-genocide hotline at 1-800-GENOCIDE. The hotline provides talking points and connects callers with their governors, senators, and representatives, enabling callers to ask them to end genocide in Darfur. In its first nine months, more than 7,000 people called their elected officials.

DC: After that trip to Darfur, I felt that if someone didn't step in, in fairly short order, the light would be going out for a lot of those kids, which is what really inspired me to combine our efforts in what we were trying to do. And that's definitely where our book *Not on Our Watch* came out of.

JP: And while we were writing the book, other things happened. You and your friends from the *Ocean's* movie series decided to do something more. How did you come up with the concept of the Not on Our Watch Foundation?

DC: Well, it was pretty interesting that George Clooney, on his own, went over to the area as well to see it with his own eyes. Brad Pitt has been there, although a lot of his focus was on water and poverty. Matt Damon as well. People asked me, "So you guys would sit around on *Ocean's Eleven* and *Twelve* and talk about Darfur and Africa?" And we said, "Yeah, a lot, actually. And about what we could do." It inspired Jerry Weintraub, our producer, to create the Not on Our Watch Foundation, and really to take advantage of this "star power."

JP: It's a nice complement to what we do at the ENOUGH Project because Not on Our Watch is able to raise significant amounts of money to support critical humanitarian priorities on the ground in Darfur and in neighboring Chad. On the other side, the ENOUGH Project tries to educate people and ensure that political will continues to increase to bring an end to the genocide.

DC: And we have to have both of those things happening. What are the goals now going forward to try to end the genocide?

JP: There are three goals we've really targeted. The first one is an effort to build a permanent constituency against genocide in the United States. For the first time since the word "genocide" was invented, over a half-century ago, there is a mass movement of people all across the United States trying to stop a genocide while it's happening. This is unprecedented. And this will, I think, remain in place over time so that we can work to prevent future ones. The second goal would be to change U.S. policy so that we're doing something about this terrible atrocity that's occurring in Sudan. We've been able to push the United Nations Security Council to authorize the largest peace-keeping mission in the history of the UN, but it hasn't deployed the force quickly enough, so people are still dying. The third is to see change on the ground in Darfur. But these are beginnings, and it takes time to construct the right ingredients to bring an end to these things. So we're pressing as hard as we can. Darfur's still suffering, but the resolve of people that we've met seems to be deepening, not diminishing.

DC: What other ideas do you have in terms of ways people can help out?

JP: I've been starting to see it as a menu, where you don't have to eat everything, but instead choose a few things that you're comfortable with. For example, join one of the organizations involved in the anti-genocide effort, whether it's Save Darfur Coalition,

STAND [A Student Anti-Genocide Coalition], or Amnesty International. They will send you a series of actions that you can take. Second is the old-fashioned bedrock of our democracy, getting in contact with your elected officials. The glaring obstacle to faster and more meaningful engagement to resolve these terrible crises in Africa is this elusive concept called "political will." Political will comes when the citizens of countries say "This matters to us," and governments respond. Sure you can write letters or e-mails, but the most effective thing is to actually visit these people. They work for you. And they're going to be much more impressed by a face-to-face meeting with a group of voters than if people send a few letters.

DC: As you were saying, even if you don't want to or can't do certain things, supporting the organizations that have committed themselves to applying political pressure to our elected officials is very important.

JP: Absolutely. Another thing is getting in touch with your local media. Media outlets have to hear from the people who actually buy the newspapers and watch the television shows that, in fact, we do want to know about these issues. Just like you'd contact your congressional representatives, you can do the same with your local NBC/ABC/CBS affiliates and the local newspapers wherever you live. What about your work with students to get the U.C. Regents to divest their money from Sudan?

DC: That came out of direct contact with a student activist organization at UCLA. The head of that movement, a student at the time named Adam Sterling, went on to spearhead this divestment that has precipitated many states around the country divesting their funds. There was a day when we went into a meeting with the U.C. Regents to try and get this divestment pushed through. First, we held a news conference, and literally there were eight people in the room. Then we began rallying, like an old-fashioned put-up-your-soapbox-and-get-out-the-megaphone. People started gathering and getting educated. We marched our way across the campus to this meeting, and by the time we got there, we had collected nearly 200 converts.

JP: About sixty universities have declared their investments to be genocide-free, and STAND has chapters in universities, high schools, and even middle schools, where young people are saying that we will not stand idly by while genocide occurs. If you look at it historically, students are always in the vanguard of social change, demonstrating their willingness to put themselves on the line.

DC: That's what happened in the overthrowing of the apartheid regime in South Africa. These were all students, who, as you said, have the energy, the desire, and the creativity to apply themselves to these things. It's extremely inspiring. I'm a father and I hope not to just talk about things that I want to see in the world, but *be* about things that I want to see in the world. Being involved, trying to see that justice is served, and trying to be about solutions that really benefit us is something we all should aspire to.

FACT

➡ In 2006 in a unanimous decision, the University of California became the first major public university system to vote to divest from companies with financial holdings in Sudan.

➡ As of June 2008, 37 states, 61 universities, 19 cities, and 18 countries have adopted or initiated Sudan divestment policies.

UNIVERSAL DECLARATION OF HUMAN RIGHTS

➡ Adopted by the General Assembly of the United Nations on December 10, 1948

No one shall be subjected to torture or to cruel, inhuman, or degrading treatment or punishment. ARTICLE 5

Nothing in this Declaration may be interpreted as implying for any State, group, or person any right to engage in any activity or to perform any act aimed at the destruction of any of the rights and freedoms set forth herein. ARTICLE 30

Everyone, as a member of society, has the right to social security. ARTICLE 22

Everyone has the right to education. ARTICLE 26

Everyone has the right to an effective remedy by the competent national tribunals for acts violating the fundamental rights granted him by the constitution or by law. ARTICLE 8

All human beings are born free and equal in dignity and rights. They are endowed with reason and conscience and should act towards one another in a spirit of brotherhood. ARTICLE 1

No one shall be held in slavery or servitude. ARTICLE 4

Everyone has the right to freedom of movement and residence within the borders of each state. ARTICLE 13

Everyone has the right to a nationality. ARTICLE 15

All are equal before the law and are entitled without any discrimination to equal protection of the law. ARTICLE 7

Everyone charged with a penal offence has the right to be presumed innocent until proved guilty according to law in a public trial. ARTICLE 11

Everyone has the right to own property alone as well as in association with others. ARTICLE 17

Everyone has the right freely to participate in the cultural life of the community, to enjoy the arts, and to share in scientific advancement and its benefits. ARTICLE 27

Everyone has the right to rest and leisure, including reasonable limitation of working hours and periodic holidays with pay. ARTICLE 24

Everyone has the right to freedom of thought, conscience, and religion. ARTICLE 18

Everyone has the right to work, to free choice of employment, to just and favorable conditions of work, and to protection against unemployment. ARTICLE 23

Everyone has the right to seek and to enjoy in other countries asylum from persecution.
ARTICLE 14

Everyone has duties to the community in which alone the free and full development of his personality is possible.
ARTICLE 29

Everyone is entitled to all the rights and freedoms set forth in this Declaration, without distinction of any kind, such as race, color, sex, language, religion, political or other opinion, national or social origin, property, birth, or other status. ARTICLE 2

Everyone has the right to a standard of living adequate for the health and well-being of himself and of his family. ARTICLE 25

Everyone is entitled to a social and international order in which the rights and freedoms set forth in this Declaration can be fully realized. ARTICLE 28

Everyone is entitled in full equality to a fair and public hearing by an independent and impartial tribunal, in the determination of his rights and obligations and of any criminal charge against him. ARTICLE 10

No one shall be subjected to arbitrary interference with his privacy, family, home, or correspondence, nor to attacks upon his honor and reputation. ARTICLE 12

Everyone has the right to freedom of peaceful assembly and association.
ARTICLE 20

Everyone has the right to take part in the government of his country, directly or through freely chosen representatives.
ARTICLE 21

Everyone has the right to life, liberty, and security of person. ARTICLE 3

Men and women of full age, without any limitation due to race, nationality, or religion, have the right to marry and to found a family. They are entitled to equal rights as to marriage, during marriage, and at its dissolution.
ARTICLE 16

Everyone has the right to recognition everywhere as a person before the law. ARTICLE 6

No one shall be subjected to arbitrary arrest, detention, or exile. ARTICLE 9

Everyone has the right to freedom of opinion and expression. ARTICLE 19

JACQUELINE MUREKATETE

On Genocide Prevention

Jacqueline Murekatete

*A survivor of the 1994 Rwandan Tutsi genocide, Jacqueline Murekatete is the founder and director of **Jacqueline's Human Rights Corner**, a genocide-prevention education program under the umbrella of **Miracle Corners of the World**, a New York–based nonprofit organization.*

➜ *miraclecorners.org/programs_partner_jacqueline*

What does a young girl do when her innocence is taken away, her whole world is changed, and she finds herself in an environment in which she is told that she is no longer a human being, a child, but an enemy of the state, a cockroach needing to be exterminated? What does a young girl do when her childhood is shattered, her parents, siblings, uncles, aunts, friends murdered by their neighbors, and she finds herself in an environment in which more than a million innocent men, women, and children are murdered simply because of their ethnicity?

When I was just nine years old, in 1994, the Tutsi genocide in my country exposed me to horrors that no child or adult should ever have to see. During the approximately 100 days of Tutsi massacres, I was forced to watch as men, women, and children were dragged down the streets on their way to be murdered, to listen to the screams of toddlers and infants whose arms or legs had been hacked off with machetes, and to get up not knowing whether I would live to see the next day. The genocide in my country exposed me firsthand to the worst of man's inhumanity toward man, and the worst human-rights violation that there is—the violation of every man's basic right to exist. My life would never be the same again.

The period after the genocide was a very difficult one, as I struggled to understand what had happened in my country. I spent many days crying for the parents, six siblings, aunts, uncles, cousins, and friends whom I would never see again, and at night I was haunted by nightmares. For six years after the genocide I found no words to express the horrors that had occurred in my country, and I was unable to talk about how my family had died. After arriving in the United States at the end of 1995, I kept to myself, and spoke very vaguely about my previous life in Rwanda to my new classmates and friends.

The turning point for me, the moment when I made the transition from victim to activist, came at the beginning of high school. I began learning about the Holocaust and how other countries had gone through genocides. I was struck by the similarities between these genocides and the one in my country, and I was appalled to learn that the silence and indifference displayed by the international community as my people were being massacred was the same type of silence and indifference that had been the response to other genocides, before Rwanda.

After I learned about the Armenian genocide, the Holocaust, the Cambodian genocide, and the Bosnian genocide, it became clear to me that what had happened in Rwanda in 1994 was not unique to Rwanda, that genocide had happened before and could happen anywhere. I realized it was a cycle that would continue to repeat itself for as long as we permitted it by our silence, indifference, and lack of actions to prevent it. Genocide can be prevented, but it requires the collective effort of all human beings around the world.

The genocide in my country exposed me firsthand to the worst of man's inhumanity toward man.

And so, in 2001, after listening to the experiences of David Gewirtzman, a Holocaust survivor who has since become a good friend and mentor to me, I made the decision to create awareness about the genocide in my country. I knew that sharing my experience and speaking out would not be easy, but that it was work that had to be done.

One important thing that people often fail to realize about the work of genocide prevention and human rights is that while we are often overwhelmed by the number and variety of human-rights violations

GET INVOLVED

There exist numerous things that each of us can do to help advance the work of genocide prevention and human rights. As an individual and a citizen of any country, make a daily effort to be aware of the various injustices and major human rights violations that go on in our world. Be aware of the precedents of genocide, such as state-sanctioned discrimination, dehumanization of certain groups of people, racism, anti-Semitism, and hate, among other precedents. And, aware of these injustices, make an effort to mobilize others and begin a collective effort to fight these things, whether in your school, community, or in a distant country.

MODERN DAY GENOCIDES

Armenian Genocide
(1915–1923) caused
1.5 million deaths.

The Holocaust
(1933–1945) caused the
deaths of an estimated 6 million Jews, at least 1.5 million
non-Jewish Polish citizens,
200,000 individuals with
mental or physical disabilities, approximately 10,000
homosexuals, and 20,000
Roma or Gypsies.

Cambodian Genocide
(1975–1979) The Khmer
Rouge killed approximately
2 million people.

The Rwandan Genocide
(April–July 1994) caused
more than 1 million deaths.

The Darfur Conflict
(2003–present) has caused
an estimated 400,000 deaths
to date.

The Srebrenica Massacre
(July 1995) Serbian forces
killed an estimated 8,000
Muslims in Bosnia.

Genocide can be prevented, but it requires the collective effort of all human beings around the world.

around the world, and while we often feel paralyzed by the enormity of it all, all it takes to end major violations and to have a positive impact on the world is the hard work, determination, and efforts of ordinary individuals who use ordinary resources like their voices and time.

When I began my activism in genocide prevention and human rights, I did not know that I, a girl of sixteen, could make a difference. But as a result of the more than 300 presentations I have delivered in the past seven years, my genocide-prevention education work has been embraced by hundreds of U.S.–based schools, universities, and faith-based communities, and by diverse groups of people all over the world. As a result of my decision to make a positive impact on the world, others have followed my lead, investing their resources in my work and joining me to educate people, young people in particular, as to how to transform hate and achieve personal goals in ways that foster peaceful coexistence among all human beings. My team has grown to include students, global leaders, entertainers, educators, and noteworthy Holocaust/genocide scholars and human-rights activists worldwide.

There is no doubt that many significant improvements have been made in genocide prevention. More than ever before, human beings are realizing how interdependent we are and are finally waking up to the fact that a more peaceful world can be achieved only through the collective efforts of individuals. And whether change is institutional, such as the creation of the UN's Office of the Special Advisor on the Prevention of Geno-cide or of an international-relations concept like the Responsibility to Protect (both of which were conceived in an effort to determine the best way to intervene and deliver aid to people in grave conflicts around the world), or change is effected by the involve-ment of young people in student anti-genocide organizations and clubs like STAND or the Genocide Intervention Network, I and other human-rights activists know that progress is being made, that our time and daily efforts are not being wasted.

Unfortunately, with hate crimes continuing to take place in the United States, child soldiering and crimes against humanity in northern Uganda and Congo, and religiously and ethnically motivated violence in the Middle East and the Balkans, we also know that our work is anything but done. Even in the twenty-first century, genocide or the intent of governments to commit genocide remains a reality that we cannot afford to ignore, as the current situation in Darfur illustrates. The work of genocide-prevention education is more necessary than ever.

I remain optimistic that a world without genocide is possible. Genocide is not a crime that arises in a vacuum or happens overnight, as I often tell my audiences. There are warnings, and thus there are always opportunities for us to intervene, by fighting the conditions that allow genocide to take place. Before being systematically murdered, a group is usually victimized by state-sanctioned discrimination, prejudice, dehumanization, and individual murders, with impunity for the murderers. This was the case for Rwandan Tutsis before the genocide in 1994, as it was the case for the Jewish people before the Holocaust and for other victims of genocide before Rwanda.

Therefore, in seeking to create a world without genocide, we must look out for these conditions, these warnings, in our own countries and in the world at large. We must speak out against these injustices whenever and wherever we identify them, and every day each and every one of us must work to create more equitable, democratic, and tolerant societies around the world. Only by doing this can we really hope to transform the "never again" said after the Holocaust from promise into practice, from hope into reality.

RESPONSIBILITY TO PROTECT

In 2005 the World Summit adopted the Responsibility to Protect doctrine, agreeing that when crimes against humanity are committed and a state is unable or unwilling to protect its people, the international community through the UN has an obligation to intervene.

MIA FARROW

→ On Activism + Darfur

Mia Farrow

Actor and activist Mia Farrow has gained worldwide recognition beyond the silver screen for her humanitarian efforts. As part of her campaign to help end violence in Sudan's Darfur region, she has challenged world leaders and mobilized public opinion to focus on ongoing human-rights atrocities. She is a special representative of the **United Nations Children's Fund (UNICEF)** *and regularly travels to Africa to visit Darfur and neighboring Chad.*
→ *miafarrow.org; unicef.org; sudandivestment.org*

This is surely a defining moment for each of us.

More than five years have passed since the Sudanese government and its proxy killers, militia known as janjaweed, launched their genocidal campaign upon the non-Arab civilian populations of the Darfur region of Sudan. I first heard of Darfur in 2004—in an article commemorating the tenth anniversary of the Rwandan massacre. I remember it was a knee-buckling moment. I thought, "Not again."

We can only despair at our inaction during those 100 days when one million Rwandans were slaughtered. Collectively and individually we must bear the burden of our abysmal failure to protect the innocent victims; the United Nations failed, the United States failed, and all the nations of the world failed the people of Rwanda, even as we failed our essential selves. And what were we in the United States doing while that unimaginable rampage was ongoing? We were watching the O.J. Simpson murder trial.

In 2004 I visited a typical Darfuri village. I saw homes with thatched roofs and walled gardens and mature fruit trees. There were animals and fields and pottery and food stores. Children played and went to school, people tended their fields and brought their goods to market and traded with neighboring villages. There were celebrations, weddings, traditions. By the time I returned in 2006, ninety percent of Darfur's villages were ashes. In terror, two and a half million people had fled their burning villages and found their way to squalid camps that formed across Darfur, eastern Chad, and finally, the Central African Republic too. Hundreds of thousands of innocent men, women, and children have died. It is all the more appalling that we cannot yet with any accuracy count the dead. And the dying continues. In the camps everyone has lost loved ones. Water, food, education, and medical care are insufficient to nonexistent. Hope, too, is in short supply. Fourteen thousand aid workers are struggling to sustain millions of fragile lives, but they themselves are being attacked. Despite their heroic efforts, rising levels of violence have left an unprecedented two million people out of reach of humanitarian assistance.

I met a woman named Halima who described the day that changed her life. She had been holding her infant son when planes and helicopters flew low and bombs began to fall, and the janjaweed swarmed her village. On camels and horseback they came, shouting racial slurs and shooting. They tore her baby from her arms and bayoneted him before her eyes. Three of her five

UNDERSTANDING THE DARFUR CRISIS

Who: The ethnically Arab Sudanese government and the janjaweed, an Arab militia from northern Darfur, are allied against rebel groups fighting in the region, including the Muslim forces of the Sudan Liberation Movement (SLM) and the Justice and Equality Movement (JEM), which represent mostly the non-Arab farmers of southern Darfur.

What: The janjaweed, backed by the Sudanese military, are carrying out the widespread killings, abductions, and rapes of non-Arab Sudanese civilians. Though it denies it, the Sudanese government has been providing military supplies to the janjaweed, which have moved south to take over rebel territory. So far, an estimated 400,000 have died from violence, disease, or starvation, and more than 2.5 million have been displaced. Villages have been bombed and burned, water sources poisoned, and means of food production destroyed. As of July 2007, a UN peacekeeping force of 26,000 troops had been placed in Darfur to protect civilians and aid workers. Despite its being one of the most dangerous places in the world for relief workers, with more than a dozen killed, many groups are still going in and doing what they can to help.

DARFUR   SUDAN

When: February 2003 to
the present.

Why: Drought, desertification,
and overpopulation have
increased the competition
between Arab nomads and
black African farmers for
fertile land. Some suspect
the attempt at eradication is
motivated by the possibility
of oil in Darfur, and the Sudanese government's desire to
explore drilling possibilities
there. Sudan's existing $6
billion oil industry is fueled
mostly by demand from
China, which historically has
ignored many international
human-rights laws. Rebels
say they need water and
peace to survive and are not
concerned with oil.

children were similarly killed that day, and
her husband too. "Janjaweed" she told me,
"they cut them and threw them into the
well." Then she clasped my hands and
said, "Tell people what is happening here.
Tell them we need help." That was 2004.

Halima's story is similar to those of countless women I have spoken with over my nine
journeys to Darfur and across its porous borders in eastern Chad and the Central African
Republic—a triangle of suffering. I carry their stories of loss and terror, of torture and rape; of homes
and fields in flames and of lives destroyed.

The late Senator Paul Simon said that if just a hundred people from every district had
contacted their representatives during the Rwandan massacre, the U.S. Government
would have taken action to stop the genocide. In 2004 our government first used the
word genocide to describe the atrocities in Darfur. Since then the very word Darfur has
become synonymous with suffering. We are seeing the most significant civic response
to an African atrocity since apartheid. But it has not produced the political will to end
the genocide. I tell my own children that with knowledge comes responsibility. But the
world's leaders do not, for the most part, reflect this at all. So we must push harder.
Write more letters. Call 1-800-GENOCIDE to contact your elected officials. Urge them
to do more. Push them and the members of the UN Security Council to stand up to the
Sudanese government—insist that the Sudanese regime cease their ongoing aerial
bombardments and ground attacks upon civilians and admit the full deployment of the
26,000 peacekeepers authorized by the United Nations in July 2007.

Halima and countless courageous women in the Darfur region continue to plead for
protection. It is past time that the nations of the world step up to accept our common
responsibility to protect this anguished and imperiled population.

This is surely a defining moment for each of us.

LUCY LIU

On Global Volunteer Work

Lucy Liu

*In 2005 Lucy Liu was appointed a UNICEF Ambassador. Her work with **UNICEF** has taken her to Pakistan, Lesotho, Ivory Coast, and the Democratic Republic of the Congo, where she has witnessed the devastation caused by violent conflict, natural disaster, lack of clean water, and HIV/AIDS.*
➡ *unicef.org*

I called UNICEF because I wanted to see what it did, how it dealt with emergency situations, and how it used its money. Since then I've been on a mission with UNICEF every year, sometimes twice a year. I am amazed by the level of belief in the people behind UNICEF. There's a commitment from their hearts that keeps them in areas of emergency.

My last trip was to the Democratic Republic of the Congo, where the disaster isn't a natural one—it's man-made. Human beings are committing the violence and atrocities.

UNICEF

The United Nations created UNICEF in 1946 to meet the emergency needs of children facing famine and disease in postwar Europe. Today its mandate is to address the needs of women and children in all developing countries. The organization works in 191 countries around the world.

DRC

UNICEF IN THE DRC

A 2003 peace accord ended the six-year civil war in the Democratic Republic of the Congo, but armed conflict still exists in parts of the country, and poverty, violence, and lack of basic services continue to affect the nation's children.

➡ UNICEF has provided shelter and household items to 100,000 families affected by armed conflict and natural disasters in the DRC, created 86 centers to provide emergency nutrition to more than 45,000 children, and provided medical care and counseling to more than 15,000 survivors of sexual violence.

➡ UNICEF has also rehabilitated classrooms, trained hundreds of teachers, and distributed school supplies to 200,000 internally displaced children during their continued campaign in the country.

UNICEF has a temporary camp set up for internally displaced persons. Because of military insecurity, they've been driven out of their own villages. Many have been killed, women have been raped, and children have been taken as slaves or soldiers.

It's horrifying to think that these things are happening—that a completely vulnerable, completely innocent child can be so violated and damaged. When these people look into your eyes, not knowing or caring who you are, and plead with you to send help, there is a sense of helplessness. It's really difficult to take the information you've gathered back to wherever you're from. When I first got home, I was unable to talk to my friends or even my family about what happened.

We can't just continue to bandage the situation. I don't know if people have given up on the DRC, just forgotten about it, or assume it's hopeless. But helping is not a matter of being motivated—it's a matter of being a human being and knowing that just because problems have subsided in one area doesn't mean everything is okay. A lot of people think that because it's happening on the other side of world it doesn't affect them. The perfect example is September 11, 2001. If there is conflict in the Middle East involving Osama bin Laden, then it shouldn't affect us at all—but it has, hasn't it?

If you look at it from a broader perspective, you tend to lose hope. But you can't change the world immediately. You have to walk ahead and hope that your footsteps will encourage other people to follow. I give ten percent of everything I make to charity. It shouldn't matter whether you make $500 or $500 million. People often say to me, "I just don't know where the money is going." It's a valid point, and people should make it, but they should go a level above that and investigate. You don't have to travel to Africa, China, or Pakistan. But get involved any way that you can. That's how people are going to learn—by being truly involved.

I saw an amazing movie recently that showed that happiness is only real when shared, and I think that's really true. You can go about life doing all the things you want to do, but if you don't share it with someone, you haven't really accomplished anything.

You can't change the world immediately. You have to walk ahead and hope that your footsteps will encourage other people to follow.

HOW TO... SOME TIPS ON HUMAN RIGHTS

TIME

⏱ **Join a human-rights organization** such as Amnesty International or Human Rights Watch, and use your social-networking sites to alert your connections to human rights abuses and collect signatures on electronic petitions to stop the abuses.

⏱ **Assist refugees.** The United States has a long tradition of offering refuge to those fleeing persecution and war. The International Rescue Committee (www.theirc.org) has many volunteer opportunities for you to help refugees become culturally oriented to life here.

⏱ **Host a Human Rights Movie Marathon.** Enlighten your guests with the various causes and struggles around the world. Have a discussion afterward, addressing ways you can help. Suggested screenings: *Hotel Rwanda* (2004), *The Killing Fields* (1984), *Schindler's List* (1993), *Tsotsi* (2005).

⏱ **Become a domestic volunteer.** Or intern at a humanitarian NGO. While many humanitarian crisis agencies seek specialized, skilled labor for operations abroad, there are also opportunites to work domestically without having gone to medical school. Organizations like the American Red Cross (www.redcross.org) have a wide variety of opportunities you can explore.

ITEMS

📦 **Subscribe to *PEN America*,** a journal published by the world's oldest human rights organization. PEN (www.pen.org), founded in 1921, works to dispel national, ethnic, and racial hatreds, and promotes understanding among all countries.

📦 **Make a donation without spending any cash.** If you've received a retail gift card, and either aren't planing on using it or have a leftover sum, you can fill in a form at www.donateagiftcard .com and choose from several charities and organizations to make donations to—including UNICEF, ProLiteracy Worldwide, and the International Medical Corps. After mailing in your card, DGC exchanges it for the cash value and sends the money to whichever cause you've chosen.

📦 **Sign up with Working Assets Long Distance** for your phone service. With every call you make, Working Assets (www. workingassets.com) donates 1% of your charges to nonprofit groups, such as Human Rights Watch. Since 1985, they've raised over $50 million for groups working for peace, human rights, economic justice, and a clean environment.

📦 **Introduce a book that touches on human rights issues to your next book club reading.** For example, *A Long Way Gone: Memoirs of a Boy Soldier* by Ishmael Beah, *Refugee Sandwich: Stories of Exile and Asylum*, by Peter Showler, *Iran Awakening: A Memoir of Revolution and Hope*, by Shirin Ebadi with Azadeh Moaveni, and *Not on Our Watch* by Don Cheadle and John Prendergast.

EXPERTISE

💼 **Be a good corporate citizen.** As a business owner, you can directly influence the economies of places that have yet to address human rights abuses. Ensure that your company's policies and practices promote and safeguard human rights. Review the corporate principles set forth by the United Nations Global Compact (www.unglobalcompact.org), a corporate citizenship initiative.

💼 **Put those Spanish classes to work.** Human rights is a cause that knows no borders. Today language skills ranging from Urdu to Portuguese are in high demand to translate news, reports, and even witness statements. Organizations like Boat People SOS (Korean, Vietnamese), SANMA (Hindi), and Mujeres Iniciando en las Americas (Spanish) all have desperate needs and are good places to start.

💼 **Volunteer to be an international, emergency response medical staff member.** In times of disaster, many organizations need highly trained medical staff for their emergency response rosters. Volunteers need to be willing to travel and be available long-term (up to a year) or more short-term with rapid deployment—usually within 72 hours. Contact Doctors Without Borders (www.doctorswithoutborders.org) or the International Medical Corps (www.imcworldwide.org).

DOLLARS

$ **Become an informed traveler.** While some have decided to boycott travel locations with terrible human-rights abuses, others are calling for boycotts of entire countries, such as Myanmar (Burma). Be more aware when deciding to support tourism industries where human-rights abuses are rampant, whether it means not patronizing government-run hotels, restaurants, or other businesses, or avoiding the destination altogether.

$ **Raise funds as a grant writer.** Despite their groundbreaking work, many human rights groups suffer from very limited funding. If you have strong research and writing skills, consider volunteering to write grants for a nongovernmental nonprofit organization (NGO) like Fight for the Children (Africa), Antares Foundation (Kazakhstan), or Nivasa Foundation (Sri Lanka) and help make an impact on the people they serve.

$ **Drink tea.** When you order a $45 gift set of organic Rescue Tea (www.rescuetea.org), 50% of the purchase price goes to the International Rescue Committee, a humanitarian relief organization that helps people escaping from the horrors of war and persecution.

$ **Personally divest.** Research mutual funds or companies that have operations in Sudan and consider switching your investment dollars. The Sudan Divestment Task Force (www.sudandivest-ment.org) can assist you in creating a genocide-free portfolio.

WHERE TO... SOME PLACES ON HUMAN RIGHTS

→ **1-800-GENOCIDE**
www.1800genocide.com
This first ever anti-genocide hotline that provides callers with up-to-date information on how to end genocide.

→ **AMERICAN FRIENDS SERVICE COMMITTEE**
www.afsc.org
Founded by Quakers in 1917 to provide conscientious objectors with an opportunity to aid civilian war victims, AFSC carries out service, development, social justice, and peace programs throughout the world.

→ **AMNESTY INTERNATIONAL**
www.amnesty.org
Amnesty International is a worldwide movement of people who campaign for internationally recognized human rights for all. The organization has more than 2.2 million members in more than 150 countries; visitors to the Amnesty International site can become members or supporters.

→ **CENTER FOR CONSTITUTIONAL RIGHTS**
www.ccrjustice.org
The Center for Constitutional Rights is dedicated to advancing and protecting the rights guaranteed by the United States Constitution and the Universal Declaration of Human Rights.

→ **CENTER FOR JUSTICE AND INTERNATIONAL LAW**
www.cejil.org
CEJIL's principal objective is to achieve the full implementation of international human rights norms in the member States of the Organization of American States.

→ **CODEPINK**
www.codepink4peace.org
Codepink is a women-initiated grassroots peace and social justice movement working to end the war in Iraq, stop new wars, and redirect resources into health care and education.

→ **ENOUGH PROJECT**
www.enoughproject.org
ENOUGH is dedicated to ending genocide and crimes against humanity, specifically focused on Darfur.

→ **FACING HISTORY AND OURSELVES**
www.facinghistory.org
Facing History and Ourselves is an international educational and professional development organization that examines racism, prejudice, and anti-Semitism to promote the development of a more humane citizenry.

→ **FREE THE SLAVES**
www.freetheslaves.net
Free the Slaves works to end slavery worldwide by liberating slaves around the world, helping them rebuild their lives, and researching real-world solutions to eradicate slavery forever.

→ **FREEDOM HOUSE**
www.freedomhouse.org
Freedom House helps focus the world's attention on core issues of freedom and democracy through public events, press releases, and opinion articles.

→ **FUND FOR GLOBAL HUMAN RIGHTS**
www.globalhumanrights.org
The Fund for Global Human Rights works to ensure a strong, effective human rights community worldwide through a strategic grant program.

→ **GENOCIDE INTERVENTION NETWORK**
www.genocideintervention.net
Created by students in 2004, GI-Net provides tools for individuals to help stop genocide through advocacy and fund-raising.

→ **HOLOCAUST MEMORIAL & TOLERANCE CENTER OF NASSAU COUNTY**
www.holocaust-nassau.org
The Center educates about the atrocities of the Holocaust and promotes awareness of the dangers of prejudice and intolerance.

→ **HUMAN RIGHTS CENTER**
www.hrcberkeley.org
The Human Rights Center investigates war crimes and other serious violations of human rights and international humanitarian law. The Center offers empirical studies that recommend specific policy measures, courses, and student fellowships.

→ **HUMAN RIGHTS EDUCATION ASSOCIATES**
www.hrea.org
Human Rights Education Associates works to implement human rights education programs. HREA provides curricula, materials, training, and research.

→ **HUMAN RIGHTS FIRST**
www.humanrightsfirst.org
Human Rights First is a human rights advocacy group that seeks justice through the courts.

→ **HUMAN RIGHTS WATCH**
www.hrw.org
Human Rights Watch is an independent, nongovernmental organization that works to prevent discrimination, uphold political freedom, investigate human rights violations, and hold abusers accountable.

→ **INSTITUTE FOR POLICY STUDIES**
www.ips-dc.org
The Institute for Policy Studies works to strengthen social movements with independent research, visionary thinking, and links to scholars and elected officials.

→ **INTERNATIONAL CRISIS GROUP**
www.crisisgroup.org
The International Crisis Group is recognized as a leading independent, nonpartisan source of analysis and advice to governments and citizens on the prevention and resolution of deadly conflict.

→ **INTERNATIONAL HUMAN RIGHTS LAW GROUP**
www.hrlawgroup.org
The International Human Rights Law Group trains legal professionals across ethnic lines around the world to promote justice and human rights.

→ **INTERNATIONAL LABOR RIGHTS FORUM**
www.laborrights.org
ILRF is an advocacy organization dedicated to achieving just and humane treatment for workers worldwide.

→ INTERNATIONAL LEAGUE FOR HUMAN RIGHTS
www.ilhr.org
ILHR provides information and news on human rights developments around the world.

→ INTERNATIONAL RESCUE COMMITTEE
www.theirc.org
A global network of humanitarian relief workers, first responders, health-care providers, activists, and volunteers, the International Rescue Committee provides emergency relief for those uprooted or otherwise affected by violent conflict and oppression.

→ JACQUELINE'S HUMAN RIGHTS CORNER
www.miraclecorners.org/ programs_partner_jacqueline
Jacqueline's Human Rights Corner is a Miracle Corners of the World project that aims to work with governments, educational institutions, businesses, and NGOs to raise awareness of genocide.

→ MEDIA 4 HUMANITY
www.mediaforhumanity.org
Media 4 Humanity is a group of media professionals and students combating child slavery.

→ NELSON MANDELA FOUNDATION
www.nelsonmandela.org
Dedicated to the values and vision of its founder, the Foundation promotes social justice by fostering global dialogue and creating strategic partnerships.

→ NOT ON OUR WATCH
www.notonourwatchproject.org
Drawing on the powerful voices of artists, activists, and cultural leaders, Not on Our Watch generates humanitarian assistance and protection for the vulnerable, marginalized, and displaced.

→ OPEN SOCIETY INSTITUTE
www.soros.org
The Open Society Institute aims to shape public policy to promote democratic governance, human rights, and economic, legal, and social reform.

→ POLARIS PROJECT
www.polarisproject.org
Polaris Project has been providing a comprehensive and community-based approach to combating human trafficking and modern-day slavery since 2002.

→ PROGRAM FOR TORTURE VICTIMS
www.ptvla.org
The Program for Torture Victims works to alleviate the suffering and health consequences of torture through psychological, medical, and social services to victims of state-sponsored violence.

→ RESPONSIBILITY TO PROTECT
www.responsibilitytoprotect.org
Responsibility to Protect promotes concrete policies to better enable governments, regional organizations, and the UN to protect vulnerable populations.

→ RFK MEMORIAL
www.rfkmemorial.org
Since 1968, the Memorial has worked to fulfill the legacy of RFK by promoting human rights around the world, developing programs that help the disadvantaged and build the next generation of leaders.

→ SAVE DARFUR COALITION
www.savedarfur.org
An alliance of more than 100 faith-based, humanitarian, and human rights organizations, the Save Darfur Coalition inspires action and raises awareness on behalf of the people of Darfur.

→ STAND—A STUDENT ANTI-GENOCIDE COALITION
www.standnow.org
A grassroots student organization with more than 700 chapters around the globe, STAND provides students with creative and effective national campaigns, resources, policy and advocacy training, and a network of informed and active peers.

→ SUDAN DIVESTMENT TASK FORCE
www.sudandivestment.org
Sudan Divestment Task Force provides support for individuals, governments, and asset managers with divesting from companies with problematic operations in Sudan.

→ SURVIVOR CORPS
www.survivorcorps.org
An organization dedicated to establishing international standards for survivor and disability rights around the world, improving health, economic opportunities, laws, and policies for survivors of war and conflict.

→ UNICEF
www.unicef.org
UNICEF provides long-term humanitarian and developmental assistance to children and mothers in developing countries.

→ UNITARIAN UNIVERSALIST SERVICE COMMITTEE
www.uusc.org
UUSC supports programs and policies that promote workers' rights and advance the human right to water.

→ UNITED NATIONS HUMAN RIGHTS WEBSITE
www.un.org/rights
The United Nations Human Rights website provides up-to-date information on international human-rights laws and issues. The site also features links to nongovernmental organizations dedicated to protecting human rights around the world.

→ UNIVERSAL DECLARATION OF HUMAN RIGHTS
www.udhr.org
The Universal Declaration of Human Rights sets forth the inalienable rights and fundamental freedoms of every person on earth as originally conceptualized by Eleanor Roosevelt.

→ WITNESS
www.witness.org
Witness uses video and other technology to fight for human rights by documenting abuse and collecting evidence.

→ WORLD ORGANIZATION AGAINST TORTURE
www.omct.org
World Organization is a coalition of international nongovernmental organizations fighting torture, executions, and enforced disappearances.

CIVIL LIBERTIES
LIFE, HAPPINESS, AND THE
CIVIL PURSUIT OF LIBERTY

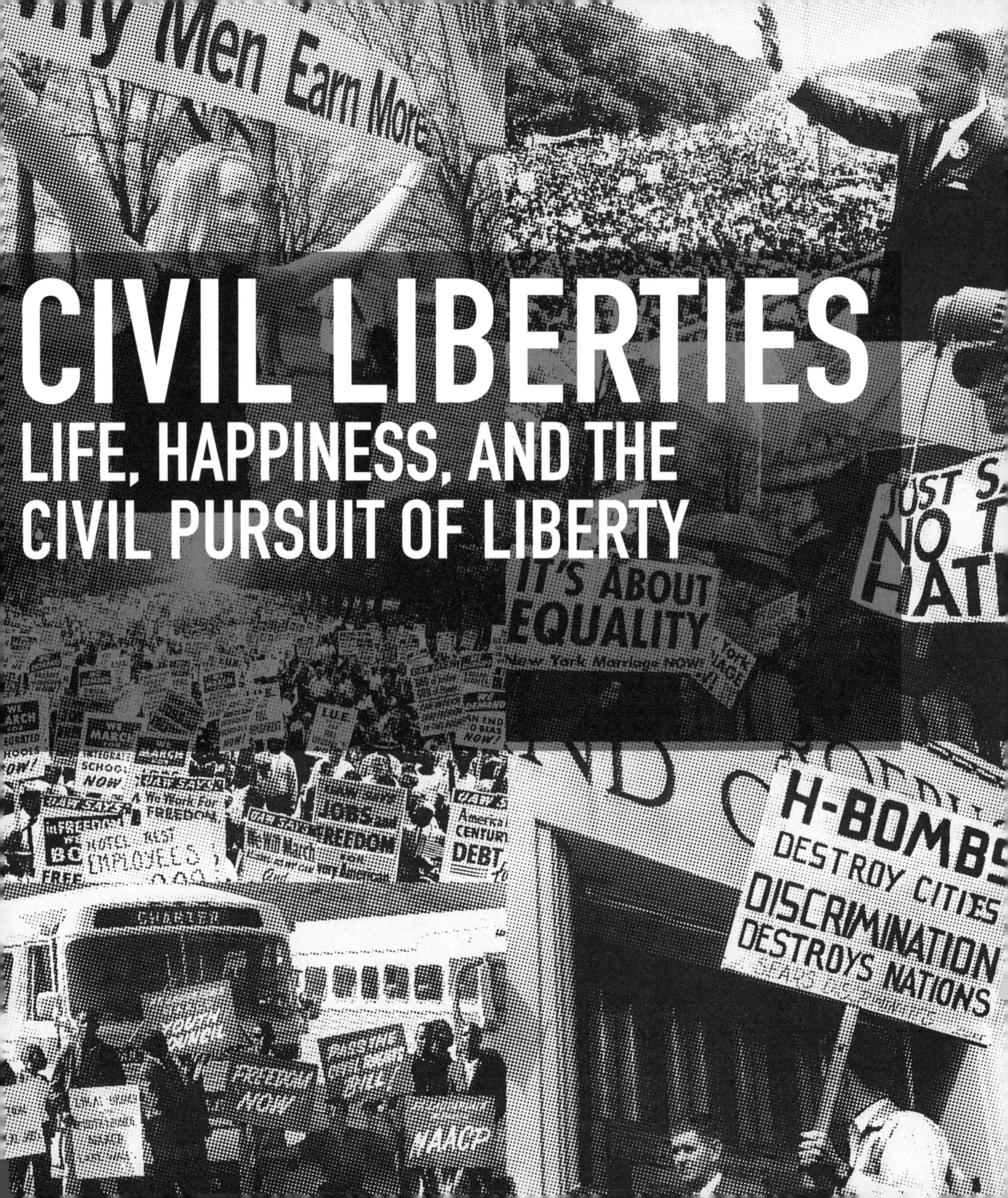

hy Men Earn More

JUST S
NO
HA

IT'S ABOUT
EQUALITY
New York Marriage NOW

H-BOMBS
DESTROY CITIES
DISCRIMINATION
DESTROYS NATIONS

In reading the essays that follow, one can't help but note how we, as a society, strive to treat all people with respect, dignity, and social equality (albeit often unsuccessfully). Whether marching on Washington, or simply marching to the beat of one's own drum, we have the right to both stand up for ourselves and advocate on behalf of others (which we are more inclined to do if the "others" agree with "us"). We have our expected messengers: our elected leaders, religious leaders, and well-known activists. Then we have the unexpected: those who inadvertently become leaders by delivering a message through their music, art, or even blog. These individuals, by showing courage to live life on their own terms, send a resounding message that empowers others to do the same. Most of the world believes in the same one God, even if they call Him by different names and worship Him at different times of the year and in different languages. He is generally a God of acceptance, of inclusion, and of peace. Yet most of our wars and global struggles are rooted in our inability to approach other individuals on those terms. ➜ **If humans are 99.8 percent the same at the genetic level, why do we insist on defining ourselves by the 0.02 percent that makes us different from one another? —Kenneth Cole**

MARTIN LUTHER KING III

On Community Building

Martin Luther King III

*The eldest son of Rev. Dr. Martin Luther King, Jr., is a human rights advocate and social activist. Martin Luther King III is the chairman and CEO of **Realizing the Dream**, an organization founded to continue the work of his parents to promote justice, equality, and nonviolent conflict resolution.*

➡ *realizingthedream.org*

Perhaps the most famous of all my father's speeches is the "I Have a Dream" speech that he delivered at the Lincoln Memorial in Washington D.C. I believe it's time to not just have the dreams, but to actually realize them. Dr. Martin Luther King, Jr., promoted the building of the "Beloved Community," where equality for all means that people have decent jobs with decent pay, the highest caliber education, affordable and quality health care, and equal treatment under the law. In 2006 I founded Realizing the Dream to continue my parents' legacy and work toward nonviolent social change. Our mission at Realizing the Dream focuses on conflict resolution, youth leadership training, and economic development.

If we had more people connected with housing issues, and more involved in addressing the drug and educational system crises in our nation, then we would see a dramatically changed America.

Nonviolence is at the very core of my father's vision of the "Beloved Community," and it is also the foundation for everything that we do at Realizing the Dream.

There are six steps of nonviolence that my father championed. In any conflict, regardless of the nature or size, the first step is Information Gathering. Thorough research is necessary before you can effectively address any conflict. The second step is Education. Both parties must be clearly educated and aware of the issues on both sides of the conflict. Third, both sides must make a Personal Commitment to being ready to work toward a resolution. The fourth step is Negotiation. Most conflicts that my dad and his team faced could be resolved within those first four steps. If the issues weren't resolved by then, he and his team went on to the fifth step, Direct Action, where you take specific action such as nonviolent civil disobedience to bring about a resolution to the conflict. The final step is Reconciliation. The goal is to peacefully bring the community back together so it can move forward from a position of unity and mutual respect.

Two other important principles that my father championed were service and love. A part of Realizing the Dream was most certainly inspired by the dedicated example of my mother, Mrs. Coretta Scott King. As a child, she took me to her undergraduate school, Antioch College. On the campus grounds is a statue of the educator Horace Mann, with a poignant quote beneath it that states: "Be ashamed to die until you've won a victory for humanity." That may sound grandiose, but you don't necessarily have to make a contribution to our world, our country, or to our city. Perhaps you can win a victory in your neighborhood, in your school, or in your church. I believe that civic engagement continues to be an effective form of direct action. Every year during the King holiday, people all over the country and the world engage in acts of service. The problem is that it may be only one act, on one day, once a year. I believe if we had a hundred million people engaged in acts of service year-round, if we had more people connected with housing issues, and more involved in addressing the drug and educational system crises in our nation, then we would see a dramatically changed America.

In 1956 my family's home was bombed in Montgomery, Alabama. In 1968 I lost my dad to an assassin's bullet. In 1974 an assassin killed my grandmother as she played the church organ. Yet I learned from my grandfather and my parents how to forgive and move forward without bitterness, because retaliation was not going to bring them back. My grandfather said to me, "The price of hatred is too great a burden to bear. I refuse to allow any man to reduce me to hatred—not the man that killed my lovely wife, nor the man that killed my son. I love every man. I'm every man's brother." He set a very powerful example by how he conducted himself. Nonviolence teaches us how to live on a higher level with higher standards. The nonviolent principles of service and love are the bricks and mortar that we need in order to build the "Beloved Community" and realize my father's dream.

1997
26%

2007
43%

FACT

→ A 1997 Gallup poll found 26% of Americans say all or most of the goals of Martin Luther King, Jr., and the 1960s civil rights movement have been achieved. In 2007, 43% of Americans believed it.

→ The National Office of the March on Washington for Jobs and Freedom articulated the six goals of the civil rights protest as: "meaningful civil rights laws, a massive federal works program, full and fair employment, decent housing, the right to vote, and adequate integrated education."

RUSSELL →SIMMONS

Russell Simmons

*As chairman of the **Foundation for Ethnic Understanding**, the entrepreneur, philanthropist, and activist Russell Simmons has worked to reduce bigotry and promote greater understanding between people of different religions and cultures through direct, face-to-face dialogue. His many philanthropic concerns also include **Rush Philanthropic Arts Foundation**, the **Diamond Empowerment Fund**, and the **Hip-Hop Summit Action Network**, among others. They all address, in some way, Simmons' dedication to fighting poverty and ignorance on the planet.*
➡ *ffeu.org; rushphilanthropic.org; diamondempowerment.org; hsan.org*

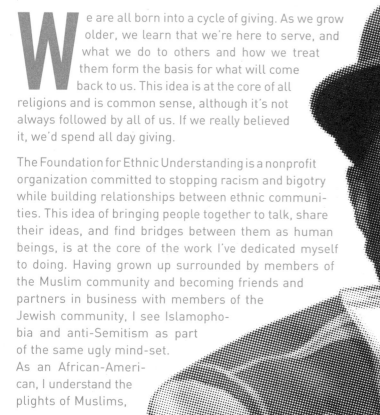

We are all born into a cycle of giving. As we grow older, we learn that we're here to serve, and what we do to others and how we treat them form the basis for what will come back to us. This idea is at the core of all religions and is common sense, although it's not always followed by all of us. If we really believed it, we'd spend all day giving.

The Foundation for Ethnic Understanding is a nonprofit organization committed to stopping racism and bigotry while building relationships between ethnic communities. This idea of bringing people together to talk, share their ideas, and find bridges between them as human beings, is at the core of the work I've dedicated myself to doing. Having grown up surrounded by members of the Muslim community and becoming friends and partners in business with members of the Jewish community, I see Islamophobia and anti-Semitism as part of the same ugly mind-set. As an African-American, I understand the plights of Muslims,

Jews, and other discriminated-against people, so I go to work for them. The quality of our freedom is a direct result of the freedom we create for others.

I don't know which person is considered better, the one who administers the drugs to heal people in Africa or the one who gives significant amounts of money to help buy the medication. The point is, it doesn't matter how much you do; what matters is that your intention is good and you find a way to serve. Ultimately, the only goal I have for my philanthropic work is the empowerment of people, spiritual empowerment, and raising consciousness in the world. Just ask yourself what resources you have, where you can make the greatest impact with what you've been given.

Ask yourself what resources you have, where you can make the greatest impact with what you've been given.

The organizations I've created or am involved with can always make good use of help. Rush Philanthropic Arts Foundation, the Diamond Empowerment Fund, the Foundation for Ethnic Understanding, the Hip-Hop Summit Action Network, the Happy Hearts Foundation—any of these places would welcome your support. For example, Rush Philanthropic funds roughly 80 programs that provide disadvantaged urban youth with exposure and access to the arts while providing exhibition opportunities for underrepresented artists and artists of color. If you're an artist, you could help teach these programs at the gallery we own. If you're a poet, you can help other poets. If you're a rapper, you can help with the Hip-Hop Summit Action Network. If you do community service, you can teach tolerance. Early in 2008 the Foundation for Ethnic Understanding filmed a TV commercial to condemn bigotry against Muslims and Jews and promote tolerance between the two. If you're a producer, you could have helped us produce it.

God gives everyone resources, and if we hold on to them instead of utilizing them, we're not living. We're stagnant. The less tightly we grasp, in general, the freer and less fearful we are, the better off we are. Whatever it is you possess, your talent or whatever you have to give, you have to learn to make it useful. That's what we all need to do.

FACT

➡ The Foundation for Ethnic Understanding was founded in 1989 by Rabbi Marc Schneier and the late Joseph Papp, head of the Public Theater. In 2007 the Foundation organized the first National Summit of Imams and Rabbis. Twenty-four religious leaders from 11 U.S. cities spent half a day in a synagogue and half a day at a mosque in an effort to foster a greater understanding between their faiths.

➡ In 1995 Rush Philanthropic Arts Foundation was founded by Russell Simmons and his brothers Danny and Joseph "Reverand Run" Simmons. The organization provides access to the arts and supports artists of color through the Rush Arts Gallery and Resource Center.

➡ The Hip-Hop Summit Action Network is the largest coalition of major figures in the hip-hop community. It uses the popularity of hip-hop culture and music to promote social change and address a range of issues that impact young people, including youth vote, financial literacy programs, and additional funding for public education.

MATISYAHU

On Music, Religion, and Charity

Matisyahu

*Orthodox Jewish reggae rapper Matisyahu challenges people to break boundaries and embrace the unconventional with his unique fusion of music and religion. He is currently launching his foundation **Something From Nothing** to encourage kids in the arts.*

➜ *matismusic.com*

Before I became religious, I remember playing some of my music for a record company. In one song, I made a reference to slavery, to which the A&R responded, "I guess that's cool...but who wants to hear a white Jewish kid rap about slavery?" He was ultimately right, especially if you look at Jews in the world today without having the historical perspective. But the truth is that Jews were the original people to break out of slavery, overthrowing the power in Egypt and leaving to start their own nation.

I've always been attracted to realness. So for me, it's never been a question as to whether or not I should deny myself and make my identity less extreme. As I've changed, so have my clothes, but none of it has been as a result of trying to conform. What was always important was to find my true identity and allow my music to stem from there. That's not to say I wasn't afraid to make different decisions, but because I believed in the music, I knew that people would embrace it. As it turned out, my differences worked to my advantage. Much of the initial press I received was based on having the surprise element of being a guy who looked a certain way, but then does this music. It's a classic example of "don't judge a book by its cover." The music was striking a chord with people and breaking down barriers.

In my religion, there's a law called *tzedakah* where you're supposed to give ten to twenty percent of the money you make to charity. And as I grew up, my parents, who are secular, taught me that doing something meaningful with our lives and dedicating our lives to helping in some way—whether by donating money or spending a day working with people—was the most important thing. The God thing is up for grabs, whether it's real or not real, but the true thing a person can do with their life is to help another person. The only way I could really do this *mitzvah* and feel good about it was to start my own program. My foundation Something From Nothing helps kids that have some talent, whether it's developed or not, and some inner spiritual turmoil to create their own music and arts. Using the connections I make in the arts industry, I am able to call on everyone from filmmakers to guitar players and drummers to help develop the artistic talents of these children.

To have the ability to really change the world and affect it in a positive way is such an amazing thing. I just hope my life is centered around that and centered around doing good things. There's another concept in Hebrew called *tikkum olam,* which literally means "fixing of the world." The world is cracked. God created the world with this essential rift, which exists in God, and the job of humans is to somehow fix it, fix the world, and, in a sense, fix God. The most that people can do is spiritual work. Don't be afraid to feel the madness, the insanity, the darkness of this world. Because it can be so overwhelming, people often distract themselves with their own lives. Before you write a check to some foundation, you have to open yourself up to knowing what's going on. From there, turn on the news and pay attention to what's happening, whether it's a fire somewhere or someone being killed, or fighting going on in Crown Heights between blacks and Jews. Whatever it is, see it, hear it, feel it, and act from there.

FACT

➡ In observance of the Jewish Sabbath, Matisyahu refrains from holding performances on Friday nights. Although it is commonly observed on Saturdays, the "day of rest" is observed from sunset on Friday until three stars appear in the sky the following night. On a certain, rare Friday evening in 2007, when he was on a tour in Fairbanks, Alaska, the sun did not set until 2 a.m. locally. Therefore, he was allowed to put on a show.

➡ Matisyahu has performed concerts that benefit the homeless, AIDS awareness, and the crisis in Darfur.

> I've always been attracted to realness. For me, it's never been a question as to whether or not I should deny myself and make my identity less extreme.

SONNY CABERWAL

On Being Sikh in America

Sonny Caberwal

Entrepreneur Sonny Caberwal is a practicing Sikh who grew up in a small town in North Carolina. He promotes acceptance of diversity on a daily basis, living by example and speaking out against racial stereotypes. He appeared in Kenneth Cole Productions' "We All Walk in Different Shoes" advertising campaign in the spring of 2008.
→ *kennethcole.com; sikhcoalition.org*

Being Sikh and an American plays a big role in my overall sense of identity. My external appearance not only represents my spiritual commitment as a Sikh and the proud history and traditions of my forefathers, it also provides me with a certain amount of resolve and strength. By consistently being an individual, I feel more confident and empowered to do what I believe, even if that's not the most popular decision. And, of course, the way I look makes me instantly identifiable and unique in nearly any social environment. However, that unique identity also makes me an obvious target for discrimination.

We've seen throughout the course of history—both in the United States and beyond—that hatred and ignorance create significant conflict, pain, and suffering. Yet even in the most accepting of societies such as ours, it persists rampantly. I've faced discrimination because of my turban, certainly—in many ways and to different degrees. Unfortunately, others who maintain the Sikh identity in the United States have faced even greater discrimination, which has led to violence, hate crimes, and even murder—all because of misconceived notions about what the turban represents. Often, discrimination doesn't even stem from ignorance—it comes from a desire to express control, and is practiced by those who feel disempowered. The only way to limit discrimination and make significant improvements in a world as diverse as ours is to work together to foster understanding and acceptance in an environment of tolerance.

There's a quote by Pastor Martin Niemoller I remember reading when I was a child, relating to the inaction of German intellectuals following the Nazi rise to power and systematic purges of various communities. He said:

> 66 *They came first for the Communists, and I didn't speak up because I wasn't a Communist.*
>
> *Then they came for the Jews, and I didn't speak up because I wasn't a Jew.*
>
> *Then they came for the trade unionists, and I didn't speak up because I wasn't a trade unionist.*
>
> *Then they came for the Catholics, and I didn't speak up because I was a Protestant.*
>
> *Then they came for me, and by that time no one was left to speak up.* 99

As unimaginable as it may seem, this is how I feel now—I need to speak up, because I am the one whose rights are disappearing. I'm amazed that so few people care—not because they should care about me, but out of self-interest that one day it could be them. Groups such as the Sikh Coalition make broad-based appeals to society with this principle in mind: We must help fight for justice and what's right. We've stood by and watched various groups—from Japanese-Americans to African-Americans to Sikh-Americans—lose rights that we all hold dear. If we don't all join together, one day it could be your rights and freedoms that are quietly swept away.

My participation in the Kenneth Cole campaign celebrating diversity has created immense interest both within the Sikh community and in the greater South Asian diaspora. The reactions have at times been overwhelming, with most people proud that their identity was chosen to be portrayed in a positive, nontraditional way. It is representative of the fact that Sikhs—and South Asians in general—feel underrepresented in mainstream media outside of very traditional stereotypes. Hundreds of people have reached out to me from all over the globe to share their pride and excitement and their stories of facing discrimination—it is quite an amazing honor and a very humbling experience.

One of my goals is to help change perceptions of Sikhs, and the campaign has, in no small way, helped make that possible. However, it will take much more effort and meaningful media exposure to truly create widespread understanding and acceptance of the Sikh identity. Even beyond the Sikh and South Asian community, I want to demonstrate to everyone who feels that they have great obstacles to overcome that anything is possible. Like much of life, a unique identity can either be an obstacle or a tool—it's simply what you make of it.

FACT

The FBI Hate Crime Report has documented more than 115,000 hate crimes since 1991. In 2006, 7,722 hate crimes were reported. Almost 52% were motivated by racial bias, 19% by religious bias, 15.5% by sexual orientation bias, and 12.7% by a national origin bias.

I need to speak up, because I am the one whose rights are disappearing.

JOANNA AND NICOLETTA TESSLER

On Being Ourselves

Joanna and Nicoletta Tessler

The Tesslers met in May 1997. In 2006 they formed a civil union in Vermont and a domestic partnership in New York. Joanna gave birth to their daughter, Ruthie, in May 2006. Nicoletta gave birth to their second daughter, Kate Stevie, in May 2008.

We have been fighting for gay rights simply by being ourselves and living our lives. We are defying the stereotypes, which so many people have accepted, of what it means to be gay. We are two hardworking professionals. We have been together for more than ten years in what many individuals tell us is the most loving and respectable relationship they know. We had a wedding with 175 guests. We have the same last name. We have two adorable daughters. By living example, we demonstrate that gay individuals cannot be pigeonholed, that the perceptions that society has of our population are often inaccurate.

We want everyone to see us as a family unit, two parents raising our delicious daughters. People ask, "Well, who is the real mommy?" And this often comes from people who are very accepting of us, or of gay individuals in general. Even though it can be hurtful, we have to remember that they are not always aware of how it may feel to us when they make these remarks. Our response is "We are both their mommies. There is no difference between us—we are both obsessed and in love with our girls."

We believe the best way to fight stereotypes is to show by example that they are inaccurate. Therefore, we stand every day as living proof that lesbian relationships are just as valid as heterosexual ones. Even more important, all successful relationships include the same ingredients—respect, love, compromise, and loyalty—and all can be difficult and trying at times.

As far as what others can do to fight for gay rights, what really matters is what you do on a daily basis. It is the small stuff that can make a real difference. People should be curious when they're with their friends who are gay, asking questions and enhancing their understanding of what has been inaccurately portrayed in our culture. A willingness to take risks and not conform or stay quiet out of fear is the single most important thing a person can do for the gay community. It's important to realize that because of the magnitude of diversity, our world has more depth and meaning. Generalizations have no place in our lives.

FACT

➡ According to a 2007 Urban Institute study, more than half of gay men and 41% of lesbians want to have a child.

➡ More than 1 in 3 lesbians have given birth.

➡ 1 in 6 gay men have fathered or adopted a child.

> **We stand every day as living proof that lesbian relationships are just as valid as heterosexual ones.**

ALAN CUMMING

On Demanding Equal Rights

Alan Cumming

Alan Cumming's tireless activism and charity work for civil rights and sex education causes have earned him several humanitarian awards. He has worked with GLAAD, the Human Rights Campaign, Bailey House, and the Creative Coalition, among others.
➡ *glaad.org; hrc.org; baileyhouse.org thecreativecoalition.org*

suppose I have always been outspoken about my sexuality, although I've never really seen it that way. I am outspoken about my rights to be the person I am and have the same protections as any other human being. We all have a tendency to focus on the sexuality part rather than the glaring injustices perpetrated against queer people. But it is about so much more than what we do with our genitals.

In the mid-'80s I joined the committee of an organization called CRUSAID, which helped raise money for people living with AIDS but also worked to change people's perceptions of the disease and how it is spread. It was the first public thing I did to ask for change in the way gay people are treated. But before that, in some of my work, particularly a stand-up show I did called "Victor and Barry," the material was pretty provocative, so maybe that was my first gay political stance.

There are great organizations—such as Empire State Pride Agenda, the Human Rights Campaign, GLAAD, the Hetrick-Martin Institute, and the Trevor Project—that work in different ways to help fight the prejudice we feel as queer people. I try to do as much as I can for them. I go to events, I speak out on their behalf, I send them things to auction off (including myself!), and I send cash. It is a great feeling to be able to reach an audience and change its members' minds, or at least challenge their thinking.

We should not sit back and accept the "all social change takes time" adage. Why the hell should it? It is time for change. People aren't fully cognizant of the lack of rights queer people have. If you were to replace gay with Jew or black and then tell everyone what rights and protections we are denied, there would be a revolution!

I think even a lot of queer people don't actually know how badly they are treated. We have to educate the straight world about what is going on, but we shouldn't take for granted that the LGBT community knows everything. The fight for gay rights is not just about the ability to get married. It is a civil rights struggle. It is about a section of society demanding to be treated justly.

Being a spokesperson is a job for life. I am doing it because of who I am. But anyone can get involved. Just start spreading the word. It doesn't cost anything to e-mail your friends about the equal rights struggle or something else you feel strongly about. Don't forget to give them a link to a website, so they can see for themselves and contribute in some way too. Getting the word out and educating people is the most important part of supporting any cause you believe in. Volunteering is fun. You meet great people, you make great friends, and you make a difference.

I think even a lot of queer people don't actually know how badly they are treated.

MAYOR GAVIN NEWSOM

On Challenging the Status Quo

Gavin Newsom

*As mayor of San Francisco, Gavin Newsom has built a reputation as an innovator on issues from homelessness to the environment, health care to education. In 2004 he took a bold step for equality in America by championing same-sex marriage. His groundbreaking initiatives also include **Project Homeless Connect**, which gathered 20,000 citizens to volunteer to assist the homeless. The program has since been adopted as a model by 160 cities.*

➡ *sfconnect.org*

Although not sanctioned by the state, four years ago I directed San Francisco's county clerk to issue marriage licenses to same-sex couples. Ensuring equality for all people is a significant part of my job as an elected official in America. So even though it was perceived as politically risky at that time, I had to challenge a status quo that was no longer viable. The right to marry the person one loves is a treasured and sacred one. To withhold it from same-sex couples is a blatant offense against the U.S. Constitution, which maintains that all people are equal and deserve equal treatment.

Marriage equality has become the major civil rights issue of our age. As with any movement, our effort has witnessed both high and low points. Recently, the California State Legislature embraced marriage equality only to have Governor Schwarzenegger veto the measure. Despite such setbacks, support for marriage rights has steadily grown. As I'm writing this, the California Supreme Court has affirmed that excluding gay couples from marriage violates the state constitution. The battle surrounding the issue will continue. It is, in many respects, begun anew. But make no mistake: It is a battle that we can win.

To ensure our success, we need to keep the issue in the public eye. There are three simple things anyone can do to help. The first is to become thoroughly educated about the details of marriage equality. The second is to share that knowledge with family, friends, and peers. The third is to seek out local and national organizations, such as Freedom to Marry, the Human Rights Campaign, and GLAAD, and lend your support by any means available. If enough people take these three vital steps, we will establish it as a fundamental right that same-sex couples can join in marriage.

A lack of time or money shouldn't prevent anyone from getting involved. There is truly no contribution too small when it comes to ensuring that every person in this country enjoys the same rights and protections. Simple and effective ways you can lend your support include setting up blogs, writing letters to editors of local and national newspapers, and discussing important issues with those around you.

I am continually inspired by the groundbreaking programs that are dedicated to the betterment of our society. A few years ago, I challenged city agencies to do something different for our community. That challenge culminated in the launch of SF Connect, a program that mobilizes residents to build a stronger San Francisco. SF Connect's volunteer-based subprograms have drawn on the individual strengths of its volunteers to address issues ranging from homelessness and the environment to technology and youth development. The character of these programs rests on the idea that partnership is essential to solving the problems we face. And they provide everyone with the opportunity to be a part of the solution.

We all have to take an active role in improving our community. Volunteering is a powerful illustration of civic pride and spirit.

> **There is truly no contribution too small when it comes to ensuring that every person in this country enjoys the same rights and protections.**

Every act of volunteerism is equally important and inspires others to act. The rewards derived from the selfless contribution of your time for the benefit of society are ones we ultimately all share. Volunteers display courage, perseverance, and a passion for helping others. Their actions represent the core of the sense of community that drives our society forward. The people, elected and not, who lend themselves to the task of creating a better society are constant sources of energy and inspiration to me in my role as the mayor of San Francisco.

FACT

→ The California Supreme Court struck down the state's ban on same-sex marriage in May 2008. The majority opinion stated that sexual orientation, like race or gender, "does not constitute a legitimate basis upon which to deny or withhold legal rights."

→ There are five countries where same-sex marriage is legal: Belgium, Canada, the Netherlands, South Africa, and Spain.

→ There are six countries where same-sex intercourse is punished by death: Saudi Arabia, Iran, Mauritania, Northern Nigeria, Sudan, and Yemen.

MARRIAGE EQUALITY AND CIVIL UNION RIGHTS

➡ In the past 40 years, public support for the lesbian, gay, bisexual, and transgender (LGBT) community has grown exponentially. One of the keys to the gay rights movement has been a steady buildup of success on local and state levels. This will hopefully lend itself to change on the federal level, where they have yet to pass a single piece of legislation prohibiting discrimination based on sexual orientation or gender identity. Twenty states and D.C. have laws protecting gays, as do the majority of Fortune 500 companies, many of which offer domestic-partner benefits. In 2008, California joined Massachusetts as the two states to issue marriage licenses to same-sex couples.

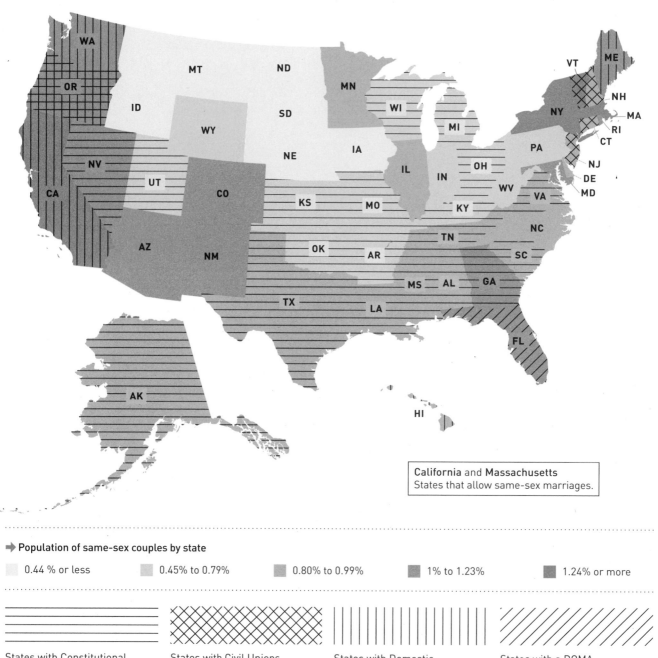

California and **Massachusetts**
States that allow same-sex marriages.

➡ Population of same-sex couples by state

| 0.44 % or less | 0.45% to 0.79% | 0.80% to 0.99% | 1% to 1.23% | 1.24% or more |

States with Constitutional Language Defining Marriage

States with Civil Unions

States with Domestic Partnerships

States with a DOMA Constitutional Amendment on the Ballot in 2008

JESSICA VALENTI ➡ On the Power of the Blog

Jessica Valenti

*Writer Jessica Valenti began the blog **Feministing.com** to fill a void in the mainstream women's movement. She is a co-founder of the **Real Hot 100**, a list that honors young women who are breaking barriers, fighting stereotypes, and making a difference in their communities, and the author of* Full Frontal Feminism *and* He's a Stud, She's a Slut...and 49 Other Double Standards Every Woman Should Know.

➡ *feministing.com; therealhot100.org*

The Real Hot 100 was created to push back against the idea that young American women are politically apathetic and shallow—all the things the mainstream media and celebrity culture promote. The young women we knew were active and committed, not this "Girls Gone Wild" stereotype. So we wanted to create something that would not only show off these amazing women but would also give them the kudos they deserve. What we learn from those in the Real Hot 100 is that change is possible anywhere—in your community, in your state, even in your home. It's just a matter of finding the place where you can make the most difference.

I started blogging because I didn't think younger women's voices were necessarily being heard in the mainstream feminist movement—we're given a lot of lip service but not a lot of decision-making positions. So I wanted to start a blog that would not only give younger women a forum to speak out but also show feminism for what it really is: not just political but fun, funny, and cutting-edge. With all the anti-feminist myths still out there, I thought it was important. Blogging gives any woman with something to say a platform—you no longer have to work for a feminist organization or be in a protest to make real feminist change. It is the grassroots activism of today.

Blogs have changed the way we do feminism—they allow people to become politically engaged on whatever level makes them comfortable. That can mean anything from reading a blog so it informs your life, contributing to the discourse, or taking online action. Our readers frequently write to legislators to speak out against sexist legislation, or to companies about their sexist products. And we get results! It's really a wonderful tool.

The most important thing young women and men can do to be involved and learn more about feminism is to become critical thinkers. Because once you see the world in a different way—through feminism, for example—activism just follows naturally.

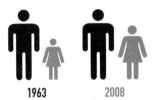

1963   2008

MEN VS. WOMEN: THE WAGE GAP

In 1963, when the U.S. government passed the Equal Pay Act, women were making 59 cents to every dollar that men were earning. Since 1982 women have outpaced men in earning bachelor's and master's degrees. Yet women still earn an average of only 77% of what men are paid, own fewer businesses, and are more likely to live in poverty.

WATCH THE GAP

MEN'S SALARY/ WOMEN'S SALARY

Median income
$40,668/$30,724 ➡ $9,944

Over the course of the average female high school graduate's lifetime?
➡ More than $700,000

...the average female college graduate's lifetime?
➡ More than $1.2 million

...the average post-secondary grad's lifetime?
➡ More than $2 million

Number of countries where women's wages are equal to men's ➡ 0

EVE ENSLER

On Atrocities Against Women

Eve Ensler

The award-winning playwright, performer, and activist Eve Ensler is the founder of V-Day, a global movement to end violence against women and girls.
➡ *vday.org*

W hen I started performing *The Vagina Monologues*, women would line up to talk to me. At first I thought I was going to hear fantastic tales about their wonderful sex lives, but instead, ninety-five percent of them were telling me that they'd been beaten or abused or been victims of incest. It was awful. I felt so irresponsible for not doing something about it.

So ten years ago I got together a group of activists in New York and said, "How can we use this play to end violence against women?" We came up with the idea of V-Day, which stands for Valentine's Day, Ending Violence Day, Victory Over Violence Day, and Vagina Day. Our first event was life-changing. Twenty-five-hundred people showed up, including some of the greatest performers in the world, from Whoopi Goldberg and Glenn Close to Susan Sarandon and Lily Tomlin. You could feel something shift politically and spiritually in the room that night. Since then, V-Day has spread to 120 countries and has raised $60 million. We are basically a decentralized grassroots movement in which people use the play, our tools, and our staff support to empower themselves and their communities to end violence against women and girls. The impact has been unbelievable. There's a growing community of women throughout the world who've broken taboos, shattered the silence, and changed laws. We've helped end violence in some places; opened safe houses in Kenya, Congo, Egypt, Haiti, India, and Native American lands; held summits in Kabul.

The longer I do this, the more I understand how fundamentally important it is to end violence against women. If women are made to feel they have no value, how will their children feel that they have value? How will their sons grow up to value their lovers and wives? I can tell a story about a girl in the Congo who at eight years old was taken by militias and raped for two weeks, her body made incontinent by fistula. This brilliant, beautiful girl is full of shame. And although hers is an extreme case, the same hopelessness is manifest in thousands and thousands of people's lives.

Many of the women I meet in my travels have suffered the worst atrocities imaginable, but rather than inflicting pain on others as retribution they devote their lives to making sure what happened to them doesn't happen to other people. So I'm not meeting just women who are "victims" or "survivors" but ones who have transformed their experiences and become some of the most powerful women in their communities—true leaders, or what we like to call "Vagina Warriors." I have seen how amazing and resilient people can be. It is a joyous privilege to be a part of this. I have always felt that one of the greatest things about living a life of volunteerism is not the praise you receive or the money you are able to raise for your cause but that ineffable feeling of nurturing your soul. It is a gift to serve. You heal yourself by giving what you need the most.

Every year I hope it will be the year I get put out of business, because I want violence against women and girls to end. I tell my staff at V-Day, "Hope this is your last year employed here; work hard so it is."

FACT

Not only do women make up more than half of the world's population, they also comprise the majority of people suffering from basic human rights abuses.

➡ In the United States, more than three women are murdered every day by their boyfriends or spouses, and approximately half of the female homeless population is fleeing domestic violence.

➡ In conflict, women make up 32 million of the world's 40 million displaced and are consistently victims of sexual violence by warring factions.

➡ Nearly 50% of all sexual assaults worldwide are against girls 15 years or younger.

ASHLEY JUDD → On Empowering Women

Ashley Judd

Well-known actor and activist Ashley Judd appeared on the cover of Ms. Magazine *in 2003 wearing a "This Is What a Feminist Looks Like" T-shirt. She has been deeply involved in a number of causes, including the* **Equal Rights Amendment Campaign** *and* **Population Services International***, and has traveled throughout Africa and Asia on behalf of* **Youth AIDS***.*

➜ *eracampaign.net; psi.org; youthaids.org*

I was radicalized as a child. I found any kind of poverty emotionally corrupting and devastating. I believe that gender inequality is the root of chronic poverty. In many areas of developing nations, women don't have enough status to get an education or own property. We must legally, economically, and sexually empower girls and women with lasting solutions to the problem of poverty. Statistically, each year a girl stays in school delays the birth of her first child by one year, and a girl who stays in school will have fewer children overall. Plus, she'll have the education and skills to earn money.

I became involved with Population Services International (PSI), a nonprofit that utilizes the private sector to help low-income groups in the developing world, when U2's Bono and PSI's Youth AIDS director Kate Roberts called me in the same week, asking me to educate myself about HIV/AIDS and advocate on behalf of the poor and vulnerable. The two calls seemed coincidence, but I believe in a power greater than myself and took them as a sign that I should look out into the wider world. My goal is to sit with people at different levels and hear their stories, and to help them get access to medically accurate sex education; prevention and treatment for malaria, TB, and pneumonia; clean water; and micronutrients.

> **Statistically, each year a girl stays in school delays the birth of her first child by one year.**

HUMAN TRAFFICKING

In 2008 Ashley Judd addressed the UN about human trafficking, an issue that came to her attention while on a 12-nation tour to promote public health.

➡ The UN estimates that 2.5 million people worldwide, most of them women and children, are believed to have been victims of a $32 billion human trafficking industry.

➡ According to the U.S. State Department's 2005 report, 600,000 to 800,000 people are trafficked across international borders each year, with 14,500 to 17,500 trafficked into the United States.

EY JUDD

We need to delay the sexual debut of young girls, and educate them about being tested for HIV/AIDS, assuring them that the process is discreet and confidential. We can also micro-finance. For instance, when I loan a poor woman five, seven, or ten dollars, she can start a small business in her home while she takes care of her kids. The loan could allow her to buy an iron, or ingredients for baking, to generate income so she doesn't have to prostitute herself. The success rates are wonderful, and the repayment rate is almost 100 percent.

There is such a backlash against women, even in our own culture, with the sexualizing of our children, the fact that talking about reproductive health is shrouded in stigma and shame. There will be liberation for everyone when we get to be on equal footing.

We need to delay the sexual debut of young girls, and educate them about being tested for HIV/AIDS, assuring them that the process is discreet and confidential.

HOW TO... SOME TIPS ON CIVIL LIBERTIES

TIME

Break a gender rule. Society says men should behave one way and women another. By subverting a basic gender stereotype, like starting your own business if you're female or deciding to be a stay-at-home dad if you're male, you are contributing to the creation of a more open-minded society in which it will be harder to discriminate against different lifestyle choices.

Notify the authorities. Act when you witness any abuses of women or girls. Victims may not contact the police themselves when they're victimized, for various reasons, but change will only happen with awareness.

Work in your community to help pass domestic-partnership laws. For example, ask your city council to enact a law to create a domestic-partnership registry or lobby businesses to provide domestic-partnership benefits.

Take part in a pride parade. Marches celebrating your culture, ethnicity, or religion help spread awareness and appreciation of diversity.

Make a pilgrimage. The concept of a pilgrimage is a part of many religions. Travel to such holy sites as Buddha's birthplace at Kapilavastu, the Holy Land in Israel, or the Vayalur Murugan Temple. Be mindful of moving at a slower pace than usual to gain as much new perspective as possible.

ITEMS

Donate your old cell phones to battered-women's shelters and cell-phone banks. It's estimated that there are 45 million unused phones sitting around. The phones can be programmed to make only calls to 911 and given away free to those who need them.

Unload your time share. Owners who feel trapped by the annual committment of a time share can donate them through a nonprofit such as Donate for a Cause (www.donateforacause.org). Each donation goes toward supporting worthy organizations like The Network Against Sexual & Domestic Abuse.

Print out copies of Martin Luther King, Jr.'s speeches. Read them (a few can also be downloaded), pass on to your friends and colleagues, and discuss. Include "I Have a Dream" and "Letter From a Birmingham Jail" from MLK Online (www.mlkonline.org).

Share your space. If you have extra room in your office, invite fledgling, civil liberties–based nonprofits that can't afford full rent to share yours. Even if your goals are not the same, it's common now for organizations to band together for the sake of efficiency and overhead savings. Arrangements like this may even result in creative solutions to staffing, fund-raising, and idea-building.

EXPERTISE

Collect and share stories of discrimination. Statistics and facts can take away from the true, compelling nature of a story told by or about a person who's suffering from discrimination. Sometimes policy makers, bureaucrats, and members of the media don't really understand a problem until they hear about an actual situation.

Plan a show of works by local minority artists. It will inspire your community and give visibility to the artists. Ask artists for help in finding a venue for the event and in planning it. Publicize it in local papers and websites. You can showcase various types of art, including paintings, drawings, photography, sculpture, prints, film, spoken word, and more.

Become a mentor for your local gay-youth community. Studies have revealed that gay teenagers are nearly four times as likely to attempt suicide as their heterosexual counterparts. Providing a positive role model for these at-risk youth will give them somewhere to turn when they face confusion and hardships as they grow up.

Share elements of your culture. Participate at your local schools during their cultural awareness days. Whether it's creating a plate of ethnic food or performing a folk dance, giving a glimpse of a different culture will teach more young students about diversity.

DOLLARS

Adopt a highway. Most states have programs through their departments of transportation that offer the chance to adopt a highway and help with its upkeep. Not only will it give your issue more everyday visibility, it will also validate your group's pride and investment in your community.

Support media. Promote culturally diverse programming, such as your local Public Broadcasting Station or National Public Radio. Very few national outlets are able to create in-depth, on-air TV programs or radio shows that go well beyond the mainstream. Give money or shop for related merchandise online at www.pbs.org and www.npr.org.

Sponsor the Wikimedia Foundation (www.wikimediafoundation.org). A nonprofit group that operates some of the largest collectively edited reference projects in the world. Your money goes to expand websites like Wikipedia that distribute invaluable, open-source content free of charge with multilingual content.

Donate while you shop online. By shopping through charitable websites such as iGive (www.iGive.com) or For Our Cause (www.4ourcause.com), you can help generate money for the women's or gay rights organization of your choice.

WHERE TO... SOME PLACES ON CIVIL LIBERTIES

→ **ADVANCEMENT PROJECT**
www.advancementproject.org
A policy, communications, and legal action group committed to racial justice, founded by a team of civil rights lawyers.

→ **AMNESTY INTERNATIONAL USA**
www.amnestyusa.org
A Nobel Prize–winning grassroots organization with more than 1.8 million members, Amnesty International works to end human- rights abuses, including violence against women.

→ **ANTI-DEFAMATION LEAGUE**
www.adl.org
Fights to end anti-Semitism and bigotry.

→ **ASIAN AMERICAN JUSTICE CENTER**
www.advancingequality.org
The Asian American Justice Center works to advance the human and civil rights of Asian-Americans through advocacy, public policy, public education, and litigation.

→ **ASIAN AMERICAN LEGAL DEFENSE FUND**
www.aaldef.org
AALDEF combines litigation, advocacy, education, and organizing to protect and promote the civil rights of Asian-Americans.

→ **ASTRAEA LESBIAN FOUNDATION FOR JUSTICE**
www.astraea.org
Astraea is an international foundation that provides critically needed financial support to lesbian-led, trans, LGBTI, and progressive organizations.

→ **BEYONDMEDIA EDUCATION**
www.beyondmedia.org
Beyondmedia Education aims to secure media tools and information equipment for women and youth to help them document and communicate their stories and influence public policy.

→ **BREAK THE CYCLE**
www.breakthecycle.org
Break the Cycle works to engage, educate, and empower youth to build lives and communities free from domestic violence.

→ **CENTER FOR REPRODUCTIVE RIGHTS**
www.reproductiverights.org
The Center for Reproductive Rights is a nonprofit, legal advocacy organization that promotes and defends the reproductive rights of women worldwide.

→ **CONGRESS OF RACIAL EQUALITY**
www.core-online.org
Founded in 1942, CORE is the third oldest and one of the "Big Four" civil rights groups in the United States. CORE is a champion of true equality for all people and a pioneer of the civil rights movement.

→ **EMPIRE STATE PRIDE AGENDA**
www.prideagenda.org
Empire State Pride is a New York–based educational and political advocacy organization working toward equality and justice for lesbian, gay, bisexual, and transgendered people.

→ **EQUAL RIGHTS AMENDMENT CAMPAIGN**
www.eracampaign.net
The ERA Campaign works to include a guarantee of equal rights on the basis of sex within the United States Constitution.

→ **EQUAL RIGHTS CENTER**
www.equalrightscenter.org
The Equal Rights Center engages in civil rights education, outreach, and advocacy for all legally protected groups in relation to all aspects of fair housing, fair employment, and equal access to public accommodations and services.

→ **FAIR FUND**
www.fairfund.org
FAIR Fund works internationally to engage youth, especially young women, in civil society in prevention of human trafficking, domestic violence, and sexual assault.

→ **FEMINIST MAJORITY FOUNDATION**
www.feminist.org
The Feminist Majority Foundation works for social, political, and economic equality for women through research and education.

→ **FEMINISTING**
www.feministing.com
Feministing provides a platform for young women to speak on their own behalf on issues that affect their lives and futures.

→ **FOUNDATION FOR ETHNIC UNDERSTANDING**
www.ffeu.org
The Foundation for Ethnic Understanding is a nonprofit dedicated to strengthening relations between ethnic communities through direct, face-to-face dialogue.

→ **FREEDOM TO MARRY**
www.freedomtomarry.org
Freedom to marry is a gay and non-gay partnership working to win marriage equality nationwide through litigation, legislation, direct action, and public education.

→ **FUTURE LEADERS OF AMERICA**
www.latinoleaders.org
Future Leaders of America provides leadership training and educational experiences to promote the personal development of Latino youth.

→ **GLAAD**
www.glaad.org
GLAAD is dedicated to promoting fair, accurate, and inclusive representation of people and events in the media as a means of eliminating homophobia and discrimination.

→ **GREENLINING INSTITUTE**
www.greenlining.org
Greenlining is a multi-ethnic advocacy, research, leadership development, and public policy organization whose ultimate goal is to increase the role that low-income and minority people play in the civic arena.

→ **HETRICK-MARTIN INSTITUTE**
www.hmi.org
The Hetrick-Martin Institute is a New York City–based nonprofit organization serving the needs of LGBTQ youth and a leading professional provider of social support and programming for at-risk youth.

➡ HUMAN RIGHTS CAMPAIGN
www.hrc.org
The Human Rights Campaign works for lesbian, gay, bisexual, and transgender equal rights by lobbying the federal government, mobilizing grassroots supporters, educating Americans, investing strategically, and partnering with other LGBT organizations.

➡ HUMAN RIGHTS WATCH
www.hrw.org
Human Rights Watch protects human rights around the world by investigating and exposing violations.

➡ LEADERSHIP CONFERENCE ON CIVIL RIGHTS
www.civilrights.org
The Leadership Conference on Civil Rights is the nation's premier civil rights coalition, and has coordinated the national legislative campaign on behalf of every major civil rights law since 1957.

➡ LEGAL MOMENTUM, ADVANCING WOMEN'S RIGHTS
www.legalmomentum.org
The oldest legal-advocacy organization in the United States, Legal Momentum is dedicated to advancing the rights of women and girls.

➡ MADRE
www.madre.org
Madre works with women who are affected by violence and to change the conditions that give rise to human rights abuses.

➡ MAGIC JOHNSON FOUNDATION
www.magicjohnson.com
The Magic Johnson Foundation works to develop programs and support community-based organizations that address the educational, health, and social needs of ethnically diverse urban communities.

➡ NAACP
www.naacp.org
The NAACP works to ensure the political, educational, social, and economic equality of rights of all persons and to eliminate racial hatred and racial discrimination.

➡ NARAL
www.naral.org
A leading advocate for privacy and a woman's right to choose, with more than one million members.

➡ NATIONAL CENTER FOR LESBIAN RIGHTS
www.nclrights.org
An organization committed to advancing the rights and safety of lesbians through litigation, public policy advocacy, free legal advice, and counseling.

➡ NATIONAL GAY AND LESBIAN TASK FORCE
www.thetaskforce.org
The National Gay and Lesbian Task Force was the first national LGBT rights organization and works to build the grassroots power of the LGBT community.

➡ NATIONAL WOMEN'S LAW CENTER
www.nwlc.org
Since 1972, the Center has expanded the possibilities for women and girls through litigating groundbreaking cases and educating the public about ways to make the law and public policies work for women and their families.

➡ NOW
www.now.org
NOW has been taking action for women's equality since 1966, and provides information on reproductive rights, violence against women, and economic justice—among other topics.

➡ OUT AND EQUAL
www.outandequal.org
A national organization devoted to the lesbian, gay, bisexual, and transgendered community in the workplace.

➡ PLANNED PARENTHOOD
www.plannedparenthood.org
Planned Parenthood Federation of America is the nation's leading women's health care provider, educator, and advocate, serving women, men, teens, and families.

➡ THE REAL HOT 100
www.therealhot100.org
Annual list of young women from around the country doing incredible things in their everyday lives to dispel the notion that all young women have to offer is their outward appearance.

➡ REALIZING THE DREAM
www.realizingthedream.org
Realizing the Dream promotes justice, equality, and community through economic development, nonviolence and conflict-resolution training, and youth-leadership development.

➡ SERVICE MEMBERS LEGAL DEFENSE NETWORK
www.sldn.org
Service Members Legal Defense Network provides nonprofit legal, watchdog, and policy services for military personnel affected by the "Don't Ask, Don't Tell" policy.

➡ SIKH COALITION
www.sikhcoalition.org
The Sikh Coalition works to safeguard the civil and human rights of all citizens as well as promote the Sikh identity.

➡ THIRD WAVE FOUNDATION
www.thirdwavefoundation.org
Third Wave works nationally to support women and transgendered people through grant-making, leadership development, and philanthropic advocacy to achieve economic and social justice.

➡ TREVOR PROJECT
www.thetrevorproject.org
The Trevor Project operates the only national, 24-hour suicide-prevention help-line for gay and questioning youth.

➡ U.S. COMMISSION ON CIVIL RIGHTS
www.usccr.gov
The U.S. Commission on Civil Rights investigates complaints alleging that citizens are being deprived of their right to vote by reason of their race, color, religion, sex, age, disability, or national origin.

➡ V-DAY
www.vday.org
V-Day encourages a global movement to end violence against girls and women through public performances, education, and networking.

HOMELESSNESS
+ POVERTY
"CHANGE PLEASE" [CAN YOU SPARE IT?]

When my kids were young our family lived in New York City. One day I was walking down Columbus Avenue with my three-year-old daughter and we passed a homeless man with a small cardboard sign. I asked Emily if she thought we should help him. She replied, "I don't know, should we?" Her question pointed out two issues. One being that everything we do or say (or don't do or say) teaches a lesson to our children. Secondly, her desensitization to that man's plight was unsettlingly normal, an accepted means of survival when living comfortably among fellow human beings who are clearly struggling. Even as adults, poverty and homelessness aren't easy problems to fully understand, let alone fix. My wife, Maria, who is chair of HELP USA, explains that homelessness is not so much one of society's most critical problems as it is a symptom of them. Often it is the result of deep-rooted, though treatable, realities such as mental illness, substance abuse, and the lack of sufficient assistance programs. Believe it or not, the largest segment of the homeless population is children and their single mothers who can't afford the childcare that would allow them to work. → **We promote prosperity and well-being in this country, but are we really doing all we can to stop the proliferation of cardboard signs? — Kenneth Cole**

JON BON JOVI
MARIA CUOMO COLE

On Rethinking Homelessness in America

Jon Bon Jovi

Musician, father, philanthropist, and professional sports team owner Jon Bon Jovi is a motivating force on the issue of affordable housing and poverty in America. His partnerships with Project HOME, HELP USA, Habitat for Humanity, and Kenneth Cole Productions have helped create new homes for low-income families from Louisiana to Pennsylvania. As co-owner of the Philadelphia Soul Arena Football team, Bon Jovi introduced a new type of philanthropy, making it the team's mission to make a difference in their community.

➜ *projecthome.com; habitat.org; philadelphiasoul.com*

Maria Cuomo Cole

Maria Cuomo Cole is the chairperson of HELP USA, the nation's largest nonprofit builder, developer, and operator of permanent and transitional housing with on-site services for the homeless. Founded in New York by her brother Andrew Cuomo in 1986, the organization under her leadership has grown nationally, providing services in job training, domestic violence, and affordable housing.

➜ *helpusa.org*

MCC: Jon, you have used your celebrity and resources to benefit others throughout your career. What inspired you to address the complex issues of poverty and homelessness?

JBJ: It's a timeless, classic problem. It was just realizing that this was something that can affect anyone at any time, from all walks of life. Urban blight is something that you can keep turning your head away from and eventually the structure that was lower- to middle-class neighborhoods is not going to survive. The sad part is that first it is going to crumble. That doesn't mean that there still is not pride in those who are living in these circumstances. So I have begun my education on the issue, and for the last five years, I think we have begun to make a difference.

> **Having the opportunity to give back in a meaningful way is the greatest thing I can share with anyone. —JBJ**

As an owner of the Philadelphia Soul Arena Football team, the way to differentiate ourselves from what we would consider the big four—baseball, basketball, football, and hockey—was to be very involved in the community. So from day one, before we sold a ticket, before we played a down, we took the first $100,000 we had and found four worthwhile charities. In time we focused our efforts on the homeless issue and were introduced to Sister Mary Scullion, who works with Project HOME. They deal in every aspect of homelessness, from helping people with mental illness and alcohol problems to getting them legal and medical advice, but what excited me most of all was their job training and service providing. It was the old adage of giving a man a fish or teaching him how to fish. I liked the idea and the concept very much, and asked how the Soul Foundation could make a difference. Sister Mary said, "It would be great if after so many years, you guys could contribute enough to build a house here on this street." My focus wasn't one home; it was on bringing back the whole block. With the help of local and state government, private donations, and our donations, both personally and from our foundation, we were able to succeed. Since then, we have provided twenty-one families in Philadelphia with a place to call home and more recently have begun a major renovation on an adjacent homeless shelter in the neighborhood for veterans. We now plan to use that as the model going forward to bring what we've done to other organizations such as HELP USA.

MCC: We agree that the most effective way to revitalize communities is by bringing the investment of private and public sectors together to create needed housing and services. How have your fans and the communities you have contributed to responded?

JBJ: Having the opportunity to give back in a meaningful way is the greatest thing I can share with anyone. It doesn't need to be measured in dollars to have meaning. Volunteering in your community for a cause that moves you has true lasting meaning and is more rewarding than just about anything you can do. And then, when you meet someone like Sister Mary or yourself, Maria, with all you and your family have done with HELP USA, it's inspiring.

MCC: By your example and reminding us all that "Volunteerism is hip," hopefully more people will become aware of these issues and try to get personally involved. There are so many ways for children and adults to help in their own communities by organizing supply and clothing drives for local shelters or giving personal time by hosting a recreational activity, serving meals, and sharing special skills.

JBJ: In this day and age of technology and the Internet, you can find little pieces of the puzzle that help to make the piece a whole. If you don't have the time to go down to Louisiana, for example, to help on a build, you could do something as simple as locating a grassroots organization, like the Angel Network, which is Oprah's charitable arm, that you can help. If you wanted to just donate the placemats for one of the twenty-eight houses that we built, that truly would make a difference and be appreciated.

MCC: With our country's wealth, technology, and resources, it seems unfathomable that the number of sheltered and unsheltered homeless in urban and rural areas across the country is increasing. We know that in addition to contributing factors such as mental illness, chronic substance abuse, and domestic violence, lack of employment and livable income are the major causes of this growing population. We need more than bricks and mortar to address these issues.

> It's not a disease. This is something that we, the collective we, can really take hold of and make a difference. —JBJ

JBJ: I agree. This isn't anything other than a social issue. It's not a disease. This is something that we, the collective we, can really take hold of and make a difference. I don't have to be a scientist or pray for that scientist to develop the cure. The cure is here—it is in our education, money, effort, and desire. We can help educate. We can help build. All it takes is that power of We...

SOUL
CHARITABLE
FOUNDATION

CHRIS GARDNER

→ **On Giving + Getting Second Chances**

Chris Gardner

Chris Gardner's struggle to overcome homelessness was the subject of the 2006 film The Pursuit of Happyness, *based on his memoir by the same name. Now the owner and CEO of **Christopher Gardner International Holdings** and a highly successful stockbroker and entrepreneur, he is also a committed philanthropist and speaker, working with a number of organizations to help the homeless, including **Glide Memorial Church** and **CARA**, among others.*

→ *glide.org; thecaraprogram.org.*

I am living proof that a few small decisions, mixed with some bad luck and bad timing, can mean the difference between having a home to sleep in at night and being homeless. In the early 1980s I was a single parent caring for my son, Chris, Jr., in San Francisco. I was employed, working hard, and doing all I could to care for my child, but like so many people I slipped through the cracks. We lost our rental apartment and my son and I had no choice but to sleep in the park or sometimes a locked public bathroom. Then I learned about Glide Memorial Church and Reverend Cecil Williams, who runs its shelter, kitchen, health-care services, job training center, and other resources for the poor and disenfranchised. He saved our lives. I know for sure there wouldn't be a Chris Gardner today if there wasn't a Reverend Williams back then. Glide is truly an oasis in a desert of hopelessness, a place where old, destructive ways are thrown out and new ones created. They serve over a million meals a year and provide the services that get people back on their feet.

I live in Chicago now, where I work with the CARA program, which assists the homeless and at-risk populations with comprehensive job training and placement. I believe in CARA's philosophy of second chances and helping people who are trying to help themselves by giving them the necessary tools and skills. In fact, one of my most trusted employees is a graduate of CARA.

I never could have imagined that telling my story in the book and movie *The Pursuit of Happyness* would help others. I am humbled that people all over the world write to tell me that I've given them hope. And I'm proud to have put a face on homelessness—and it's not the face of a drug addict or a convict. It's the face of a workingman who lost everything except the will to survive, succeed, and make a better life for his children. It is estimated that twelve percent of the homeless population in the United States is employed; in some communities that estimate is as high as 30 percent. There is often a fine line between getting by and not having anything.

While it's important to make donations to reputable organizations like Glide, CARA, and others I support such as HELP USA, Covenant House, and Common Ground, I try to give my time and reach out to others so they become involved too. I do everything from speaking at events for Glide, attending counseling sessions, and donating clothes and shoes. A little goes a long way with people who have nothing. When I'm traveling, I try to see if I can make contact with a local church or shelter. I know that sometimes just shaking a man's hand or hugging a child, telling them that they will make it, is the push they need to get through the day. It doesn't cost a dime or take any time to acknowledge them and make them feel human. I try to give back however I can, because I was fortunate enough to receive help when I desperately needed it.

> **I'm proud to have put a face on homelessness—and it's not the face of a drug addict or a convict.**

FACT

Today Chris Gardner is involved with homelessness initiatives assisting families to stay intact, and assisting homeless men and women who are employed but still can't get by. He helped fund a $50 million project that created low-income housing and opportunities for employment in the notoriously poor Tenderloin area of San Francisco, where he was once homeless.

GEORGE McDONALD

On Providing Opportunity

George McDonald

*Former business executive George McDonald launched the not-for-profit **Doe Fund** in 1985 to help address New York City's rapidly escalating homeless crisis. The **Doe Fund**'s award-winning **Ready, Willing & Able (RWA)** program empowers homeless and formerly incarcerated individuals to become self-sufficient and independent by offering housing in conjunction with paid work opportunities, job skills training, and counseling.*

➡ *doe.org*

There wasn't a single event that made me say, "I'm going to help the homeless," but rather a confluence of events over time. I attended Catholic school as a boy, and the nuns taught me that "other people's miseries are your miseries." Later in life, I entered the business world—seizing opportunities and working hard. But there were others for whom a productive and responsible life didn't seem possible. I would walk out of $200 business lunches and have to step over people lying on the street.

The combination of my upbringing and what I was seeing on the streets prompted me to begin giving out sandwiches to homeless people in Grand Central Terminal, and I fed them for 700 nights in a row. A refrain began to emerge from my conversations with these men and women that flew in the face of conventional perceptions. They appreciated the sandwich, but what they really wanted was "a room and a job to pay for it." They weren't asking for a handout, they were asking for a hand up, an opportunity to build better lives.

Then, on Christmas Eve in 1985, one of the women I had befriended in Grand Central froze to death after being forcibly ejected from the terminal. She was known only as "Mama"—Mama Doe—and it was from her death that the Doe Fund was born.

The concept behind our Ready, Willing & Able program is quite simple:

> They weren't asking for a hand*out*, they were asking for a hand *up*, an opportunity to build better lives.

Work works. It works to break the cycles of homelessness, substance abuse, and incarceration. My wife and partner, Harriet Karr-McDonald, and I recruited the first participants for RWA right from the floor of Grand Central. In 1991 we won a contract to put them to work renovating city-owned low-income housing and a separate contract to purchase and renovate a building for them to live in. Over the years we have grown tremendously, and because we are social entrepreneurs, we have not depended on donations or on government alone to do so. We offer paid transitional work, coupled with social services, counseling, adult-educational opportunities, vocational training, job placement, and career services. RWA focuses on the root causes of homelessness and criminal recidivism, offering people a real opportunity to get back on their feet—and so far, more than 3,300 men and women have seized that opportunity, graduating from RWA into permanent employment, self-supported apartments, and lasting sobriety.

The first thing any New Yorker can do for RWA is to take notice. Look at the "men in blue" of RWA and say "hello" or "good job," because they need encouragement just like everyone else. Donations, of course, are always important, and we have many volunteer opportunities. One of the most popular is our Mock Interview evenings, which allow business professionals to help our trainees practice for the interviews they must go on to secure those all-important first jobs. RWA is about the fulfillment of dreams. Nazerine Griffin, the program director at our Harlem Center for Opportunity, is the fulfillment of one of my personal dreams. He is the first man to have "pushed the bucket," graduated from the program, and become a top executive at the Doe Fund. Now he helps other men make their way toward their own dreams.

This cause is my life's work. I started the Doe Fund because I couldn't stand to see human lives being wasted. The greatest love you can show someone is to *expect* something of them. And that's the only way the cycles of homelessness, dependency, and incarceration will ever be broken.

DOE FUND VENTURES

Social entrepreneurship is at the heart of the Doe Fund. The organization has opened several businesses to get graduates of their programs better-paying jobs and to generate additional revenue for RWA.

➡ Their latest venture, RWA Resource Recovery, was launched in December 2006. Resource Recovery collects waste cooking oil from New York City restaurants free of charge and sells it to convert into biodiesel fuel. They have gone from collecting less than 3,000 gallons to more than 35,000 in May 2008 alone. And trainees participating are given the opportunity to earn a commercial driver's license.

THE NEED FOR AFFORDABLE HOUSING

➡ An estimated 13% of the homeless are working. For many Americans, having a job isn't enough to escape poverty. According to a 2008 report by the National Low Income Housing Coalition, affordable housing for many low-income families remains out of reach. The average minimum-wage employee needs to work more than 100 hours per week to afford a two-bedroom, fair-market apartment in fifteen states.

4 jobs
160hrs/wk
Hawaii

3.4 jobs
136hrs/wk
Maryland

3.2 jobs
128hrs/wk
New York

3.1 jobs
124hrs/wk
New Jersey,
Virginia

3 jobs
120hrs/wk
California,
New Hampshire

2.9 jobs
116hrs/wk
Massachusetts,
Nevada

2.8 jobs
112hrs/wk
Connecticut

2.7 jobs
108hrs/wk
Florida,
Rhode Island

2.6 jobs
104hrs/wk
Alaska, Texas

2.5 jobs
100hrs/wk
Louisiana

2.4 jobs
96hrs/wk
Georgia,
Minnesota

2.3 jobs
92hrs/wk
Arizona, Colorado,
Delaware, Utah

2.2 jobs
88hrs/wk
Illinois, Indiana,
South Carolina

2.1 jobs
84hrs/wk
Idaho, Kansas, Maine,
Nebraska, North
Carolina, Tennessee,
Vermont, Wisconsin

2 jobs
80hrs/wk
Alabama, Kentucky,
Michigan, Mississippi,
Oklahoma, Pennsylvania,
Washington, Wyoming

1.9 jobs
76hrs/wk
Missouri, Montana,
New Mexico, Ohio,
South Dakota

1.8 jobs
72hrs/wk
Arkansas,
North Dakota

1.7 jobs
68hrs/wk
Oregon,
West Virginia

1.6 jobs
64hrs/wk
Iowa

➡ There is not a single state in the country where a person working a full-time minimum wage job can afford to house a family.

STANLEY TUCCI

On Hunger in America

Stanley Tucci

*Acclaimed actor, director, and producer Stanley Tucci is a long-time spokesperson and board member of the **Food Bank for New York City**. He has also been a supporter of **Hollywood for Habitat for Humanity**, the **James Beard Foundation**, and **amfAR**, among others.*

➡ *foodbanknyc.org*

A charity event called Canstruction, in which teams of architects, engineers, and students compete to build the most amazing structures out of cans of food, is what first got me involved with the Food Bank for New York City. The number of people who help and the amount of food they're able to bring together in a single night are incredible. One year it was 90,000 cans. At the end, all the cans are donated to the local food bank. In the fifteen years since the program started, it has grown to include more than 100 different competitions around the country, and ten million pounds of food have been donated in the fight against hunger.

It is shocking to hear statistics about people who can't afford to feed themselves. People think it's the guy on the street who goes to the soup kitchen. That's often the face that is given to the hungry, but we know it's not just homeless people. The Food Bank for New York City sends out twelve to fourteen tractor-trailers daily, providing a quarter of a million meals, so imagine how many people there are who need this food. We know there are not a quarter of a million homeless people in New York, so who are they? It's the elderly. It's the disabled. It's single parents and their children. It's someone who just lost a job. It's people who are living on the edge and need an extra few bags of groceries a week to feed their kids. More than two million people across New York City are at risk of going hungry. It is our absolute moral obligation to do everything we can to stop it.

With soaring food prices and cutbacks in funding from federal programs, donations are extremely important to provide needed meals. Every $25 donation to the Food Bank provides 125 meals, with ninety-seven cents of every dollar going toward food acquisition, distribution, and programs. Realize it's something you can do as a family. Perhaps once a month, go to a soup kitchen, visit the elderly, or help package food for a food bank. On a larger scale, you can conduct a food drive by registering with the Food Bank, where you can learn the steps to a successful drive and about getting your community together—whether you are part of the Boy Scouts, schools, companies, or churches. There is so much you can do.

It is shocking to hear statistics about people who can't afford to feed themselves.

JEFFREY D. SACHS

→ On Carrying Each Other

Jeffrey D. Sachs

*Pre-eminent economist Jeffrey D. Sachs is at the forefront of the challenges of economic development, poverty alleviation, and enlightened globalization. He is the director of the **Earth Institute at Columbia University**, special advisor to former UN Secretary-General Kofi Annan on the **Millennium Development Goals**, and co-founder of the **Millennium Promise**, a non-profit organization aimed at ending extreme poverty.*

➡ *earth.columbia.edu; un.org/millenniumgoals; millenniumpromise.org*

We can be the generation that ends extreme poverty. Given our generation's wealth, technology, and global interconnectedness, extreme poverty is an extreme anachronism. It can be banished by the year 2025 if we each do our part. Small but world-changing efforts from each of us will coalesce to a global force for historic change.

The poorest of the poor already know the need to carry one another. I witnessed an amazing and heartening illustration of the profound human will toward volunteerism in support of others. It happened like this.

One year after Sauri, Kenya, became Africa's first Millennium Village, the village celebrated a bumper harvest. The project had enabled the village's long-forlorn farmers to obtain fertilizer and high-yield seed, and the industrious community promptly repaid the opportunity with a tripling of food output. We were taken on a walk through the village to see the benefits of the bumper crop, including several improved places to draw safe drinking water. We were led into a clearing to face several newly constructed houses, with their adobe walls and corrugated tin roofs.

"Do you know what these are, Professor Sachs?" our guide inquired. "No, what are they?" I replied. I was astonished by the answer. "These are newly built houses for the village poor. We villagers volunteered to build them in honor of the bumper harvest." So this was the village's new "low-income housing," a voluntary offering by the community to several destitute widows and HIV-infected individuals who could not meet their own housing needs.

I have marveled at this generosity ever since that visit. From my vantage point at the time, even with a trained eye for the village's economy, everybody in Sauri was extremely poor. After all, at the outset of the project there was no clinic, or mosquito nets to fight malaria, or fertilizer to achieve a harvest sufficient to feed the community much less to earn cash income. Yet the first impulse of this poor community, following its surplus harvest, was to give some of it back to the poorest of the poor amongst them.

FACT

➡ There are approximately 2.6 billion people—40% of the world's population—living on less than $2 a day, set as the global level for poverty in developing nations.

➡ Approximately one billion people live in extreme poverty on less than $1 a day.

➡ The Millennium Villages project is an innovative model for helping reduce extreme poverty in sub-Saharan African communities. Through targeted investments in agriculture, health, education, and infrastructure, each village is moving toward becoming sustainable and self-sufficient.

Small but world-changing efforts from each of us will coalesce to a global force for historic change.

The Millennium Villages School 2 School program uses the Internet to connect a grade school classroom in Ruhiira, Uganda with counterparts at the Whitby School in Greenwich, Connecticut. Students are able to share their life experiences through a variety of interactive lessons using text chat, video blogs, and emails to educate youth living in vastly different parts of the world about the similarities shared by all, facilitating a sense of global responsibility.

I've now seen this many times. When our team worked with the government of Malawi to implement a special program to help its two million smallholder farmers obtain fertilizer and seed, thereby doubling the country's production, one of the first steps of the government, jubilant at having broken the back of famine, was to give food aid to some of the neighboring countries. The very poor came to the rescue of the famine-ridden.

There are many practical lessons from our experience in the African Millennium Villages Project, an effort which currently helps half a million people in a dozen countries to escape from extreme poverty. Some of the lessons are technical. Fertilizers work to double food yields, or more. Anti-malaria bed nets cut down malaria transmission and children's deaths. School feeding programs attract kids to school and help them to learn when they are present. De-worming costs a few cents per schoolchild per year and can restore vitality, nutrition, and scholastic achievement.

These efforts must be scaled up. Each of us can be a contributor, a volunteer, and thereby a lifesaver. A gift of $10 can save a life, by enabling an African child to be protected with an anti-malaria bed net. A philanthropist's gift of $300,000 per year can enable an entire Millennium Village of 5,000 people to escape from extreme poverty. And just 0.7 percent of the rich world's annual income could enable extreme poverty to be banished from the planet by 2025. Each of us can volunteer for this global effort, as individuals, professionals, members of churches, businesses, schools, and community groups.

The very poor, of course, know full well what it means to be on the edge of survival, and therefore understand the need for such efforts. Sadly, it is the rich who sometimes forget. Too many are prone to blame the poor or their governments for the impoverishment. It is not easy for those in the rich countries to understand the consequences of soils depleted of nutrients, or huts filled with malaria-transmitting mosquitoes, or local climates which are increasingly prone to droughts.

Ours will be the generation that ends extreme poverty on Earth.

Religious traditions called on the religious community to tithe —that is, give ten percent of income—for the poor. Now as a global society we are so rich that even less than one percent of our income, indeed around 0.7 of one percent, can be sufficient. With that modest sum, invested properly, with expertise, and in the spirit of cooperation, ours will be the generation that ends extreme poverty on Earth. As Bono sings about our good fortune as human beings, "We get to carry each other."

MILLENNIUM GOALS

➡ At the Millennium Summit in September 2000, the largest-ever gathering of world leaders, the UN Millennium Declaration was adopted, committing to achieve the following goals by 2015.

1.
ERADICATE EXTREME POVERTY AND HUNGER

2.
ACHIEVE UNIVERSAL PRIMARY EDUCATION

3.
PROMOTE GENDER EQUALITY AND EMPOWER WOMEN

4.
REDUCE CHILD MORTALITY

5.
IMPROVE MATERNAL HEALTH

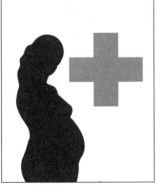

6.
COMBAT HIV/AIDS, MALARIA, AND OTHER DISEASES

7.
ENSURE ENVIRONMENTAL SUSTAINABILITY

8.
DEVELOP A GLOBAL PARTNERSHIP FOR DEVELOPMENT

LAUREN BUSH

On World Hunger

Lauren Bush

*Former model, activist, and presidential niece Lauren Bush is an honorary spokesperson for the **UN World Food Programme**. She created the **FEED bag** with the idea that a reusable bag can feed the world.*

➡ *feedprojects.org; wfp.org*

From the time I was young, the idea of giving back and serving others has been a very important theme in my life. I've learned that it's about jumping in and doing it. My work as an honorary spokesperson for the UN World Food Programme (WFP) started when I was in college. They were looking for a young spokesperson who could help rally students in the fight against world hunger. The first part of my education involved a trip with the WFP to see their operations in Guatemala firsthand. Despite its relative proximity to the United States, Guatemala is a vastly different world. Many people live in rural, mountainous villages where steep hills make it difficult to farm sustainably. As a result, most of the population suffers from chronic malnutrition. When I visited the schools, I noticed that the children were all genuinely excited to be there. I then found out that one of the reasons for their attendance was the free daily lunch provided by WFP. That was the moment when I fell in love with WFP's School Feeding Program, and realized how powerful food can be in encouraging education and getting these kids into school and out of the poverty cycle. This school lunch is sometimes the only meal these kids will receive all day, and it is a wonderful incentive for kids to get even a primary school education.

Food, water, shelter, and schooling are top priorities, even if many of us take them for granted. But in developing countries, education falls somewhere near the bottom of the list. In many developing countries I visited, women suffered the most from their impoverished situations. However, girls who attend school and receive even the most basic education are more likely to have less children; and as a result, their children are better fed, educated, and cared for. Essentially, educating women improves the next generation's chances of escaping poverty. The School Feeding Program is an incentive for boys and girls alike to attend school, and has helped improve attendance rates up to ninety-three percent. While the locals build land terraces to make farming easier, the WFP provides food aid. This frees people to do community planning and set up a proper farm system. It's not a quick fix for a situation that's just going to perpetuate itself, but a process toward self-sufficiency.

World hunger is a massive, seemingly intangible issue, but in fact it kills more people than AIDS, malaria, and TB combined. Even though there is enough food in the world to feed everyone, there are such inequities in the food systems in our backyards and abroad. Figuring out a solution to these issues is a huge undertaking, but an important one. If you're sick, access to medication is ineffective if you are undernourished. And if you do have food, but that food is not healthy, then there are also huge health consequences. Food issues really intersect with everything in human life.

After traveling with the WFP, I would come home inspired by the people I had met and want to make a more tangible difference in their lives. In 2005 I conceptualized a reusable shopping bag that would support WFP's School Feeding Program. Designing the FEED 1 bag was a fun way to combine my love for design with my passion to help fight world hunger. Initially, I was on my own, but then I partnered with Ellen Gustafson, whom I met at the UN. Together we started FEED Projects, a small company with a mission of creating good products that feed the world. Since April 2007 we have fed 240,000 children in school for a year. Each FEED 1 bag purchased feeds one child in school for a year. The FEED bag allows consumers to give in a way that is measurable and makes a direct impact on kids' lives around the world. The newest creation is the FEED 100 bag. Through the sale of this reusable grocery bag, we are encouraging the use of reusable bags instead of plastic, as well as giving 100 school meals to kids in Rwanda.

I always try to encourage young people to incorporate their humanitarian goodwill with their talents and passions on a daily basis to create change. Get involved locally and globally on your campus or in your neighborhood. My younger sister Ashley, for example, has started the first Student FEED Club at her school—they host lectures, have bake sales to benefit WFP, and volunteer at soup kitchens. Everyone can do their part on a daily basis. It's up to us, as citizens of the world, to find innovative solutions.

FACT
More than 850 million people around the world are unable to meet their basic nutritional needs, causing the deaths of more than 9 million people each year. Despite the billions of dollars in food relief given annually to areas in need by rich governments, malnutrition continues to be one of our most critical international health issues.

Get involved locally and globally on your campus or in your neighborhood.

KIRSTEN CLARK

On Becoming a Change Agent

Kirsten Clark

*Kirsten Clark participated in the second **Kenneth Cole Fellowship on Community Building and Social Change** program at Emory University in 2003. She now works with **World Vision**, a Christian humanitarian organization dedicated to working with children, families, and their communities worldwide to reach their full potential by tackling the causes of poverty and injustice.*
→ *worldvision.org*

GET INVOLVED
World Vision is an active advocate for the poor. Their 30 Hour Famine is an international youth movement that empowers and equips teens to raise awareness and funds to fight hunger. The program challenges those who participate to experience for just over a day what too many children experience for a lifetime.

My parents always encouraged me to volunteer whether it was singing Christmas carols at our local nursing home or helping with our neighbor's lawn. I think that was partially why the Kenneth Cole Fellowship program was so appealing to me. I was able to combine my interest in political science with my passion for community outreach. The program was an opportunity to learn, volunteer, and then learn through volunteering. It opened my eyes to the idea of lasting change through empowerment and helped me better understand the science behind development. I learned that true enrichment and empowerment come through partnership rather than leadership.

I now work at World Vision, a Christian organization that acts within communities around the world to attack the root causes of poverty. Motivated by my faith in God and using what I learned in the Kenneth Cole Fellowship, it is my goal to change the culture of charity in the United States by instilling a spirit of compassion for our neighbors in need, here and around the world. I work with students who, despite setbacks, have and share hope. Youth groups in the South Bronx, one of the poorest neighborhoods in the United States, give what little they have by fund-raising for starving children in Ethiopia. Many of the children in these groups come from broken homes and nearly all are below the national poverty level, but they are aware of their collective power to create change. They still have food, they still have hope, and they want to share this. Students at Columbia and Princeton Universities raised more than $50,000 for children of war in Gulu, Uganda. They understand that you do not have to wait until you enter the corporate world to make a difference. These kids and young adults, they get it and they are sharing their knowledge with their parents, faculty, and communities. I do what I do because I want to show people the power they have to make a difference just as my professors showed me. If I can inspire the leaders of tomorrow to become "change agents" in their communities, together, we can make a lasting difference around the world.

SHEILA C. JOHNSON

On Raising Women From Poverty

Sheila C. Johnson

*Philanthropist Sheila C. Johnson, CEO of **Salamander Hospitality**, president of the WNBA's **Washington Mystics**, and co-founder of **Black Entertainment Television (BET)**, fights the underlying causes of poverty working as an ambassador for **CARE**, an international relief and development organization.*

➡ *care.org*

I am a global ambassador for CARE, an organization that has spent over a half century waging a war on Third World poverty. CARE has recently determined that the only sustainable way to win that war is to empower women. By treating women as little more than livestock or property, Third World cultures all across the globe have been systematically cutting the pool of potential civic, business, and cultural leaders in half, while at the same time engendering a sense of male entitlement that serves only to maintain the status quo and perpetuate the poverty. Women constitute seventy percent of the poorest people in the world. Women produce half the world's food but own only one percent of its farmland. Of the 876 million illiterate adults in the world, two-thirds are women. And in some Third World countries, women are more likely to die in childbirth than reach the sixth grade. My work with CARE has been incredibly fulfilling and life-affirming, but at the same time it has been an extremely sobering experience.

The global village is quickly becoming a reality, and every day the world seems to be getting smaller. The Information Age is bringing people across the planet from each other together in ways most of us would never have thought possible. And now problems in places like Asia, Africa, and South America, which seemed so far removed from the United States just a few years ago, are striking a little closer to home.

Giving your time to those in need does to one's soul what throwing the windows open on the first warm day of spring does to one's home. I'd like to do what anyone with children ultimately wants to do: leave the world in better shape than I found it. For every dollar donated to CARE's "I Am Powerful" campaign, I donated a dollar, raising $8 million total, and I encourage everyone to continue giving and fighting for marginalized women across the globe.

BLAKE MYCOSKIE

On Giving Back as Good Business

Blake Mycoskie

Social entrepreneur and globetrotter Blake Mycoskie is the founder, designer, and "chief shoe giver"
of **TOMS Shoes for Tomorrow,** *which, for every pair of shoes purchased, donates a pair to a child in*
need. Originally hoping to sell 250 pairs of shoes, Mycoskie has since given away 60,000.
➡ *tomsshoes.com*

I competed on a TV show called *The Amazing Race* on a team with my sister, Paige, and for thirty-one days we hitchhiked our way around the world at breakneck speed. In the end we came in minutes shy of the $1,000,000 prize, but it was still the best thing that could have happened to me. After the show was over, I wanted to revisit all of the places I'd raced through: Belize, South Africa, and Argentina.

I spent some time volunteering in the poorer outskirts of Buenos Aires, where I developed an understanding of the effects of poverty on children as I witnessed them playing barefoot and then walking a few miles to fetch fresh water, developing cuts and sometimes life-threatening infections. There is a relatively unknown disease in Ethiopia called non-filarial elephantiasis, which affects 600,000 people. Those infected develop ulcers and boils on their feet and legs, and have little chance of going to school, finding work, or raising a family. Having shoes is a luxury that can save lives.

I realized that the best way I could help would be to create a self-sustaining business. In Argentina, I became a devotee of the traditional *alpargata*, an espadrille that is a staple for farmers and has recently become a favorite of polo players. I decided to adapt the *alpargata* for the U.S. market in the form of a slip-on shoe called Shoes for Tomorrow, or TOMS, for short. For every pair I sold I would give a pair away to a child in need. No one thought that a company could survive by giving away half its inventory, so I immediately needed to prove them wrong. With the help of a few friends and interns, I quickly found out that giving back is a business, a model that's gone more or less untapped. The interest and support we've had from the media and consumers have been immense, and I encourage all aspiring entrepreneurs to think about how they can incorporate philanthropy into their business strategies.

Too many companies approach giving back in the wrong way. They create complex formulas and percentages that people don't understand and cannot make an emotional connection to. Rather than spending countless dollars on "clever" advertising and fancy mission statements, just go out there and make the world a better place. We live in a highly integrated and 'Net-connected world. Tell great stories and customers will become your best advertisers. Keep things as simple as possible. At TOMS it is just One for One. For every pair you purchase, we give a pair away on your behalf. To date, we have given away 60,000 pairs of shoes: 10,000 in Argentina during our first year and, more recently, 50,000 in South Africa. I hope to be giving shoes away for the rest of my life.

FACT

Private giving by foundations, corporations, and individuals in the United States to poorer countries far outpaces aid provided by the U.S. government. America is the single biggest donor of foreign aid, giving $23.5 billion for poverty relief and development assistance. But a study by the Hudson Institute's Center for Global Prosperity found Americans gave $34.8 billion in private philanthropy to poor countries, four-and-a-half times more.

KRISTIN DAVIS

On Small Efforts, Big Differences

Kristin Davis

*Since the tsunami in Southeast Asia in 2004, Kristin Davis has been a passionate supporter of **Oxfam**. Her work as an Oxfam Global Ambassador has helped raise awareness for the organization's programs in South Africa and for **Oxfam America Unwrapped**, which aids poverty relief around the world.*

➡ *oxfam.org; oxfamamericaunwrapped.com*

I first became involved with Oxfam as a donor. I was impressed by the variety of issues they deal with. They take on problems that affect people around the world who are living below the poverty line—less than $2 a day. Oxfam's emphasis is on helping people become self-sufficient. But I didn't understand the full impact of their work until I traveled with them to South Africa and Mozambique for the first time.

The trip was life-changing. I learned so much about the complicated situations that lead to extreme poverty. But more than that, I was inspired by the people I met, by the joy and vibrancy they maintained in spite of lacking the most basic resources. It changed the way I read the newspaper. Faces come to mind now, not statistics. I met a woman in the mountains of Mozambique who had earned $20—the first money of her life. She bought soap, and paper, which allowed her son to go to school. You could see her pride in being able to help her family. That's all that matters.

If you think about the big picture, it can be overwhelming. There are so many people living in extreme poverty, so many facing AIDS, malaria, drought, intolerance. But my work with Oxfam reminds me how little it takes to make a difference.

At OxfamAmericaUnwrapped.com, you can send gifts to people who are living in severe poverty. These gifts range in size, from a water bucket to a schoolroom. A water bucket may not seem like a big deal, but in northern Uganda, where the malaria rate is extremely high, a mosquito carrying malaria can easily find its way into the open bowl that a young mother is using to transport water for her family. So buckets with lids and spouts to keep the water clean make a huge difference. Three of these buckets cost $18! That could mean the difference between life and death for three families. It doesn't take a lot to make a difference.

It is humbling and exciting to learn that you can be in a position to help another person. For me, it gives the fame that has come along with my job a greater purpose. I feel very lucky that doing something I love has allowed me to contribute. When I have the opportunity to talk about Oxfam's work, I'm thrilled to share the good news—lives are being changed, in ways big and small.

GET INVOLVED

Oxfam is an international relief and development organization that works in more than 120 countries. In 2008 Oxfam America and eBay Foundation launched an online fundraising initiative (www.communitygives.org) to support Oxfam in its efforts to supply clean, safe water to communities in Ethiopia and Zambia. People can either donate directly or by buying and selling items using eBay Giving Works.

I was inspired by the people I met. It changed the way I read the newspaper. Faces come to mind now, not statistics.

SCOTT HARRISON

On the Gift of Clean Water

Scott Harrison

Former event planner Scott Harrison was inspired to create the nonprofit charity: water to help bring safe, clean drinking water to communities in Africa, India, and South America. For every 200 bottles of charity: water sold in the United States, a well can be built in a developing country. To date, the organization has funded more than 624 projects in eleven nations, providing 250,000 people with clean water.
➡ *charitywater.org*

After years of success in the nightlife industry, my life was a mess. I was spiritually bankrupt. I lived arrogantly; I was one of the worst people I knew. During a vacation in South America, I realized I'd never have enough of the things I was chasing. I began praying and reading about the life of Jesus. I left New York City and committed to a year of humanitarian service on a hospital ship in Africa.

When I founded charity: water, I was trying to connect people here in the States to the people in Africa who most needed our help. The 1.1 billion people without clean water, the women walking three hours a day to get water filled with leeches, the kids waking up at 4 a.m. to haul forty-pound containers of water home from the river—they didn't choose to be born into extreme poverty. They do the best they can in horrible circumstances. I saw many of my friends in America living selfishly, like I had for years, and I wanted them to be part of changing these lives so dramatically. For years, everything was about excess—I used to sell $16 cocktails in my clubs. In Liberia, West Africa, $16 can buy a bag of rice that will feed four people for a month.

Recently, I returned from our projects in the Tigray province of northern Ethiopia. In that region alone, fifty percent of the people, about 1.5 million people, don't have clean water. We need 6,000 wells there. That's only one state in one of the eleven countries we're working in. But I also visited a village of 300 people that we helped, and another one, and another one. We were able to make all the difference to them. It's an honor to be able to do this work. More awareness has been raised. More people are talking about water. And they need to be.

If you want to contribute to this cause, the first thing you can do is learn more about the people without clean water. Then act to help them. Learn more about us, and tell our story to friends and family. And give. One hundred percent of donations to charity: water directly fund water projects. Even if you can only give $1, it means something. And whatever cause you care about, find an organization you believe in and make the time.

CLEAN WATER

A person needs 4 to 5 gallons of water per day to survive.

➡ The average American individual uses 100 to 176 gallons of water at home each day.

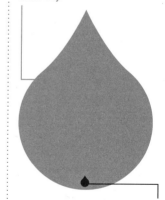

➡ The average African family uses about 5 gallons of water each day.

HOW TO... SOME TIPS ON HOMELESSNESS + POVERTY

TIME

⏱ **Get a better understanding of what poverty feels like by throwing an Oxfam America hunger banquet.** The meal simulates the different quality and quantities of food eaten around the world by income statistics. Participants draw random tickets assigning them to the various dining groups and are fed accordingly (www.oxfamamerica.org).

⏱ **Call your senators and urge them to support the Jubilee Act.** The bill, recently passed by the House of Representatives, calls for the cancellation of debts owed to the United States by impoverished developing nations. Go to www.senate.gov and find out who your senators are, then call 1-800-786-2663 and make your case. By eliminating the debt, millions of dollars are freed up to be used for vital needs like health care, education, and housing.

⏱ **Educate yourself about homelessness.** Recognize its many faces, understand that there are many different reasons for homelessness, and help dispel stereotypes.

⏱ **Take a moment to acknowledge a homeless man, woman, or child.** The smallest gesture of kindness can make a difference. It doesn't cost a dime, but will give them respect as individuals.

ITEMS

📦 **Don't let food go to waste.** Donate leftover food from your next big event, whether it is a wedding or a company party, to a food rescue organization such as America's Second Harvest (www.secondharvest.org) or City Harvest (www.cityharvest.org). They pick up excess food and redistribute it to help feed the hungry.

📦 **Make care packages for the homeless.** Hygiene is one of the biggest needs for the homeless. It's easy to put together kits of toothpaste, soap, and shampoo for regulars in your neighborhood.

📦 **Donate your business suits to individuals who are looking for a break.** Organizations such as Dress for Success (www.dressforsuccess.org), Career Gear (www.careergear.org), or Goodwill (www.goodwill.org) help provide professional attire and services to disadvantaged men and women seeking a job.

📦 **Gift livestock.** Go online and donate such as a goat or pig (which can help feed a family and fertilize crops), or even a package of bees to help pollinate plants through Heifer International (www.heifer.org) or Oxfam America Unwrapped (www.oxfamamericaunwrapped.com).

📦 **Recruit your company to donate excess inventory.** Gifts In Kind (www.giftsinkind.org) works with large and small technology, retail, and consumer companies to facilitate the distribution of products to millions of people in need around the world.

EXPERTISE

💼 **Volunteer to help build new homes.** With the lack of affordable housing, in addition to destruction from natural disasters, Habitat for Humanity organizes construction of affordable homes that are then sold to low-income buyers for no profit. Habitat has projects in all 50 states, as well as around the world, and has built over 225,000 homes to shelter over 1 million people since its inception.

💼 **Share your know-how.** Contact residential facilities and programs that help the homeless and disadvantaged and offer to host a workshop to teach them interview techniques, basic financial planning, or computer training. Even sharing hobbies such as cooking, woodworking, or photography, can empower someone to find a new direction and learn useful skills.

💼 **Get the word out.** Many people are unaware of the local shelters in their communities. Help organizations in your area publicize their services or needs for volunteers and donations by contacting community websites, newsletters, and newspapers and ask them to publish and distribute the organization's wish lists on a weekly or monthly basis.

DOLLARS

$ **Buy products certified Fair Trade.** Which means they were purchased from workers in developing nations with safe working conditions and living wages. Fair Trade items available in the United States include coffee, tea, cocoa/chocolate, sugar, rice, spices, herbs, and fruit.

$ **Support the UN-commissioned Millennium Project**, eight goals aimed at resolving various human rights issues, including eradicating poverty and hunger, by the year 2015. Adopting a "quick win" campaign such as providing bed nets to children in malaria zones to reduce the incidence of the disease can make immediate, vital changes to improve the lives of millions in need. Contact info@milleniumproject.org for more information.

$ **If you're a restaurateur, become a part of the annual UNICEF Tap Project.** Customers can donate $1 or more for a glass of tap water they would typically get gratis. For every dollar raised, a child will have clean drinking water for 40 days. In 2008 over 2,350 restaurants participated in the project.

$ **Make a microloan and support an entrepreneur in a developing country.** Kiva.org, a nonprofit microfinance organization, will help you make a loan as small as $25 to someone on the other side of the world. Kiva has funded more than $11 million worth of loans to date.

WHERE TO... SOME PLACES ON HOMELESSNESS + POVERTY

→ ACCION
www.accion.org
Established in 1961 and a leader in microfinance since 1973, Accion has over 45 years of experience in the field of international economic development and microfinance.

→ ACTION AGAINST HUNGER
www.actionagainsthunger.org
Action Against Hunger is an international organization that delivers emergency aid to people suffering from natural disasters or man-made crises.

→ BREAD FOR THE WORLD
www.bread.org
Bread for the World provides policy analysis on hunger and strategies to end it. The institute also educates its advocacy network, opinion leaders, policy makers, and the public about hunger.

→ CARA PROGRAM
www.thecaraprogram.org
The CARA program assists the homeless and at-risk populations by providing training, permanent job placement, and support services.

→ CARE
www.care.org
CARE is a leading humanitarian organization that fights global poverty and places special focus on working with poor women.

→ CENTER FOR COMMUNITY CHANGE
www.communitychange.org
The Center for Community Change works to establish and develop community organizations across the country, primarily in urban areas, by forming autonomous, citizen-based groups.

→ CENTER FOR URBAN COMMUNITY SERVICES
www.cucs.org
CUCS is the nation's largest provider of social services in supportive housing as well as a comprehensive human services agency that implements new practices so that persons who are homeless, low-income, or living with mental illness can live successfully in the community.

→ CHARITY: WATER
www.charitywater.org
Charity: water brings clean and safe drinking water into impoverished communities. In less than 2 years charity: water has founded more than 600 projects in 11 nations that will provide 250,000 people with clean water.

→ CORPORATION FOR SUPPORTIVE HOUSING
www.csh.org
The Corporation for Supportive Housing is a Community Development Financial Institution that helps communities create permanent housing with services to prevent and end homelessness.

→ COVENANT HOUSE
www.covenanthouse.org
Covenant House International is the largest privately-funded agency in the Americas providing shelter and other services to homeless, runaway, and throwaway youth.

→ DOE FUND
www.doe.org
The Doe Fund develops programs to empower formerly homeless and low-income individuals.

→ DOROT
www.dorotusa.org
DOROT enhances the lives of the elderly and brings generations together by addressing basic needs such as food and housing, health and wellness services, and life management skills.

→ FAIR TRADE FEDERATION
www.fairtradefederation.org
The Fair Trade Federation is an association of businesses committed to providing fair wages and good employment to economically disadvantaged artisans and farmers.

→ FEED PROJECT
www.feedprojects.org
The Feed Project sells FEED 1 and FEED 100 bags: simple burlap and organic cotton bags that help raise awareness and funds for child hunger.

→ FEED THE CHILDREN
www.feedthechildren.org
Feed the Children has grown into one of the world's largest private organizations dedicated to helping hungry and hurting people over the past 29 years. Feed the Children delivers food, medicine, and clothing to needy people.

→ FOOD BANK FOR NYC
www.foodbanknyc.org
The Food Bank for NYC works to end hunger by organizing food, information, and support; it provides 68 million pounds of food annually to more than 1,000 food programs.

→ GLIDE MEMORIAL CHURCH
www.glide.org
Glide Memorial Church provides a variety of social services to San Francisco's homeless population, including meals, a women's center, a walk-in center, health care, housing placement, family services, and training and employment.

→ GLOBAL FUND
www.theglobalfund.org
The Global Fund provides resources to help fight tuberculosis, HIV/AIDS, and malaria in needy countries.

→ GOOD MORNING AFRICA
www.goodmorningafrica.org
Good Morning Africa is the only U.S.-based nonprofit organization that is solely dedicated to high-growth, social entrepreneurship in Africa that will ultimately aid communities.

→ HABITAT FOR HUMANITY
www.habitat.org
Habitat for Humanity is a Christian organization that builds affordable housing in partnership with people in need.

→ HEIFER INTERNATIONAL
www.heifer.org
Heifer International provides animals and training to families living in poverty, allowing them to make lasting improvements in their quality of life.

→ HELP USA
www.helpusa.org
HELP USA is one of the nation's largest providers of housing, job training, and social services for the homeless and victims of domestic violence.

→ HOPE PROGRAM
www.thehopeprogram.org
The HOPE Program helps individuals transcend poverty by preparing them to find, keep, and grow careers.

→ HUNGER ACTION NETWORK
www.hungeractionnys.org
The Hunger Action Network of New York State is a statewide anti-hunger coalition that combines grassroots organizing with research, education, and advocacy to address the root causes of hunger.

→ HUNGER PROJECT
www.thp.org
The Hunger Project is a global movement aimed at ending hunger in Africa, Asia, and Latin America by empowering local people to create lasting society-wide progress.

→ MILLENNIUM PROMISE
www.millenniumpromise.org
Millennium Promise was created to achieve the Millennium Development Goals.

→ NATIONAL ALLIANCE TO END HOMELESSNESS
www.endhomelessness.org
The Alliance works to prevent and end homelessness by working collaboratively with the public, private, and nonprofit sectors and providing data and research to policy makers.

→ NATIONAL CENTER FOR HOMELESS EDUCATION
www.serve.org/nche
Provides research and resources enabling communities to address the educational needs of children experiencing homelessness.

→ NATIONAL COALITION FOR THE HOMELESS
www.nationalhomeless.org
The National Coalition for the Homeless is a network of people who are currently experiencing or who have experienced homelessness, activists and advocates, and community-based service providers.

→ NATIONAL COUNCIL OF LA RAZA
www.nclr.org
The largest national Latino advocacy organization in the United States works to improve opportunities and community development for Hispanic Americans.

→ ONE CAMPAIGN
www.one.org
The ONE Campaign seeks to raise public awareness about the issues of global poverty, hunger, disease, and efforts to fight such problems in developing countries.

→ OXFAM AMERICA
www.oxfam.org
Oxfam works in 26 countries in 7 regions to create lasting solutions to global poverty, hunger, and social injustice.

→ PARTNERS IN HEALTH
www.pih.org
Partners in Health provides research, advocacy, and publications related to health and poverty, and helps bring quality care to areas without access.

→ PEACE CORPS
www.peacecorps.gov
The Peace Corps began in 1960, when then Senator John F. Kennedy challenged students to serve their country by living and working in developing countries. Since then more than 190,000 Peace Corps volunteers have served in 139 countries.

→ PHILADELPHIA SOUL
www.philadelphiasoulfoundation.org
A charity for the Philadelphia Soul, the Foundation is committed to developing role models on the individual, corporate, and community levels, promoting and assisting in innovative solutions to rebuilding pride in one's self.

→ PLAYPUMPS INTERNATIONAL
www.playpumps.org
PlayPumps International raises money to buy and install special water pumps that also function as merry-go-rounds.

→ PROJECT HOME
www.projecthome.org
Project HOME empowers people to break the cycle of homelessness, address the structural causes of poverty, and attain their fullest potential as members of society.

→ ROBIN HOOD FOUNDATION
www.robinhood.org
The Robin Hood Foundation funds and supports more than 240 poverty-fighting organizations in New York City.

→ TOMS SHOES
www.tomsshoes.com
TOMS is a shoe company that donates one pair of shoes to a child in need for every pair of its shoes purchased.

→ TRICKLE UP
www.trickleup.org
Trickle Up works to empower the world's poorest people to take the steps out of poverty through micro-enterprise development.

→ UN MILLENNIUM DEVELOPMENT GOALS
www.un.org/millenniumgoals/
These eight goals focus on eradicating extreme poverty and hunger, achieving universal primary education, and combating HIV/AIDS, among other things.

→ U.S. DEPARTMENT OF HOUSING AND URBAN DEVELOPMENT
www.hud.gov
HUD is a cabinet department that was developed to execute policy on housing and cities. The website provides information on grants, community organizing, and avoiding foreclosure.

→ WORLD FOOD PROGRAMME
www.wfp.org
The World Food Programme is the United Nation's frontline agency in the fight against global hunger, working to improve nutrition and quality of life for the world's most vulnerable people.

→ WORLD VISION
www.worldvision.org
World Vision is a Christian relief and development organization that works to help children by tackling the causes of poverty.

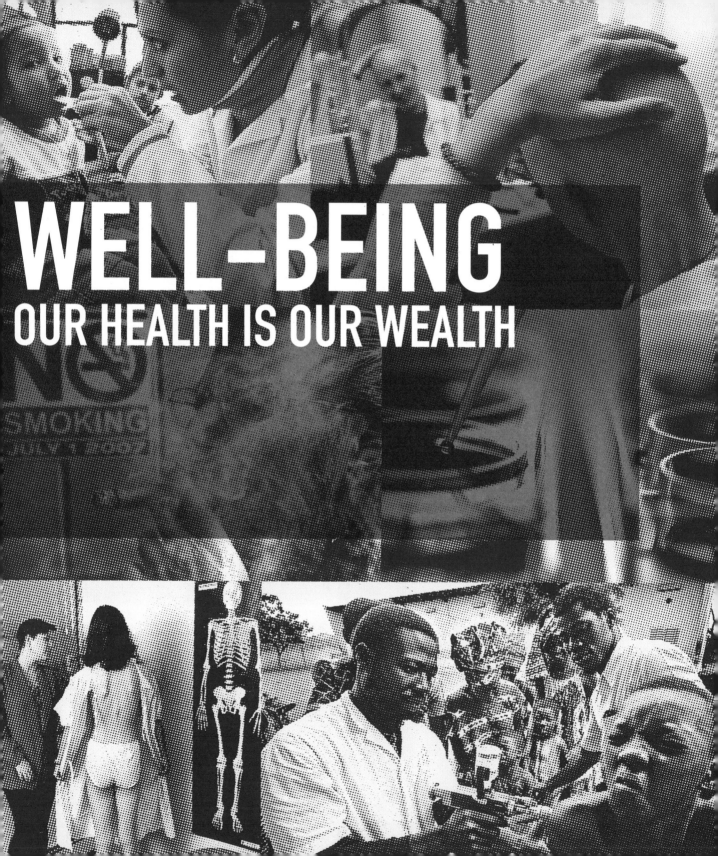

WELL-BEING
OUR HEALTH IS OUR WEALTH

Working on this book has reminded me of the many life experiences that have shaped who I am today. One that had a profound effect was a visit with my friend Christopher Reeve after the horse riding accident that rendered him instantly paralyzed. At a complete loss for words, I simply asked, "How are you doing?" His reply still amazes me. "I'm fine," he said. "But my body is not." He had such a clear understanding of what he had lost, but perhaps more importantly he understood what he still had. It is a lesson I will never forget. Chris worked tirelessly over the next nine years on rehabilitation and the support of research to raise his physical self back to the same level as his mental and spiritual self. He made tremendous progress without having what most of us take for granted, and showed us the surprising power of the mind/body connection. That is just one example of how a positive mental attitude can impact one's physical well-being. To effectively help others we need to be well ourselves. We must take care of our own physical, mental, and spiritual health before we can truly address the well-being of society—of its whole, or its parts. ➜ **But why does it so often take losing something to realize what we have? — Kenneth Cole**

MAYOR MICHAEL R. BLOOMBERG

 On Promoting a Healthy Public Policy

Mayor Michael R. Bloomberg

*A dedicated philanthropist, Michael R. Bloomberg has donated time and resources to many different causes and organizations. He has served on the boards of numerous institutions, including **Johns Hopkins University** where, as chairman of the board, he helped build the **Bloomberg School of Public Health**. As mayor of New York City, his commitment to health-care issues led to a series of bold initiatives that have positively impacted the health of millions of citizens.*

➡ *mikebloomberg.com; volunteernyc.org*

Pretending problems don't exist—or simply ignoring the facts—isn't good public health policy, and it's not how we do things in New York City.

The best piece of advice I ever got about public health is actually something I learned in my first job on Wall Street: "In God We Trust. Everyone else: Bring data." Good, solid data is the key to confronting any major health issue—because if you can't measure a problem, you can't manage it. This might seem like a given, but at all levels of government we've recently seen decades of scientific discovery take a backseat to political ideology. I like to call this phenomenon "political science." And you can see it at work in the movement to restrict federal funding for stem cell research, or to discredit the theory of climate change.

But pretending problems don't exist—or simply ignoring the facts—isn't good public health policy, and it's not how we do things in New York City. Instead, we find out what issues are facing our citizens, and we gather all the information we can. Then we attack the problems, stressing prevention wherever possible and focusing our resources where they will do the most good. A great example involves our fight against tobacco. Shortly after I became mayor in 2002, we quickly identified tobacco as the leading cause of death in our city—implicated in 10,000 completely preventable deaths every year. The science also showed that secondhand smoke kills. So later that year, we passed pioneering legislation outlawing smoking in the workplace, including restaurants and bars.

You can probably imagine that in the beginning, I wasn't the most popular person in certain parts of the city. Even some of my good friends opposed the ban—and they weren't shy about telling me. I also remember many predicting that the ban would be a death knell for our tourism industry. Some feared no one from places like Italy or Ireland would ever visit the city again. Not only have those predictions proved to be wrong, Italy and Ireland are now among more than two dozen nations that have followed our lead and banned smoking in public places. So have more than two dozen states and many cities here in the U.S. In fact, almost two-thirds of all Americans are now protected by secondhand smoke laws.

My administration has taken other steps, as well. We've mounted hard-hitting public information advertising campaigns, and expanded smoking cessation programs. We also raised the city's tax on cigarettes. Research has shown again and again that higher taxes help drive down smoking rates—and we've learned that youth are especially sensitive to cost increases. Just a few years ago, one in six teens in New York City smoked; today, the rate is one in twelve. Overall, some

FACT

On Valentine's Day 2007, the NYC Health Department announced the launch of the NYC Condom at a press conference held in the Kenneth Cole store in Rockefeller Center. It was the same condom the city had been distributing previously, but packaged in a NYC-themed wrapper. The year it was introduced, the Health Department distributed more than 36 million condoms, approximately twice the number as before. Some 900 local businesses (including Kenneth Cole stores), clinics, and nonprofit organizations now distribute the NYC Condom free of charge, helping to prevent unplanned pregnancies and the spread of sexually transmitted diseases.

FACT

➡ As of April 2008, 24 states, the District of Columbia and Puerto Rico have passed smoke-free laws covering bars and restaurants. Four other states have smoke-free restaurants.

➡ Internationally, a growing number of countries have enacted nationwide smoke-free laws, including Bermuda, Bhutan, France, Iceland, Ireland, Italy, Lithuania, New Zealand, Norway, Panama, Sweden, Thailand, Turkey, the United Kingdom, and Uruguay.

300,000 fewer New Yorkers smoke today than did in 2002. That will prevent about 100,000 premature deaths in the years to come.

Perhaps it's no surprise that the smoking ban helped earn me some less than favorable nicknames in certain circles. But frankly, if my policies are saving lives, people can call me whatever they want. That's why I have always had such great admiration for those who dedicate their lives to public health. There's no fortune or fame—but if you have the independence to look at the facts, and if you have the courage to embrace what the science says regardless of the consequences, you can make a difference in the lives of millions.

Our health-care system is in critical condition; if we're going to fix it, we need to build a system that promotes health instead of just treating the disease.

WHAT YOU CAN DO TO IMPROVE PUBLIC HEALTH
by Michael R. Bloomberg

➡ People are constantly bombarded with health advice. Lots of the information you find on TV, on the Internet, and in the newspaper is conflicting and confusing. That's why in New York City we've concentrated on ten core health issues that have the largest impact on health and identified action steps for each. We call the policy "Take Care New York." If all of us took just some of these steps, we could prevent thousands of deaths and hundreds of thousands of illnesses and disabilities each year.

1. HAVE A REGULAR DOCTOR OR OTHER HEALTH-CARE PROVIDER

2. BE TOBACCO-FREE

3. KEEP YOUR HEART HEALTHY

4. KNOW YOUR HIV STATUS

5. GET HELP FOR DEPRESSION

6. LIVE FREE OF DEPENDENCE ON ALCOHOL AND DRUGS

7. GET CHECKED FOR CANCER

8. GET THE IMMUNIZATIONS YOU NEED

9. MAKE YOUR HOME SAFE AND HEALTHY

10. HAVE A HEALTHY BABY

ELIZABETH EDWARDS

On Changing the Face of Cancer

Elizabeth Edwards

Elizabeth Edwards was first diagnosed with breast cancer in 2004 at the end of her husband John Edward's campaign for the vice presidency. She was in remission until March 2007, when she discovered it had returned. Already a passionate advocate for children and families, her courageous battle with cancer has led her to become an inspiring and powerful voice on behalf of health-care reform and cancer research.

We should rebel against the disease, but not against discussing it.

very thirty seconds, someone in this country is diagnosed with cancer. When I was the one whose number was called, I talked publicly about it, but in the way of one who has not yet traveled cancer's road might. It was terrifying, but also abstract. But it didn't last. When I looked in the mirror and saw scalp instead of hair, my reaction was to pull inward. To avoid the looks of concern and even pity—maybe to pretend it wasn't really true—I stepped out of the light. I would see someone who stepped forward and said, "This is who I am," maybe wearing a T-shirt asserting they were "Bald and Beautiful." I was, and still am, overwhelmed with admiration. It was clear that silence wasn't giving me the strength I needed. When I stepped forward, like they taught me, I found my real voice. And that is the changing face of cancer.

We should rebel against the disease, but not against discussing it. It's important to talk about cancer without cleansing the language. If you are receiving radiation, and your blisters are oozing through your clothes, just talk about it. I don't see the advantage in pretending I'm untouched by the disease. Talking frankly about cancer gives me some measure of control. For as hard as it sometimes is to imagine, we do have power over cancer. We have the power not to let it rule each day, and the power to fight it. I have heard people participating in walks that benefit research say, "I'm just one person walking, and it means nothing." That couldn't be further from the truth. Each step toward a cure builds confidence in our ability to beat this disease. One day we'll raise that dollar that finds The Cure. I think it's perfectly fine for everyone who ever joined a Walk for Life or participated in any kind of fund-raiser to believe that dollar was the dollar they raised. In a sense it will be. Everyone is responsible for getting closer to the answer.

The money raised doesn't matter unless people who need care get it. Because I had great health care I survived my first bout with cancer. In 2007 I gave a speech. Afterward, a woman whispered in my ear that she had a lump in her breast, and was a working mother with no health insurance. She was afraid to go to the doctor. With a documented preexisting condition she would never get health insurance. Our health policy had put her in this terrible catch-22. That's just not acceptable. We need universal health insurance, and we need a patient's bill of rights so a doctor and a patient can together decide on adequate care. Ask your representatives to make this a priority. Every congressman has legislative assistants who are assigned different areas, including health. Find that person and, instead of writing a generic letter, tell them what would make a difference in your life: "My insurance company denied a test, but my doctor thought it was necessary." Whatever your story, tell them. It's that constant pressure from constituents that will make the difference. If you know someone being treated for cancer, there is a lot you can do. Take their kids to the park so they can have a long bath. It sounds silly, but carry their heavy things. A lot of energy is spent in treatment, so things are hard to lift. Lobby your employers to provide health care coverage if they don't already. If you're an employer, and you're not capable of offering it, be a location for mobile testing. In the end, it is about taking care of each other.

WALKING TO END BREAST CANCER

American Cancer Society's Making Strides Against Breast Cancer
Since 1993, nearly 4 million walkers across the country have raised more than $280 million to help fight breast cancer.

Susan G. Komen 3-Day Cure
Since 2003, more than $220 million has been raised for breast cancer research through sponsors, donations, and contributions.

Avon Walk for Breast Cancer
From 2003 to 2006, the coast-to-coast series raised more than $150 million.

Revlon Run/Walk
Since 1993, the Revlon Run/Walk for Women raised more than $50 million for women's cancer research, education, and support programs.

LANCE ARMSTRONG

On Starting a Movement

Lance Armstrong

*In 1996 world-class cyclist Lance Armstrong was diagnosed with testicular cancer. After undergoing treatment, he came back from cancer to win the Tour de France seven consecutive times. As chairman and founder of the **Lance Armstrong Foundation**, he is a leading advocate for cancer survivors and the issues they face.*

➡ *livestrong.org*

In 1996 I was diagnosed with testicular cancer, and, at the time, information about it was hard to come by. I had no personal connection to cancer prior to my own illness. I had no family members nor friends who had ever suffered from it. Even so, the diagnosis comes out of the blue for everybody, regardless of their family history or whether they were smokers for forty years.

Over the last decade or so, access to information has improved drastically, in terms of our ability to search the Internet and have sites like livestrong.org at our fingertips. That was not the case back then, when you were left asking around or perhaps calling some 1-800 numbers. I was in the middle of active treatment when I asked my friends to help initiate this movement of uniting people to fight cancer, raise awareness, and empower those affected by the disease. We were just a bunch of regular guys from Austin, Texas, who didn't know what a 501(c)(3) was, let alone the rules and regulations of charities. All I knew was that I had a tricky situation that I hoped to parlay to help others, and they had a friend who was awfully sick and wanted to help others as well. We didn't think the change would be very big; we thought we'd start a small charity and reinvest into worthy programs.

In 2004 Nike asked us if they could make five million yellow bands so we could sell them as part of an effort to raise $5 million for my foundation. We all sat around and joked about what we were going to do with 4.9 million leftover yellow bands that said "LIVE-STRONG," but now, four years later, we've sold over seventy million around the world. We could not keep up with the demand. This tells me that people want to get involved.

For me, the most important thing for our organization is to try to make this disease a political issue. This is the number one killer in our country. Every time people ask why we are in Iraq or why this or why that, we should also be asking why we are still losing an American every minute to this disease. Research is only one part of the equation, and a lot of it comes long before we even need it. In fact, a lot of it should happen way before diagnoses, like with prevention.

Unfortunately, prevention is just not a sexy topic, which makes it very hard to preach to people, and therefore, difficult to get funding or attention like hard science can. But it is just as important as finding a cure because we're preventing future burdens. It's even controversial to legislate—for example, should we regulate tobacco abuse? It could be sunscreen, seat belts, or helmets. All of these things are devices we use to prevent death, illness, or injury. Nevertheless, we have to move toward a prevention-based society. You put on a seat belt or I put on a bike helmet. We have to start there. Of course, people will choose to smoke. In that case, the key is to catch the disease early, so we should diagnose every American as early as possible.

If even just a fraction of the people who bought those bands came together and demanded that cancer become a national priority, then we would see change. Change happens forever. So many people say, "I can't give x, y, z dollars, but I'll volunteer." That's the same as giving money. In fact, some argue it's more important. That's the power of the people and the reality of being active citizens. The only way to live life and to lead life is actively and as active citizens.

LIVESTRONG WRISTBANDS

In 2004 the Lance Armstrong Foundation and Nike partnered to create the Livestrong wristband in support of people living with cancer. The color yellow was chosen for the bands to symbolize strength and determination—a yellow jersey is worn by the leader of the Tour de France. By May 2005, 47.5 million wristbands had been sold, raising more than $44 million, well exceeding the initial fund-raising goals.

> The most important thing for our organization is to try to make this disease a political issue.

ALEXANDRA AND MATTHEW REEVE

On Continuing the Legacy of Christopher Reeve

Alexandra and Matthew Reeve

*Late actor Christopher Reeve was widely admired for his long history of speaking out on issues ranging from campaign finance to the environment. After his paralysis in 1995, Reeve and his wife, Dana, became powerful advocates for those suffering from spinal cord injuries, lobbying for health-care reform and research funding. In addition to his work on behalf of the **Christopher and Dana Reeve Foundation**, Reeve served on the boards of the **National Organization on Disability**, **World TEAM Sports**, and **TechHealth**, and founded the **Creative Coalition**. His three children —Alexandra, Matthew, and Will—continue his inspiring legacy.*

➡ *christopherreeve.org*

W hen you see someone with a spinal cord injury, it's so easy to think, "That could never be me." But disability touches all of us. It is so important to look beyond the wheelchair and see the person—and understand just how easily it could be you or someone you love sitting there instead.

Even in the years before our father's accident in 1995, he was very politically active. He campaigned for environmental groups and lobbied for public funding of the arts. He always had a strong sense of responsibility for others, and he instilled in us a strong commitment to serve the world beyond ourselves. After the accident, our father realized he had a platform to help other people living with disability. He recognized how lucky he was—he could work, travel, and access the best physical therapies—and he was determined to extend those opportunities to the millions of people living with disability in the U.S. and across the world.

The Christopher and Dana Reeve Foundation has been a big part of our lives since our father's injury. We used to fund-raise in school, and Matthew once spent the day in a wheelchair to raise awareness of the everyday challenges faced by people with spinal cord injuries. The Foundation works to improve quality of life for people with paralysis, funding accessibility initiatives, employment programs, voting rights campaigns, sports leagues, children's groups, and arts programs to help people live a more active life. We officially joined the board in 2006.

Growing up, the latest medical breakthrough was our nightly dinner conversation. The progress in recent years has been remarkable and gives us tremendous hope for the future. Physical therapy programs funded by the Reeve Foundation have some people out of their wheelchairs and walking. But when we talk about a "cure" for paralysis, we're really talking about many cures and many forms of recovery. Each case of spinal cord injury is unique, and small steps make a big difference. In 2001 dad was suddenly able to move his left index finger, and then his wrist, contract his arm, and eventually his leg. He also regained sensation in seventy percent of his body. Imagine after six years, being able to feel your wife's touch, your child's hug—that's life-changing. Even the slightest step forward can have a big impact on a person's life, and it makes the Foundation's work that much more important.

"You have to take action and stand up for yourself—even if you're sitting in a wheelchair."
—Christopher Reeve

How can everyday people help with disability issues? The most important change starts within ourselves: a resolution to look past the chair, and see the person. Focus on ability, not disability. Refuse to put limits on another person's potential. Our father was exceptional in his refusal to accept absolutes. Dad once said, "So many of our dreams at first seem impossible, then they seem improbable, and then, when we summon the will, they soon become inevitable." That's one of the lessons we learned from him, and we hope others learn too: to dream, and then summon the will.

FACT

➡ Almost 5 million Americans are living with paralysis caused by spinal cord injury and other diseases, disorders, or birth conditions such as multiple sclerosis, stroke, spina bifida, ALS (Lou Gehrig's disease), cerebral palsy, or transverse myelitis.

➡ Every 49 minutes an American is paralyzed due to a spinal cord injury.

➡ Since its inception, the Christopher and Dana Reeve Foundation has directed over $77 million to spinal cord injury research.

➡ The Christopher and Dana Reeve Foundation has awarded over 600 grants to scientists around the world.

JOE PANTOLIANO

On the Stigma of Mental Illness

Joe Pantoliano

*Actor and author Joe Pantoliano has been a long-time advocate for raising awareness on a variety of issues. He established **No Kidding, Me Too!** in order to eliminate the stigma attached to mental illness, and served as co-president to **The Creative Coalition**, a nonpartisan social and political advocacy organization.*

➡ *nokiddingmetoo.org*

I started No Kidding, Me Too! after I did a film called *Canvas* that deals with the effect of mental illness on a small Italian-American family living in Florida. The wife gets diagnosed with late-onset schizophrenia that basically controls the lives of her entire family. In preparation for the film, we did a lot of research and visited Fountain House, one of the clubhouses for the mentally ill that started proliferating in the 1980s to fill a void after President Reagan began shutting down federal mental health facilities. And even though I myself had been diagnosed with clinical depression, it didn't really click how widespread the problem is until I started making this film.

About five days before we started shooting the movie, my friend Charlie—who married my wife Nancy and me—called me up out of the blue to talk about Thanksgiving. We were laughing, and I asked, "How's it going?" And he said, "It's going pretty good." He wasn't auditioning much, but he was looking forward to Thanksgiving. Two days later, my wife called to say that Charlie had committed suicide. There was no indication that there was anything wrong with him.

That's the thing that really gets me. I'm clinically depressed. My depression doesn't come from anything real. When my mother died, I felt really bad. And I can recall what that feeling was—I have it every day. It can control me or I can try to deal with it. The reason why my organization is called No Kidding, Me Too! is because when I tell somebody that I live with mental illness, that's what they say: "No kidding? Me too." Our main goal is simple: Remove the stigma that is attached to mental illness through education. Schizophrenia affects one percent of the globe, which means that it's sixty times more prevalent than muscular dystrophy and AIDS combined—and that's just schizophrenia. A quarter of American adults experience mental illness in any given year. There's so many of us, and we don't have to hide anymore.

When you make a movie, you're required to get a physical because the insurance company wants to know that you're not a high risk. So, when the doctor asked me what kind of medicine I took, I told them aspirin, Lipitor for cholesterol, and anti-depressants. Afterward, my lawyer called me and said the insurance company was not going to cover me because of the anti-depressants. My option was to sign a waiver, so that if I had a nervous breakdown, I'd be financially responsible for the stoppage of the work. And I said, "Well, what if I have a heart attack?" And they said, "The heart attack's covered." That pissed me off. A lot of friends of mine in show business tell me to just not say anything. I'm not a righteous dude—I mean, I've lied about stuff. But I can't be quiet about this. I just think that the brain should have the same rights as the liver, the kidney, and the gallbladder. I shouldn't be penalized because I'm trying to improve my life by taking that medicine.

Call your congressman. Call your sister. Teach your family to embrace the disease and not hold it against people who have it. Invite your brother, who has bipolar disorder, over for dinner. Have the kids understand why Uncle Johnny might bite the family dog. Contact me at nokidding-metoo.org. Reach out to places like Fountain House.

After I went public with my depression, a lot of my anonymous friends who also live with my illness called to say that I was brave. So, No Kidding, Me Too! is an organization of ambassadors connected to the entertainment industry who will support me in talking about my illness that I use for my craft of storytelling. And what I hope to do is get more and more of my colleagues who have this in their life to come out. We don't have the luxury of anonymity.

FACT

➡ Approximately 57.7 million Americans, an estimated 26% of American adults, suffer from a diagnosable mental disorder.

➡ Approximately 14.8 million Americans—almost 7% of American adults—suffer from major depression, but 54% of people believe that depression is a personal weakness.

> **The brain should have the same rights as the liver, the kidney, and the gallbladder.**

JAMIE-LYNN SIGLER

On Body Image

Jamie-Lynn Sigler

*After a battle with borderline anorexia and exercise bulimia, actress Jamie-Lynn Sigler became a spokesperson for the **National Eating Disorder Association (NEDA)** and created the **Jamie-Lynn Sigler Foundation** to raise awareness of the dangers of eating disorders. She regularly shares her story of recovery with audiences across the nation.*

→ *nationaleatingdisorders.org*

We live in a society where we are always conscious of how we look. As a young girl, I cared about clothes, but I became body-conscious when I was about sixteen. My body was really starting to change, and when my first boyfriend broke up with me, all of a sudden I felt very insecure for the first time. Along with the pressures of schoolwork, I felt overwhelmed.

Life suddenly seemed out of control, and I turned to food and exercise as a source of control. It began by adding a twenty-minute treadmill routine to my already active lifestyle, and cutting things from my diet, like dessert. Within a few months, it snowballed into exercising three hours every day before school and eating next to nothing. I never liked the way I looked after that, but I was afraid to give up the control. I began to ignore my friends, my schoolwork, everything except exercise and dieting. It was a miserable existence, but I didn't know how to get myself out.

Things hit a wall when I started contemplating suicide. I hated living like that. It was then that I had to admit to myself that I had a problem and needed to get help. Once I was ready to tell this to my family and friends (who had tried desperately to help me), I went into therapy. Therapy was huge. It helped me understand my behavior, and I began to feel like I wasn't alone in this fight anymore—that there was light at the end of the tunnel.

It took me a while to share my disease on the set of *The Sopranos*. I was initially very ashamed and didn't think they would want to work with someone with my problems. So I put on a brave face for a long time. Nobody ever commented on my weight fluctuations during my years of recovery. It was silent support, and it meant the world to me. By the time I opened up to everyone, I could almost talk about it as a past problem, not a present one.

When NEDA approached me to work with them, I wasn't sure what I could do. I didn't want to be the "poster child" for eating disorders, but I quickly realized they wanted me to be the face of something else: hope. It's amazing that just by being candid about my life, I can help someone else going through the same thing. But it also keeps me in check. I'm constantly reminded of what I've been through, as well as what I've overcome.

As a NEDA spokeswoman, I've met people from many different walks of life suffering from the same disease. And I started my own foundation to help promote healthy body image in young women and men, and to further public understanding about the severity of eating disorders. In most of our country, insurance doesn't cover treatment, and some people, in the midst of getting help, have to stop because they can't afford it. I have heard too many stories of people losing their life to this illness. We need to bring attention to the aid that people need. It's a tough battle, but it's one we can win.

Eating disorders are an addiction in many ways, and need to be handled with care and patience.

I believe Hollywood and the fashion industry have a responsibility to show a broader spectrum of beauty. We are all different—shape, size, everything. Health is important, but what is healthy for one person can look very different on another.

Eating disorders are an addiction in many ways, and need to be handled with care and patience. As people who have been through it know, it can't be done alone. The NEDA website is a wonderful resource for anyone who wants to help.

Helping others is a duty, and we all have times where we need it ourselves. I believe that is just a part of life.

JAMIE LEE CURTIS

→ **On Children's Health Advocacy**

Jamie Lee Curtis

*Actress and children's author Jamie Lee Curtis has said, "The best use of my celebrity is to bring focus to an issue that needs it." Her active commitment to children has inspired her work on behalf of organizations such as the **Children's Hospital of Pittsburgh**, the **Children's Hospital of Los Angeles**, **Children Affected by AIDS Foundation (CAAF)**, the **Commitment to Kids Initiative**, and **Starlight Starbright Children's Foundation**.*

→ *givetochildrens.org; caaf4kids.org; starlight.org*

From a very early age, I remember my mother spending a great deal of time with a charity called SHARE, an organization for mentally handicapped children that was started by the wives of powerful people in Hollywood. She worked with them for years raising money, and I grew up thinking that's what people do. Because what else in the world are you famous for? A lot of people feel they just don't have the time, but if you expect your children to be charitable, you have to demonstrate it for them. Find something that is your passion and turn it into your advocacy. I advocate for children because they are my passion.

Most people don't know how difficult it is to have a sick child—the concentric circles of grief that envelop a family, what that does to a mother, father, or other family member. The design of youth is freedom and exploration, but illness prevents children from exploring their minds and bodies and the world around them. You just want to take the pain away and let them run free.

In 1983 I met a thirteen-year-old girl named Lori Tull who was the recipient of the first successful pediatric heart transplant. I was making a movie in Pontiac, Illinois, and the town was putting on a benefit to help Lori's family pay her medical bill (the operation had been deemed "experimental"). Our movie production got involved, and I became friends with her. When she died at age nineteen, I arranged to have the Sony Corporation put video machines in her name in all the rooms at the Children's Hospital of Pittsburgh, and later became chair of their fund-raising. As a gesture of gratitude, the hospital named a chair of pediatrics and transplantation after me, which is the highest honor I've received.

Be the change, don't preach the change. Call your local children's hospital and ask, "What can I do?" Have a bake sale or lemonade stand, make $10, and donate it. There are tremendous opportunities to do things that directly affect the lives of other human beings. If you know someone whose family member is sick, drop off dinner one night and say, "I know your family is going through something—all of this is ready to eat." That makes people feel like they're not alone. It connects us all.

If you expect your children to be charitable, you have to demonstrate it for them.

There's an old Greek proverb that says, "Civilization flourishes when people plant trees under the shade of which they will never sit." It's about continuing the good prosperity of the human race. We have to help other people even though we may never meet them. You're doing it because this is what civilization does for you.

FACT

The multimedia Fun Center video game systems were designed by Nintendo of America and Starlight Starbright Children's Foundation to help combat anxiety and weariness faced by hospitalized children. The portable units provide welcome distraction for children undergoing long treatment procedures and may result in a reduced need for pain medication, as well as lower levels of stress and loneliness in patients. Companies, foundations, and individuals have sponsored the placement of more than 5,000 units in hospitals throughout North America.

DR. VICTORIA HALE

On Making Medicine Affordable

Dr. Victoria Hale

*In order to develop safe, effective, and affordable medicine
for people with infectious diseases in the developing world,
Dr. Victoria Hale founded the **Institute for OneWorld Health**,
the first nonprofit pharmaceutical company in the United States.*

➡ *oneworldhealth.org*

Back in 2000 I was riding in a taxi and chatting with the driver, an African immigrant, who asked me what I did for a living. When I told him I was a pharmaceutical scientist he broke into a fit of laughter. He finally regained his composure and remarked with a shake of his head: "You guys have all the money."

That was a turning point for me. All the money, yes, but to what end? His comment crystallized the growing discomfort I felt at the imbalance of resource allocation that was so evident in my chosen field of work. The world's poorest people were dying from curable diseases, and large pharmaceutical companies were no longer making new medicines to treat the diseases of poverty. One third of the world's population lacks access to essential medicines. Millions of lives are needlessly lost to infectious diseases each year. Malaria causes more than one million deaths annually. Visceral leishmaniasis, also known as kala-azar or black fever, causes 300,000 deaths every year. The numbers are truly staggering.

I thought, "Why in the twenty-first century are there people who have medicine for any disease or complaint, while in other parts of the world, two million babies die of diarrhea every year? I am a pharmaceutical scientist and a mother. This is unacceptable!" So I quit my job, invested personally, and founded the Institute for OneWorld Health, the first U.S. nonprofit pharmaceutical company that develops safe, effective, and affordable new medicines for people with infectious diseases in the developing world.

Today, OneWorld Health has a staff of eighty working in the U.S. and India, and we've received nearly $150 million in funding from the Bill and Melinda Gates Foundation to develop lifesaving drugs for the world's most impoverished communities.

Why nonprofit? It's simple, really. The therapeutic drugs that exist today are produced by for-profit pharmaceutical companies that operate according to a very strict business model and require a certain return on investment to shareholders. Adhering to this business model leads these companies to pursue drugs for wealthy countries, focusing on heart disease, diabetes, cancer, and so-called "lifestyle" drugs. As a result, only ten percent of the $70 billion spent on health research worldwide each year is for research into the health problems that affect ninety percent of the world's population. OneWorld Health looked at this so-called "90/10 gap" and asked, "If lack of profitability is all that keeps drugs from reaching people, why not take profitability out of the equation?" Unlike for-profit drug companies that measure success in terms of profits, OneWorld Health measures success in terms of lives saved and new medicines produced. We travel to some of the most remote corners of the world to meet disease experts and people who are basically voiceless because of their extreme poverty. With the help of translators, we learn why so many people in these villages are dying. Then we talk together about solutions. To make these solutions real, we then forge innovative partnerships to complete the critical global health work.

You don't have to be a doctor or a pharmaceutical scientist—or Bill Gates—to make a real impact. First, educate yourself about the eye-opening numbers of children who die from preventable and treatable diseases. Second, enlist others to get involved and make your voice heard—through the media, government officials, or online advocacy—to champion the right of all people around the globe to have access to the essentials of good health. Third, support a global health organization whose work you admire, and contribute whatever time, money, or expertise you can offer. A little money goes a long way in the developing world. Whether you serve in another country or closer to home, on behalf of a person or a cause, you will enrich your life in unexpected ways.

FACT

One-third of the world's population lacks access to essential medicines. In the poorest regions of Africa and Asia, this figure rises to one-half. Ten million children die every year before reaching their fifth birthday, many from preventable and curable diseases.

➡ Pneumonia, UNICEF reports, kills 2 million children, more than any other disease. When properly diagnosed, pneumonia can be treated inexpensively with antibiotics.

➡ Diarrheal diseases are another leading cause of death in children under the age of 5 worldwide, killing nearly 2 million children.

➡ More than 40% of the world's population live in areas where malaria is endemic. This disease is responsible for more than 1 million deaths annually, and between 350 and 500 million people fall ill to malaria each year.

➡ Tuberculosis, a preventable and curable disease, claims 2 million victims, 90 percent of them in developing countries.

DR. ALLAN ROSENFIELD

On Social Justice + Public Health

Dr. Allan Rosenfield

*Among the first to draw attention to the health crisis in the developing world, Dr. Rosenfield is emeritus dean of the Mailman School of Public Health at Columbia University. He is considered a legend in the field of public health, and has spent forty years advancing the health and human rights of hundreds of millions worldwide through innovative programs in reproductive health, maternal mortality, and the treatment of HIV/AIDS. He has also served as a board member of the **Doctors of the World**, **Population Action International**, **EngenderHealth**, **Global Health Council**, and **amfAR**, among other organizations.*

➡ *dowusa.org;*
populationaction.org;
engenderhealth.org;
globalhealth.org

On occasion, choices that seem insignificant turn out to have a major impact on your life and the lives of many others. For me, certain decisions I made as a young man didn't appear momentous at the time, but ultimately were personally transformative. In the 1960s, I was training to be an obstetrician/gynecologist, just as my father had. I planned to go into private medical practice. But I was indelibly altered after learning about health problems in the developing world during a year spent in South Korea for the Doctor's Draft and in Nigeria at a teaching hospital.

I delayed starting my practice to accept a position with the Population Council as an adviser in reproductive and maternal health to Thailand's Ministry of Public Health. They were developing access to family planning for the entire country. At the time, when the typical household had seven children, only doctors could prescribe birth control pills, but there were very few physicians, especially in the rural areas. So I came up with an idea—why couldn't I prepare a simple checklist for midwives to use to safely distribute oral contraceptives? It was the first major program to take the pill out of the hands of the doctors and I was supported by some of the leaders of the Ministry of Public Health. By the end of the first year more than 3,000 midwives were able to provide family planning service. Eventually, the average number of children per family dropped to 1.6. I stayed in Thailand for six years, completely departing from the secure path that had lain before me. I realized I could have a greater impact by addressing the needs of populations, rather than focusing on the health of one patient at a time. I wanted to work on big issues, not in a small private practice with patients who already had access to quality medical care.

I have remained devoted to women's health issues throughout much of my career. I asked myself what could be learned from these issues, especially from the alarming mortality rate of pregnant women in resource-poor countries. Nobody was taking action to bring lifesaving services to these women, care that was commonplace in industrialized nations. Looking beyond the conventional boundaries of medicine, it was clear there was an important connection between social justice and public health. The societal disparity between men and women is at the core of the hazards against women's health, and, in turn, against the well-being of

FACT

➡ In 1985 Dr. Rosenfield and Deborah Maine penned a seminal article, "Where is the M in MCH [maternal and child health]?", arguing MCH programs in developing nations neglected mothers. They won the largest grant in Columbia University's history at the time, creating programs that increased women's access to emergency obstetric care in over 50 Asian, Latin American, and sub-Saharan African countries.

➡ In 2001 Rosenfield co-authored another paper on maternal-to-child transmission (MTCT) of HIV, gaining funding to establish the MTCT-Plus Initiative, after which UN Secretary-General Kofi Annan said: "Among all the initiatives that have been taken in the struggle against HIV/AIDS, none has done more than MTCT-Plus to focus attention on the situation faced by women in the pandemic."

The central challenge in public health is to develop systems that deliver lifesaving care to those who need it.

THE GLOBAL FUND

At the 2000 G7-G8 Summit in Okinawa, world leaders pledged to start the Global Fund to Fight AIDS, Tuberculosis, and Malaria—the first international financing of its kind. Since it officially launched in 2002, the fund has gone on to be the top monetary provider in the effort to stop the infectious diseases, saving millions of lives.

their community. If you empower women, it changes not only their role in society, but society as a whole.

We love "magic bullets" and want to see fast, impactful results. But the central challenge in public health is to develop systems that deliver lifesaving care to those who need it. While most of the fanfare goes to new technologies, we already have what we need to save millions of lives. A study on research priorities in child health estimates that only three percent of research dollars go toward improving delivery, access, and utilization of effective existing interventions. In the seventy-five most resource-poor countries, roughly 1,500 women die while giving birth every day. Most of those deaths could be avoided with care that is commonplace in industrialized nations. As my friend and colleague Dr. Mahmoud Fathalla once said, "Women are not dying because of a disease we cannot treat. They are dying because societies have yet to make the decision that their lives are worth saving."

Our world is increasingly interconnected, and it is imperative that each of us appreciates the value of collaboration, staying open-minded while growing from our interactions with people from various backgrounds. In the quest for program and policy solutions, learn to see through the eyes of others, especially the eyes of the most marginalized. I recommend doctors-in-training to get experience with low-income populations in this country, as well as in global health issues by working abroad. But even a commitment of ten minutes a day of your time can make a difference: Read an article about educating girls in Nigeria and pass it on to others, sponsor a campaign to end violence against women, or ask congressional representatives to develop policies on HIV/AIDS that are scientifically sound and actually empower and protect women and young people. Remember to challenge traditional thinking, look at problems from different angles, ask questions, be compassionate, and stand up for what you know is right. Know that you have the power to effect change.

In the quest for program and policy solutions, learn to see through the eyes of others, especially the eyes of the most marginalized.

When I first started my training, I knew very little about public health. Now I recognize the importance of dedicating my career to it. It's a choice I never took lightly, and it has provided me with enormous professional and personal gratification.

HOW TO... SOME TIPS ON WELL-BEING

TIME

🕐 **Get trained in CPR.** Organize a CPR training class at work or for your religious or community group. Ninety percent of cardiac arrest victims die before reaching the hospital. A CPR lesson often takes just a few hours, and can help you save a life.

🕐 **Volunteer at a hospital or care facility.** Hospitals often need volunteers to assist patients and caregivers with information and support. If you enjoy working with children, you can donate a few hours every week to playing games with a child battling cancer.

🕐 **Sign up to man a phone at your local crisis center or campus hotline.** Many helplines rely upon volunteers to staff phone lines. The National Suicide Prevention Lifeline website (www.suicide preventionlifeline.org) has a list of volunteer crisis centers across the country.

🕐 **Participate in any of the many rides, walks, or runs.** Join walks and runs to support medical research and advocacy programs. Not only does raising money through these events help others, but training can improve your overall health too.

🕐 **Read to the visually impaired or dyslexic.** Make recordings of printed materials for Recording for the Blind & Dyslexic (www.rfbd.org), Iowa Radio Reading Information Service (www. iowaradioreading.org), or Utah State Library for the Blind and Disabled (blindlibrary.utah.gov). Readers narrate the text of books and other periodicals, describing any visual elements.

ITEMS

📦 **As a family, help another family whose child is in the hospital.** Knit a blanket and donate it through Project Linus (www. projectlinus.org) or contact your local children's hospital and find out what items (books, toys, or craft materials) they may need.

📦 **Join the organ donor registry.** Keep an organ donor card with you at all times. There are nearly 100,000 people waiting for lifesaving transplants, with about 300 added to the list every month. Register at *www.organdonor.gov.*

📦 **Give blood.** Every 2 seconds, a person living in the United States needs blood for emergencies and other serious illnesses. Call 1-800-GIVELIFE or go to *www.givelife.org* to find your nearest blood drive, learn about donor eligibility, and discover more reasons why it's not only easy but important in saving lives.

📦 **Donate your used eyewear.** Give the Gift of Sight (www. givethegiftofsight.org) provides free vision care and eyewear to underprivileged people around the world. Organize a used glasses drive or drop off your own at a participating optical store. They will clean, repair, and deliver them to people who otherwise cannot afford vision care.

EXPERTISE

💼 **Use your medical knowledge abroad.** At least 1 billion people lack access to basic health care. Organizations such as Operation Smile (www.operationsmile.org), HealthCare Volunteer (www. healthcarevolunteer.com), and AmeriCares (www.americares. org) recruit medical professionals to help address this need.

💼 **Volunteer your skills.** We sometimes forget health and well-being nonprofits have the same needs of other organizations. Groups like the Heart Touch Project (www.hearttouch.org), and Strides Therapeutic Riding Centers (www.strides.org) all need professional skills like accounting, legal, and I.T.

💼 **Because health insurance often doesn't cover** alternative forms of therapy, such services can be in high demand at social service agencies. For example, the Charlotte Maxwell Complementary Clinic (*www.charlottemaxwell.org*) in the Bay Area looks for licensed volunteer acupuncturists to provide free acupuncture to low-income women with cancer.

💼 **Collaborate on books in progress.** The Hesperian Foundation (www.hesperian.org) is nonprofit publisher of community-based health care books and newsletters. Their first book, *Where There is No Doctor*, is considered to be one of the most accessible and widely used community health books in the world. Collaborators with any expertise or experience in community health issues can help throughout the editorial process.

DOLLARS

$ **Search the Internet and give to charity.** With each Internet search you do via GoodSearch.com, about 1 cent goes to the charity of your choice. Support your favorite health organization by simply sitting at your computer.

$ **Approach a celebrity.** Ask if they are willing to give you something of theirs to sell to help raise awareness and funds for the health charity or organization you support. Auction the item at a fund-raising event or sell it online with Charity Folks (www. charityfolks.com) or eBay Giving Works (www.ebaygivingworks).

$ **Get your company to donate matching funds.** Many companies offer to match their employees' charitable contributions dollar for dollar. Take advantage of this generous benefit and double the amount to your favorite nonprofit.

$ **Create a charity registry.** Instead of presents, ask your friends and family to contribute to finding a cure. JustGive (www.justgive. org) provides tools you can use to create a charity wish list or use their wedding center to decide on a unique and meaningful wedding registry.

WHERE TO... SOME PLACES ON WELL-BEING

→ **AMERICAN CANCER SOCIETY—MAKING STRIDES AGAINST BREAST CANCER**
www.cancer.org
Making Strides Against Breast Cancer is a premier breast cancer event that helps fight breast cancer and provides hope to people facing the disease.

→ **AMERICAN HEART ASSOCIATION**
www.americanheart.org
The American Heart Association is committed to fighting heart disease and stroke.

→ **AMERICAN RED CROSS**
www.redcross,org
In addition to disaster relief, the American Red Cross offers services that help the needy, collect and distribute blood, and offer international relief and development programs.

→ **ANGEL FLIGHT**
www.angelflight.com
Angel Flight network organizations arrange free air transportation for charitable and medical needs.

→ **BEST BUDDIES**
www.bestbuddies.org
Best Buddies is dedicated to enhancing the lives of people with intellectual disabilities by providing opportunities for one-to-one friendships and integrated employment.

→ **CHILDREN AFFECTED BY AIDS FOUNDATION**
www.caaf4kids.org
CAAF provides social, educational, recreational, and other critical support programs to vulnerable children impacted by HIV/AIDS.

→ **CHILDREN'S HOSPITAL OF PITTSBURGH**
www.chp.edu
Renowned for its outstanding clinical services, research programs, and medical education, Children's Hospital of Pittsburgh has helped establish the standards of excellence in pediatric care.

→ **CHRISTOPHER AND DANA REEVE FOUNDATION**
www.christopherreeve.org
The Christopher and Dana Reeve Foundation funds research to develop treatments and cures for paralysis caused by spinal cord injury and other central nervous system disorders.

→ **DOCTORS OF THE WORLD**
www.dowusa.org
Works where health is diminished or endangered by violations of human rights and civil liberties in collaboration with a network of affiliates around the world.

→ **DOCTORS WITHOUT BORDERS**
www.doctorswithoutborders.org
Doctors Without Borders is an international medical humanitarian organization that provides independent, impartial assistance to those most in need.

→ **ENGENDER HEALTH**
www.engenderhealth.org
Leading international reproductive health organization working to improve the quality of health care in the world's poorest communities.

→ **FOUNDATION FOR THE NATIONAL INSTITUTES OF HEALTH**
www.fnih.org
The Foundation for the National Institutes of Health fosters public health by helping to underwrite biomedical initiatives.

→ **HOLISTIC HEALTH NETWORK**
www.holisticnetwork.org
The Holistic Health Network is an online community of practitioners and patients seeking alternative health solutions.

→ **INSTITUTE FOR FAMILY HEALTH**
www.institute2000.org
The Institute for Family Health provides high-quality health care to underserved populations and sponsors innovative training programs.

→ **JAMIE-LYNN SIGLER FOUNDATION**
www.givingback.org/sigler
The Foundation promotes healthy body images in young women and men, and educates the public about the prevention and serious consequences of eating disorders.

→ **KIDNEY CANCER ASSOCIATION**
www.kidneycancerassociation.org
The Kidney Cancer Association funds, promotes, and collaborates with other cancer institutes on research projects while serving as an advocate for patients.

→ **LIVESTRONG**
www.livestrong.org
LiveStrong was founded in 1997 by Lance Armstrong. The organization provides a variety of resources for people affected by cancer, including articles, a counseling hotline, and grants to address the needs of cancer survivors. Through grassroots fundraising campaigns, the foundation has become the largest cancer support organization in the world.

→ **NATIONAL DOWN SYNDROME SOCIETY**
www.ndss.org
The National Down Syndrome Society is a national leader in Down syndrome education, research, and advocacy.

→ **NATIONAL EATING DISORDER ASSOCIATION**
www.nationaleatingdisorders.org
The largest nonprofit organization working to prevent eating disorders and provide treatment referrals to those suffering from anorexia, bulimia, and binge eating disorder.

→ **NATIONAL ORGANIZATION ON DISABILITY**
www.nod.org
Works to expand the participation and contribution of America's 54 million men, women, and children with disabilities in all aspects of life.

→ **NO KIDDING, ME TOO!**
www.nokiddingmetoo.org
No Kidding, Me Too! is an organization made up of entertainment-industry professionals working to remove the stigma attached to mental illness by generating messages of empowerment and acceptance.

➡ ONEWORLD HEALTH

www.oneworldhealth.org

As a nonprofit pharmaceutical company, OneWorld Health develops new and affordable medicines for neglected diseases.

➡ OUR BODIES OURSELVES

www.ourbodiesourselves.org

Our Bodies Ourselves is a public interest women's health education, advocacy, and consulting organization.

➡ PATH

www.path.org

PATH collaborates with diverse public and private sector partners to provide appropriate health technologies to improve global health and well-being.

➡ PHYSICIANS COMMITTEE FOR RESPONSIBLE MEDICINE

www.pcrm.org

Physicians Committee for Responsible Medicine promotes preventive medicine, conducts clinical research, and encourages higher standards for ethics and effectiveness in research.

➡ POPULATION ACTION INTERNATIONAL

www.populationaction.org

Population Action mobilizes political and financial support for population, family planning, and reproductive health policies and programs.

➡ THE SAMFUND

www.thesamfund.org

The SAMFund is a nonprofit that offers grants and scholarships to help young cancer survivors through their transition into post-treatment life.

➡ SOLVING KIDS' CANCER

www.kidcancer.org

Solving Kids' Cancer is a public charity that funds research initiatives through donations to solve childhood cancer.

➡ SPECTRUM HEALTH SYSTEMS

www.spectrumhealthsystems.org

Spectrum established one of the first therapeutic communities in the country for drug abuse treatment, and now runs more than 55 programs and serves 18,000 individuals yearly.

➡ STARLIGHT STARBRIGHT FOUNDATION

www.starlight.org

The Starlight Starbright Foundation improves the quality of life for seriously ill chidren and their families by providing entertainment, education, and family activities designed to help them cope with pain, fear, and isolation.

➡ SUSAN G. KOMEN FOR THE CURE

www.cms.komen.org

Susan G. Komen for the Cure is the world's largest grassroots network of breast cancer survivors and activists who fight to save lives, empower people, and ensure quality care for all.

➡ TAPESTRY HEALTH

www.tapestryhealth.org

Provides high-quality, affordable, confidential health services and advocacy.

➡ TECH HEALTH

www.techhealth.com

Tech Health offers efficient access to a broad range of ancillary medical services such as diagnostic imaging, home health, and outpatient rehabilitation.

➡ URBAN ZEN

www.urbanzen.org

The mission of the Urban Zen Initiative is to raise awareness about well-being, cultural preservation, and empowering children. To do this, the initiative holds forums and events on each of these three areas of interest.

➡ VENTURE STRATEGIES FOR HEALTH AND DEVELOPMENT

www.venturestrategies.org

Improves the health of low-income people in resource-poor settings by making use of local market forces around the world.

➡ WORLD TEAM SPORTS

www.worldteamsports.org

World T.E.A.M. Sports uses the universal power of sports to create soul-stirring experiences by teaming disabled athletes with able-bodied athletes.

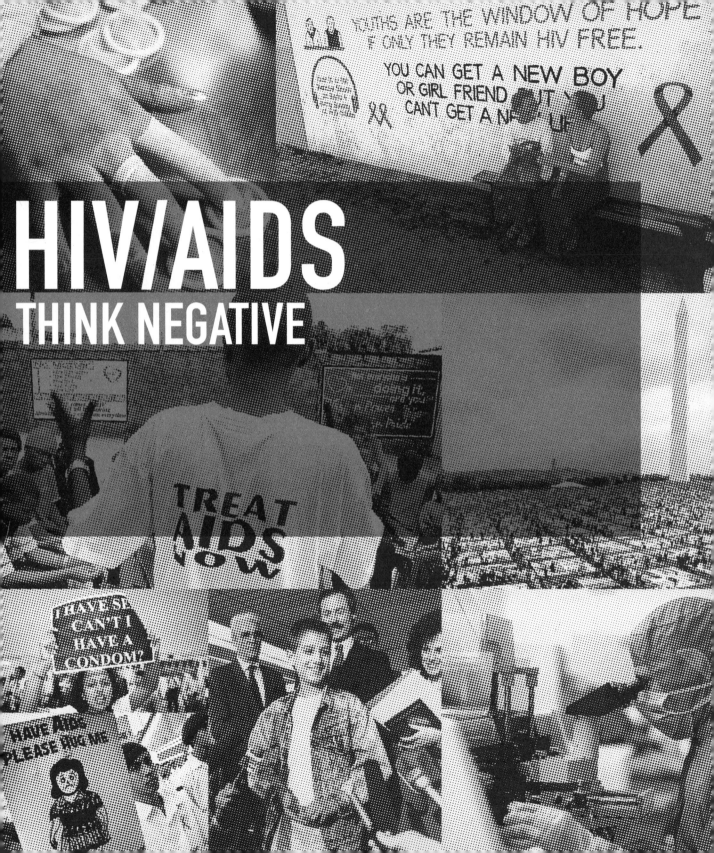

For the last twenty-five years, our company has supported AIDS-related initiatives in an effort to fight the stigma and spread of this deadly disease. Recently we launched one of the largest awareness campaigns in the history of the company, and maybe the disease. It was based on the notion that if one of us is infected, all of us are affected; the headline was, "We all have AIDS." To promote the concept we planned a public relations campaign that would generate more coverage than we could ever afford with advertising. Prior to its release, we asked certain well-known AIDS activists and celebrities to attend events wearing T-shirts emblazoned with the words "I have AIDS." We figured that once the paparazzi shot our forthcoming "messengers," the tabloids would publish speculation pieces about their lifestyle. Then, on World AIDS Day, all the activists would unite in New York to unveil the new campaign and message: "We all have AIDS (if one of us does)." Unfortunately, this never happened. No one wanted to be the first to wear the T-shirt, and some didn't want to wear it at all. Upon further reflection, I too would have declined, reluctant to subject my family to intrusive speculation. ➜ **If AIDS activists aren't comfortable with that message, it leads one to the question, "Is the stigma of AIDS as devastating, if not more, than the disease itself?" —Kenneth Cole**

PRESIDENT BILL CLINTON

On the Global Fight Against HIV/AIDS

President Bill Clinton

*After leaving office, President Bill Clinton has continued to have a positive impact on the lives of millions, working to solve some of the world's biggest challenges through the **Clinton Foundation**. He launched the **Clinton Foundation HIV/AIDS Initiative** to expand essential access to lifesaving medication and to help developing countries systematize their treatment approach.*

➡ *clintonfoundation.org; mycommitment.org*

In the early 1980s Hillary and I each lost a close friend to HIV/AIDS. I still remember sitting beside my friend's hospital bed, feeling powerless to help him and thinking we had to do something to stop all these tragic deaths.

When I was president, we greatly increased funding for AIDS care, treatment, and prevention, contributing nearly twenty-five percent of what was then being spent to fight AIDS in developing countries, and worked to create the Global Fund for AIDS, Tuberculosis, and Malaria. After leaving office, I attended the 2002 International AIDS Conference in Barcelona with Nelson Mandela, who encouraged me to do more in the fight against HIV/AIDS. My foundation began by negotiating dramatic reductions in the price of antiretrovirals (ARVs) and testing equipment, in order to make them available to the people who need them most.

A great disparity still exists between the developed and developing world in terms of access to affordable, safe, and effective treatments for HIV/AIDS and other infectious diseases. In Africa, one in four people who die this year—including a large number of children—will die from AIDS, TB, malaria, or another infectious disease, in many cases because they do not have access to the safest and most effective treatments. My foundation has negotiated new pricing agreements that have made high-quality treatments more affordable. In 2003 the Clinton HIV/AIDS Initiative (CHAI) negotiated a decrease of more than fifty percent in the price of adult first-line regimen treatments. Since its inception, CHAI has negotiated breakthrough ARV price reductions with seven suppliers on more than forty formulations and has negotiated significant price reductions with twelve suppliers for sixteen HIV/AIDS diagnostic tests. Now 1.4 million people in more than sixty nations are getting ARVs under our low-price agreements, but there are still more than seven million people in immediate need of treatment.

While lowering the cost of drugs is immensely important, we must also focus on getting treatment to the most vulnerable populations, including children. In 2005, when we started our pediatric AIDS program, two million children around the world were infected with HIV/AIDS, and more than a third needed treatment immediately in order to live. Though available, drugs for children were often far too expensive and difficult to administer. We worked with UNITAID and other donors to increase access to affordable pediatric

More than ever before, governments are recognizing the importance of taking steps to bring care and treatment to their citizens.

FACT

At the beginning of 2003, there were only about 150,000 people in the developing world (outside of Brazil) with access to the HIV/AIDS treatment they needed. Now, with the help of the Clinton Foundation, there are nearly 3 million people receiving medicines in the developing world.

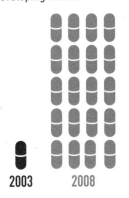

2003   **2008**

FACT

After Hurricane Katrina, former president Clinton and former president Bush established the Bush-Clinton Katrina Fund to help survivors rebuild. The Fund raised more than $130 million in two years. They had collaborated previously on relief work after the Indian Ocean tsunami.

drugs that are easier to use, and doubled the number of children getting treatment in thirty-three countries within the first two years.

More than ever before, governments are recognizing the importance of taking steps to bring care and treatment to their citizens. Additionally, the tremendous increase in the number of non-governmental organizations (NGOs) has helped supplement the efforts of governments. This cooperation has allowed my foundation to help reorganize the market for drugs and diagnostics used to treat HIV/AIDS and strengthen health systems.

The capacity for private citizens to advance the public good is greater than ever before due to several factors: the concentration of wealth in the hands of people who can make positive change, the growth of NGOs in both developing and developed countries, and the ability for people to take action using technology and the Internet. I encourage people to get involved with organizations that are fighting HIV/AIDS, whether here at home or globally, by giving time or money. Also, if you are a health-care worker or are involved in the health-care field, you can make significant impact by volunteering your services in the developing countries hit hardest by HIV/AIDS.

I am amazed at the innovative ways people are getting involved to turn the tide of this pandemic around the world. In 2005 I convened the Clinton Global Initiative (CGI) to bring together heads of state, business leaders, NGOs, philanthropists, and many others to discuss pressing global challenges, but most importantly to identify creative ways to improve global health and make commitments to take action. CGI allowed us to match people who have innovative ideas with those who can fund them, as well as with reliable partners to do the work on the ground. In its first three years, CGI has inspired nearly 1,000 "Commitments to Action," which are improving the lives of more than two million people around the world. We've expanded this model to encourage young people to make commitments to take action as well. In 2008 the first Clinton Global Initiative University meeting was held to inspire young people and give them a platform to make positive changes in their communities and around the world.

I stay motivated by the evidence that our efforts are truly making a difference.

One of the most innovative commitments came from a man in India who discovered that the only HIV/AIDS prevention booklets available in his community were printed in Hindi, but the local dialect is Telugu. He began translating these pamphlets so that everyone could have access to this potentially lifesaving information. This simple idea will have a major impact on his community.

In 2007 CGI launched MyCommitment.org, an online portal to encourage people to make a commitment to give in any way they can. The site has a wealth of information on how to put your unique talents into action, and in its first six months, visitors from more than 185 countries collectively pledged more than 92,000 volunteer hours, $1.5 million, and more than 40,000 items to those in need.

I stay motivated by the evidence that our efforts are truly making a difference. While touring a hospital in Lesotho, I met an adorable, lively little girl named Arietta. When we met, she took my hand and started dancing with me, right there in the clinic's hallway. Without her AIDS medication, Arietta wouldn't be alive today. Thanks to these treatments, she's not just alive—she can dance and play like any other child. I've met lots of children like her in Africa, Asia, and the Caribbean—that's more than enough motivation for anyone.

FACT

In 2008 UNITAID and the Clinton Foundation HIV/AIDS Initiative announced new agreements with generic drug manufacturers that made available new and more affordable child-friendly HIV/AIDS medication.

DR. MATHILDE KRIM

On the Search for a Cure

Dr. Mathilde Krim

*Soon after the first cases of AIDS were reported in 1981, geneticist and activist Dr. Mathilde Krim dedicated herself to increasing the public's awareness of the disease and to finding a cure for it. As founding chairman of **amfAR**, she has been recognized with the Presidential Medal of Freedom for her tremendous efforts to increase the pace of AIDS research and to protect the rights of all those affected by HIV/AIDS.*

➡ *amfAR.org*

When I was eighteen, I saw a documentary on the liberation of German concentration camps by Allied soldiers. I was horrified not only by the fact that some people had perpetrated such terrible crimes, but that millions of others had stood by and said nothing. I swore to myself that I would never tolerate injustice and would speak up whenever I saw it.

Decades later, in early 1981, I had a research lab at New York's Sloan-Kettering Institute when cases of a condition that came later to be called AIDS were first seen in this city. Some of us soon recognized that something serious was happening but medical knowledge was not sufficient at the time to understand the new disease, let alone treat it. Intensive research on AIDS needed to be urgently and widely undertaken; people with AIDS desperately needed care and support and the public at large needed information on how to protect itself and to contain the further spread of AIDS. There was a broad and heavy agenda before us.

Those few who took it upon themselves to venture into such an endeavor soon discovered, to their dismay, that because the early cases of AIDS had been found among members of the gay community, much of the public's reaction to the issue of AIDS was one of indifference and lack of empathy. The attitude of most members of Congress reflected that of the public that had elected them and a similar reaction among people in the executive branch of government delayed by some five years significant funding for AIDS research. All this created a disconcerting and very painful reality, one that came to cost many lives. It so reminded me of how murderous all prejudice and callous indifference can be.

It is volunteerism that first created and first sustained AIDS appropriate social and medical services and even prompted valuable AIDS research initiatives supported by private funds. To this day, however, plenty remains to be done. In particular, there is a growing and persistent need for the public to receive and absorb information that is "evidence based," i.e., that is logically derived from the observation and study of biomedical realities, not from myth and bias; there is also an enormous need for economic assistance and for nonjudgmental, comprehensive, and humane care among afflicted communities around the world.

In the United States, volunteerism has already resulted in the establishment of institutions that competently deal with the grave ill-health, as well as the psychological, economic, and human rights problems that face all people with HIV/AIDS. Such capabilities do not exist as yet in most of the world's resource-poor countries. The global epidemic of AIDS thus continues to offer would-be volunteers a wealth of gratifying opportunities to serve in various capacities, including those of caregiver and educator.

Indeed, even in the United States where the vast majority of people have heard of HIV/AIDS and know how to prevent being at risk for it, there remain dangerous misconceptions. Young people often hold, for example, that since it takes on average of ten years for HIV infection to result in "full-blown" AIDS, they don't need to worry anymore about becoming HIV infected because there surely will be a cure ten years from now. Neither are our political authorities exempt from enduring misguided thinking. For example, injection drug users are at very high risk of acquiring HIV through sharing syringes because the purchase of sterile syringes is prohibited by law on the assumption that it would encourage drug use. It has been amply demonstrated that the most effective way to prevent the transmission of HIV among injection drug users (and from them to their partners and children) is to let them have easy access to sterile syringes and needles that cost a few cents apiece when bought in large amounts. Instead, most of our governmental and religious authorities have decided that giving clean needles to addicts would encourage drug use...as if wearing a seat belt encouraged drivers to speed.

Whether human societies will wisely solve such issues will largely be determined by the level of concern, understanding, and dedication that volunteers will impart upon others and the extent to which the compassion that they exemplify will inspire others.

amfAR

Since its founding in 1985, amfAR has invested almost $260 million in AIDS research, HIV prevention, treatment education, and the advocacy of sound AIDS-related public policy.

➡ According to a recent amfAR study, nearly 40% of respondents had not been tested for HIV. And 80% of those people indicated that they did not need a test either because they "knew" they did not have HIV or because they didn't think they needed to be tested. However, 65% support making HIV testing as part of standard routine health care.

SIR ELTON JOHN

On Giving Back

Sir Elton John

*Established by Sir Elton John in 1992, the **Elton John AIDS Foundation (EJAF)** is a leader in supporting innovative HIV/AIDS prevention education programs and direct care and support services to people living with HIV/AIDS. **EJAF** has raised more than $150 million for programs in fifty-five countries around the world.*

➡ *ejaf.org*

n the 1980s there was so much misinformation surrounding HIV/AIDS. People were genuinely terrified, and there was a great deal of stigma surrounding the disease. During this time, I became involved with the fight against HIV/AIDS because I was inspired by Ryan White and his family. People shut him out of school, shot bullets at his home, and spread lies about him. But Ryan didn't hate them. He knew they were just uninformed and afraid. Ryan and his family were such positive and forgiving people, despite the horrific prejudice they encountered.

The United States government was disgracefully slow in doing anything toward the fight against HIV/AIDS. There were no antiretroviral drugs at that point; insurance companies showed prejudice toward gay men in their AIDS treatment policies. So many people would lose their jobs after being diagnosed with the disease, and then lose their homes because they had no financial support.

In 1992 I decided to bring focus to all of my AIDS-related work by establishing the Elton John AIDS Foundation. After years of reckless behavior and drug addiction, I felt a huge responsibility to make up for lost time and give back to anyone living with or affected by the disease. The goals of EJAF are education, awareness, and direct care and support. Our efforts are concentrated on the most highly marginalized and vulnerable populations living with the disease. Awareness has improved massively in the Western world, but there is still more work to be done. Lately we seem to be losing ground as a new younger generation of people becomes infected with the disease. And in the developing world there is even more work ahead of us.

I feel my greatest strength is in the area of fundraising. I am able to use my celebrity to bring people together and help them understand the desperate need to support the fight against HIV/AIDS. I am particularly motivated whenever I make visits around the world and see the difference our foundation is making in the fight against the disease. Despite the staggering worldwide numbers associated with the disease, even the smallest amount of money can make a huge difference. People shouldn't be intimidated by the statistics surrounding HIV/AIDS. Everyone can make a difference. Write a check! No amount is too small. We constantly hear stories from people across the United States that participate in AIDS Walks, run in races, and host lunches to raise money. They simply called up their local AIDS organizations and got involved. It's not just grand fund-raising dinners that are important, it's the people in every city and town speaking in their churches and schools to continue to raise awareness and dispel stigma and prejudice wherever it exists.

I have a very special, a very rich life, but when I see the gratitude people have for the little we've given them, I feel I've got to do more. Until the day I die I'll continue getting out there and raising money for people with AIDS.

RYAN WHITE

In 1984 13-year-old Ryan White was diagnosed with AIDS after contracting the virus through a blood transfusion. Given six months to live, he asked to continue to attend school. Ryan and his family were forced to battle discrimination from their community as well as the Kokomo, Indiana, school board after Ryan was barred from the classroom. His fight gained national attention and Ryan soon became a spokesperson for greater AIDS awareness. His story touched the hearts of the entire country, including celebrities such as Elton John, Phil Donahue, Greg Louganis, and Michael Jackson, all of whom offered their support to the teen. After a 5-year battle, Ryan White died of AIDS-related complications. At his bedside were his family and his friend Elton. Soon after his death, Congress passed the Ryan White CARE Act to provide federal funding for treatment and education for people affected by HIV.

> **The United States government was disgracefully slow in doing anything toward the fight against HIV/AIDS.**

Sir Elton John and David Furnish hold a baby who was born HIV-negative at the Site B Hospital, Khayelitsha in South Africa.

LOVE HEALS

On the Legacy of Ali Gertz

Stefani Greenfield, Victoria Leacock Hoffman, and Dini von Mueffling, co-founders of Love Heals

*Alison Gertz was infected with HIV through a sexual encounter when she was sixteen. After discovering that she had AIDS, Ali shared her story in an effort to help others and became an internationally recognized spokesperson for AIDS prevention. After her death, Ali's best friends continued her mission by founding **Love Heals**, the Alison Gertz Foundation for AIDS Education. Love Heals has reached more than 350,000 young people through their Speakers Bureau and educational programs.*
➡ *loveheals.org*

We did not know a great deal about AIDS prior to Ali's diagnosis. It was not, in our opinions at the time, a potential threat to any of us. When Ali was diagnosed with HIV in 1988, she already had full-blown AIDS. She had been hospitalized in critical condition for weeks before it even occurred to someone to test her for HIV, as she was a white, heterosexual woman in a monogamous relationship.

After Ali was diagnosed, she did everything she could to ensure that others had the information they needed to protect themselves from HIV infection—information that could have saved her. We saw the strength it took for Ali to speak out; when she became a public speaker, many people were concerned that she could pass the virus to them just by being in the same room. Parents of the young people she spoke to warned them not to get too close to her. The irony was that her immune system was so compromised that she was the one at risk of contracting something from them! But Ali handled all of this with grace.

Combating HIV means combating stigma. The most important thing we can do is make sure that everyone has access to HIV/AIDS education.

Another issue Ali faced was criticism for having been sexually active as a teenager. In reality, she was responsible and mature enough to take what she understood to be the necessary precautions before engaging in sex. HIV and AIDS simply weren't on the radar for a teenager in 1982. It wasn't even called AIDS then! Once more, Ali handled the criticism well. Time and time again, she was willing to put herself out there to educate others. She was determined to do this.

Ali's death in 1992 was devastating and shocking. She was twenty-six; this was not supposed to happen. When it came to starting Love Heals, we did not have a choice. Being her best friends—and being healthy—we were in a unique position to further Ali's work. We started with only one goal: to one day go out of business, meaning that a cure had been found or, at the very least, that comprehensive HIV/AIDS education had been mainstreamed into schools' health curricula.

The mission of Love Heals remains the same as it did when we started fifteen years ago: to empower young people in the fight against HIV by giving them the tools they need to protect themselves. The Love Heals Speakers Bureau is made up of more than twenty HIV-positive speakers and trained health educators who visit hundreds of schools, community groups, churches, and prisons annually. Our speakers make HIV real. Their strength and bravery are amazing, standing up in front of thousands of young people every year, telling and retelling their stories. What happened to them does not have to happen to others: HIV is 100 percent a preventable disease. Information saves lives.

Everyone can help in the fight to eradicate HIV/AIDS by donating money and time to organizations that work to educate people or support those who have already contracted the disease. Combating HIV means combating stigma. The most important thing we can do is make sure that everyone has access to comprehensive HIV/AIDS education. The younger it starts, the better. People who want to help should know that anything at all makes a difference, whether it's a dollar or an hour. The rising tide lifts all ships.

CAROL GERTZ
Mother of Alison Gertz

" After she got over the initial shock of her diagnosis and was recuperating in the hospital, Ali said to me, "Mommy, I know I'm going to die and I would like to help others so that they don't get AIDS like I did." We thought that this was wonderful, but we were so concerned with her illness that we didn't pay too much attention. A few months later, the New York Times ran a series of articles about AIDS that focused exclusively on gay men and intravenous drug users. I became more upset each day reading these articles, as there was no mention of women being infected. After discussing it with Ali and getting her okay, I called Bruce Lambert, the writer of the articles, and told him our story. A few days later, the Metropolitan section of the Times devoted most of the front page to an article about Ali, "The Girl Next Door Gets AIDS." When the story broke, I started getting calls from other mothers saying, "We thought we were the only ones." There were many young women out there who were too ashamed to come forward, as the virus was known to be sexually transmitted and that was—and still is—a taboo subject. Ali was asked to talk to students in universities and high schools all over the country about her experience and the realities of HIV and AIDS, and continued to do this as long as she was able.

Ali was on the cover of People, she was chosen as "Woman of the Year" by Esquire, and was interviewed on television. It made people open their eyes to the fact that anyone can get AIDS. Even members of Congress took notice, realizing that this could affect their own daughters too! Suddenly, they started allocating more money for AIDS research. In June of 1992 Ali was recognized for "Exceptional Achievement in Public Service" by the Department of Health and Human Services. She died August 8 of that year. Even today when I meet people, they tell me that when the Times article ran, they all cut it out and sent it to every young girl away at college that they knew. "

PETER STALEY

On Acting Up

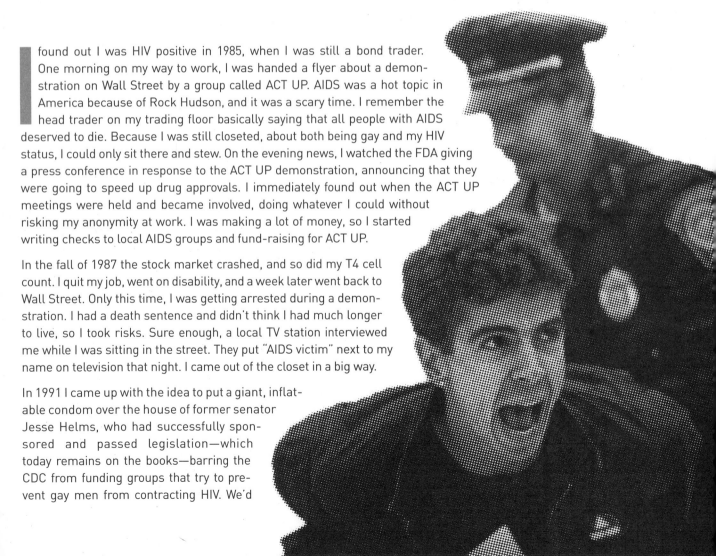

Peter Staley

*Peter Staley is a founding member of **Treatment Action Group (TAG)**, an early leader of **ACT UP New York**, a street activist, an **amfAR** board member, and founder of **AIDSmeds.com**. He is a leading voice in AIDS research and treatment advocacy.*

➜ *aidsinfonyc.org; aidsmeds.com*

I found out I was HIV positive in 1985, when I was still a bond trader. One morning on my way to work, I was handed a flyer about a demonstration on Wall Street by a group called ACT UP. AIDS was a hot topic in America because of Rock Hudson, and it was a scary time. I remember the head trader on my trading floor basically saying that all people with AIDS deserved to die. Because I was still closeted, about both being gay and my HIV status, I could only sit there and stew. On the evening news, I watched the FDA giving a press conference in response to the ACT UP demonstration, announcing that they were going to speed up drug approvals. I immediately found out when the ACT UP meetings were held and became involved, doing whatever I could without risking my anonymity at work. I was making a lot of money, so I started writing checks to local AIDS groups and fund-raising for ACT UP.

In the fall of 1987 the stock market crashed, and so did my T4 cell count. I quit my job, went on disability, and a week later went back to Wall Street. Only this time, I was getting arrested during a demonstration. I had a death sentence and didn't think I had much longer to live, so I took risks. Sure enough, a local TV station interviewed me while I was sitting in the street. They put "AIDS victim" next to my name on television that night. I came out of the closet in a big way.

In 1991 I came up with the idea to put a giant, inflatable condom over the house of former senator Jesse Helms, who had successfully sponsored and passed legislation—which today remains on the books—barring the CDC from funding groups that try to prevent gay men from contracting HIV. We'd been fighting the spread of HIV with one hand tied behind our backs because of Senator Helms, and I thought it was time to let him know the free ride was over. Congress doesn't like full-frontal attacks, so I thought the best way to do it was with some humor. We spent $5,000 to have the condom made. It said: "A CONDOM FOR UNSAFE POLITICS, HELMS IS DEADLIER THAN ANY VIRUS." It was all over national news. Senator Helms went on the floor of the Senate and railed against us, saying that radical homosexuals had trespassed on his property, but he never got another piece of anti-gay AIDS legislation passed. After he left his office, he admitted that a lot of what he said about AIDS was wrong and joined the religious-right movement to stop AIDS in Africa. The challenge for activists these days is being creative and figuring out how to garner interest from the news media, which has become pretty jaded about traditional activism. My last political act made the greatest impact of anything I did. I came out as a recovering crystal meth addict in late 2003. The drug was damaging the lives of many gay men in New York, yet nobody was talking about it. One day, after going to a twelve-step meeting, I saw these sexy advertisements on phone booths in Chelsea for gay.com, targeting the neighborhood's large gay community. No recovering addict had ever bought his own ads with a political message. I bought six ads on three phone booths for $5,000 and spent another $1,000 on a publicist. It became a huge story, and within two months, the city health department and various AIDS organizations responded by appropriating money for more ads.

Anger can be a very positive emotion, and has actually fed the best activism I've ever done and that I've seen others do. There's a lot of injustice in the world, and when you get angry, you get motivated to take risks. However, I would always argue against things that might deeply offend a larger audience and turn the public against you. When your actions become the story rather than message, you're really not doing anybody any good.

Volunteerism can be incredibly empowering, but it should only be done in a very serious, determined way. First off, don't foist yourself on an organization that doesn't have a volunteer program. Pick a place where volunteers play a crucial role. Start by letting people know you're personally invested in a situation: Telling your friends and family that something is important to you is a form of activism. If you have your own blog or Facebook page, create something to let people know you care about it. It changes social norms when you're willing to publicly say, "This matters to me."

The challenge for activists these days is being creative and figuring out how to garner interest from the news media.

DIRECT ACTION

In 1989 Peter Staley showed up at the Burroughs Wellcome headquarters in Research Triangle Park, North Carolina with fellow ACT UP members to protest the pharmaceutical giant's exorbitant pricing of the AIDS cocktail, AZT, which came to $8,000 a year at the time. Dressed in business suits, the men used power drills and metal plates to barricade themselves inside a room. A few months later, after the company refused to change the cost, ACT UP shut down the New York Stock Exchange at the opening bell in another publicity-grabbing stunt. Three days later, Burroughs Wellcome lowered the price by 20 percent—the first, and last, time an AIDS drug price has been reduced in the U.S.

MAGIC
JOHNSON

On the Campaign to End Black AIDS

Earvin "Magic" Johnson

*In 1991 sports legend Earvin "Magic" Johnson, Jr., announced his HIV-positive status, immediately becoming one of the most prominent crusaders for AIDS awareness. The **Magic Johnson Foundation** supports a number of educational and prevention programs, including the award-winning "I Stand With Magic" campaign to end AIDS in the African-American community.*

➡ *magicjohnson.com*

There is no handbook passed out to those diagnosed with HIV/AIDS. I could have the best care, but it was up to me to educate myself.

verything in my life changed seventeen years ago, the day I shared the news of my HIV status. I was in the prime of my career and, like most young people, felt invincible. So being told I was HIV-positive was a shock. While I'd heard of the disease, I didn't know much about living with it—back then it was perceived as more of a death sentence. I had to change my thinking and focus on the future and on living with the disease.

The hardest part was telling my wife, Cookie, who was pregnant with our son. I said I would understand if she didn't want to stay with me. That was the toughest moment. But she assured me that we were going to beat this together, and I felt that with her by my side, I could find a way to live with HIV.

There is no handbook passed out to those diagnosed with HIV/AIDS. I could have the best care and resources in the world, but it was up to me to educate myself. By working with my doctors to find the right medication and regimen, and by eating healthier and staying active, I've taken control of the disease instead of letting it take control of me. I maintain a positive frame of mind and wake up every day feeling blessed to be alive.

Prior to my diagnosis, I was aware of the disease and knew of others, such as Elizabeth Glaser and Arthur Ashe, who had contracted it. I admired Ashe because he never let HIV stop him from living or from working to increase awareness of the disease and of the importance of efficient health care. Elizabeth Glaser inspired me to take action and understand that my story could help others. By starting the Magic Johnson Foundation in 1991, I've been doing my part to encourage young adults to know their status and stay protected.

On December 1, 2006, internationally known as World AIDS Day, I launched the "I Stand with Magic" program, part of the "Campaign to End Black AIDS," in partnerships with Abbott, a global health-care company. The program seeks to reduce the stigma of HIV in the African-American community and increase awareness of testing, prevention, and treatment methods. Ultimately, my hope is to reduce the rate of new HIV infections among African-Americans.

The African-American community is the hardest hit in the United States when it comes to HIV/AIDS. Although they make up only thirteen percent of the population, they account for almost half of the estimated number of HIV/AIDS cases diagnosed in 2006. As alarming as the numbers are for all African-Americans, they are even

FACT

The Magic Johnson Foundation has provided free HIV/AIDS testing to more than 38,000 Americans in 16 major cities. Additionally, the program has educated nearly 280,000 people about HIV and helped patients receive access to doctors/medicine through four AHF Magic Johnson Healthcare Clinics.

FACT

➡ **64% of women living with HIV/AIDS in 2005 were African-American.**

➡ **74% of them contracted HIV through unprotected heterosexual sex.**

more shocking for African-American women. A resounding 64 percent of women living with HIV/AIDS in 2005 were black, and HIV is the leading cause of death among black women aged 25 to 34 years. Those statistics have to change.

The strongest barrier to getting tested is often our own fear. We should be more afraid of being HIV-positive and *not knowing it*. Getting tested is the only way we can stop the spread of the disease.

Seventeen years ago we couldn't speak openly about HIV/AIDS without encountering tremendous fear and discrimination. That is changing. Today, our youth want to know the facts, and telling them the truth will motivate them to abstain, use protection, and get tested. I want to encourage young adults to be comfortable talking about sex and HIV/ AIDS. I hope that by visiting schools and colleges, I help young adults understand that they have to take responsibility for their own health.

Although African-Americans make up only thirteen percent of the population, they account for almost half of the estimated number of HIV/AIDS cases.

DR. MONICA SWEENEY

➡️ **On Pushing Legislation**

Dr. Monica Sweeney

*Dr. Monica Sweeney fights AIDS as a doctor in the heart of the inner city. She helped lobby for the passage of the "Baby AIDS Bill" in New York City, served as chair of the Prevention Subcommittee for the **Presidential Advisory Council on HIV/AIDS**, and is the **New York City Health Department**'s Assistant Commissioner of HIV Prevention and Control.*

➡️ *pacha.gov*

In the beginning of the HIV/AIDS epidemic I felt paralyzed by helplessness. No doctor wants to make a diagnosis and follow it by saying, "I know what's wrong with you, but there's nothing I can do." I can still see the face of the first patient—a young gay man, a marathon runner that was admitted to the hospital on Friday and died by Monday from Pneumocystis carinii pneumonia (PCP). I didn't have to see that repeated too many times before the question arose: Since it can't be treated, how can it be prevented? So prevention became and remains my passion.

For many years, I worked to stop the epidemic through direct patient care, recruiting and educating community-based doctors to accept and treat infected patients, and by speaking openly at any venue that would let me, whether it was for two, 200, or 2,000 people. In the '90s I met Nettie Mayersohn, a New York State assemblywoman who had sponsored a bill, now known as the "Baby AIDS Bill." There was such opposition; she was a lone voice crying in the wilderness. I joined forces with her to get that legislation passed, which it was in 1996. That piece of legislation has been responsible for saving the lives of more babies than any single intervention before or after. Many people are unaware that there are still laws that prevent public health/medical professionals from doing all that they can do to stop the epidemic. In the '80s, when these laws were passed, they served an important function. Now that AIDS is a chronic disease, these laws can be barriers to early diagnosis and treatment. If more people were aware of how current legislation impedes HIV testing, they would demand change.

GET INVOLVED

1 Lobby your legislators to remove all the barriers that tie the hands of those working to end the epidemic.

2 Get tested and know your HIV status. If you are negative, stay negative. If you test positive, get treatment, stay in treatment, and do not infect others.

3 Raise awareness. Use every opportunity in any venue. If you belong to an organization or a club, put HIV/AIDS on the agenda of the next meeting. Give a few facts; invite someone to a meeting that will help dispel myths and stereotypes. Hug a person publicly known to be infected and help overcome the stigma.

4 Find an organization whose goals and mission match something you can support and give according to your means. Check the organization's annual report to be sure that the majority of contributions are going to programs instead of operations.

5 Use your professional position in the media, retail sites, corporations, or small businesses to make changes. Make personnel policies that support privacy and HIV testing the way that blood drives are supported by many places of employment.

NATASHA RICHARDSON

On Stigma

Natasha Richardson

*Actress Natasha Richardson has been an AIDS activist since the death of her father of AIDS-related causes in 1992. She has spearheaded numerous fundraisers, participated in events and symposia, and currently serves as an **amfAR** board member.*
➡ *amfAR.org*

At some point during the 1980s, my father, the filmmaker Tony Richardson, contracted the AIDS virus. Public awareness had been increasing, but until I witnessed the rapid deterioration of his health, my relationship to the epidemic was only of passive sympathy and concern. Of course, when he died, everything changed and I felt a tremendous responsibility to do something.

My father was not open about having AIDS. He would talk about certain individual illnesses, but not call it AIDS. Frankly, he would've covered it up in the same way had he gotten cancer, which does not carry a stigma. He was just determined to fight the disease, carry on, and not be treated like a sick person. I wish I had that courage.

When it was close to the end, I came out to L.A. to look after him with my sisters, mother, and stepmother. The AIDS ward at the hospital was a very isolated area with cautionary signs everywhere. There was tremendous fear about being in contact with anyone with AIDS; it was like leprosy. The nurses would even wear moon suits. But if you did a little research, you knew you were absolutely fine.

When Magic Johnson announced he was HIV-positive in November of 1991, my father was no longer cognizant. But for my family and I, it was a joyous celebration. We had T-shirts printed up with Magic's picture on the front and the words "Magic, we love you" on the back. It was such positive reinforcement. We wore them to the hospital every day. A week later, my father passed away.

In family discussions, we worried that if we released the news that his death was AIDS-related, he would only be remembered for that. But we also knew the importance of being open about it, so we made the decision to tell the truth. Afterward, I really started to think about ways that I could help other than just sending a check. I concluded that the most urgent need was to find a vaccine or cure, and that I'd be most helpful in fundraising for research. If my father had the kinds of antiretroviral drugs that are available today, he'd probably still be alive.

One of the first fundraisers I did for amfAR was a gala premiere of *Blue Sky*. It was the last film my father made before his death, and it was a way to bring the focus on him for his work, and on the disease to help others. But the biggest event I put together came after I'd seen the hugely successful charity auction of Princess Diana's dresses. It made me think of Hollywood and the public's fascination with all the gowns that get made for the Oscars. Despite the enormous help of my co-chair Anna Wintour and *Vogue*, not to mention the staff at amfAR, organizing the auction proved to be an enormous undertaking. The event raised a great deal of money, so our hard work paid off.

The biggest obstacles in fighting HIV/AIDS are still the practical ones: the prevention of the spread of the disease; making medications affordable, available, and understandable; and most vital, creating the vaccines to prevent people from getting it. I continue to educate myself about the epidemic. You don't have to spend your life researching. I get my information how most people do: I read newspapers. I talk to friends and doctors. I listen. The other day I learned that the number one cause of death for twenty-four- to thirty-four-year-old African-American women in the United States is AIDS. It was deeply shocking to me. But it doesn't make me lose hope. Instead, it makes me feel that we can do something about it, that AIDS is absolutely preventable through education, awareness, medication, and access to that medication.

Everyone can help in different ways. You can send money. You can work in kitchens or deliver meals to patients. You can run in a fundraising marathon. What I really love is coming up with ideas, even though it's like conceiving a great movie idea—it doesn't happen every day. Any major charity would be delighted to hear about your suggestions. All you need to do is contact the organization you care most about and say, "Here's an idea." The most important thing to remember is that every little bit helps. They are pinpricks in the darkness; the more people help, the lighter and brighter the sky will become.

HIV/AIDS OBSTACLES

Stigma and fear.
HIV/AIDS is still often mistakenly perceived as a "gay disease" or one that only intravenous drug-using heterosexuals or prostitutes can contract. This not only leads to discrimination of those with HIV or AIDS, but it prevents people from admitting to being HIV-positive or getting tested and seeking medical treatment.

Complacency.
Health advocates are worried that because HIV has been around for so long, it's become normalized to the point where the public is not taking precautions like they used to. There is even a misconcpetion among some that a vaccine or cure is already available.

Lack of access to treatment.
Antiretroviral drugs can be prohibitively expensive. Fortunately, in recent years, advocates have helped increase access to the drugs. Yet difficulties persist in proper dissemination and, with developing nations in particular, not having enough qualified health workers to administer treatment.

Lack of prevention education.
We have known how to prevent the spread of HIV/AIDS since the 1980s, but until every person is educated, HIV/AIDS will continue to proliferate with tragic consequences.

MARK SELIGER

→ **On Art for Good Causes**

Mark Seliger

*Award-winning photographer Mark Seliger co-founded the non-commercial gallery **401 Projects** to provide exhibition space to unique artists and photographic campaigns. Every exhibit at 401 Projects celebrates a different charity. Seliger's own nonprofit work includes the Vote or Die campaign, **Keep A Child Alive**, amfAR, and the **Michael J. Fox Foundation for Parkinson's**.*

→ *401projects.com*

Whenever Kenneth puts his name on something, I've come to expect that the project will always be a meaningful one. So a few years ago, when he approached me to photograph a new AIDS awareness campaign, there was no hesitation on my part.

Our concept was to shoot celebrities, doctors, and researchers putting their footprints in concrete, like on Hollywood Boulevard, with the slogan: "We all have AIDS." It was a very bold statement that captures the six-degrees-of-separation idea of the disease and how pervasive it is. The idea of the footprint was not just about taking your shoes off and taking a step forward, but also symbolically making an imprint in society in terms of AIDS awareness and turning it into a thing of the past. It was a great cam-

FACT
Launched on December 1, 2005, the "We All Have AIDS" campaign was the biggest AIDS public service announcement in the history of the disease. Some of the world's greatest AIDS activists including Elizabeth Taylor, Nelson Mandela, Elton John, and Archbishop Desmond Tutu were photographed by Mark Seliger.

paign to be a part of because amfAR has been known as the leading, grassroots group of AIDS research, HIV prevention, and treatment education.

One of our most memorable subjects was Nelson Mandela, whom we photographed in a town called George, a few hundred miles east of Cape Town, South Africa. Mr. Mandela was there for a concert commemorating the anniversary of his imprisonment, and was staying at the hotel where we had set up the shoot. I'll never forget the guests and employees who were in tears as they gathered around outside the building. It was very moving. Although he did not speak very much, he was very charming and affable.

As I've been incredibly fortunate in my career, it has been important for me to give back by shooting other public service campaigns. Another, more personal way of contributing is through my nonprofit gallery, 401 Projects, which serves as a vehicle for important work you would not typically see in a normal art gallery. We produce six to eight photography shows a year—four of them are based on social issues and social documentary, and the other two or three are more fun. It has a salon-style approach where we attach a charitable organization as well as a special program, like a roundtable discussion or lecture, to each show. Developing 401 Projects was a result of finding my voice in a way I could. It helps me reconnect with what I've always loved about photography and has the capacity to tell stories more effectively than any other medium.

FACT

On December 1, 2006, 401 Projects debuted Bloodline: Aids and Family, an intimate look at the reality of the AIDS pandemic in sub-Saharan Africa by photojournalist Kristen Ashburn. The exhibit helped raise funds for Keep a Child Alive and Mashambanzou Care Trust, organizations working to combat the disease in Africa.

It was a very bold statement that captures the six-degrees-of-separation idea of the disease and how pervasive it is.

MILESTONES IN THE FIGHT AGAINST HIV/AIDS

➡ The U.S. Centers for Disease Control and Prevention releases first reports on "Gay-Related Immune Deficiency." In New York, activist Larry Kramer holds the first AIDS fundraiser.

➡ HIV is isolated by the Pasteur Institute in Paris and the National Institutes of Health in the United States. A hundred-thousand lesbians and gays march at the Democratic National Convention, demanding an increase in federal AIDS spending.

➡ In October, Surgeon General Koop releases an AIDS report urging sex education and condom use. Jon Parker, a former drug addict, begins the first needle exchange in the United States

➡ *Cosmopolitan* magazine publishes an erroneous article telling women that "most heterosexuals are not at risk." It further states that it is impossible to transmit HIV using the "missionary position."

➡ The Ribbon Project is launched. It becomes an international symbol of AIDS awareness. In November, L.A. Laker Earvin "Magic" Johnson announces he is HIV-positive and retires from pro basketball.

➡ The FDA approves the first female condom but refuses to test it for anal sex because sodomy is illegal in many states. Sexual transmission surpasses IV drug use as the number one cause of HIV infection among women.

1981	**1982**	1984	**1985**	1986	**1987**	1988	**1990**	1991	**1992**	1993	**1994**

➡ AIDS, acquired immunodeficiency syndrome, is first used as a term. The first federal funding of $5.6 million is given to AIDS medical research.

➡ The start of the AIDS Vigil in San Francisco, where activists camp out in tents and continue a constant vigil that lasts until 1995. Dr. Mathilde Krim and Dr. Michael Gottlieb found amfAR. Actor Rock Hudson dies of AIDS in October, putting a famous face on the disease for the first time. AIDS Project Los Angeles holds the world's first AIDS Walk, raising $673,000.

➡ ACT UP holds its first mass demonstration on Wall Street. In October, hundreds of thousands of gays and lesbians join the Second National March on Washington for Lesbian and Gay Rights, demanding government action in the fight against AIDS.

➡ AIDS patient Ryan White, whose school prevented him from attending after discovering his diagnosis, dies at 18. In July, the Americans with Disabilities Act is passed to protect people with disabilities, including people with HIV, from discrimination.

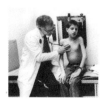

➡ Magic Johnson and Arsenio Hall host the Malcolm–Jamal Warner-directed public service video "Time Out: The Truth About HIV, AIDS, and You," a free Blockbuster rental that serves as the MTV generation's 42-minute introduction to AIDS awareness.

➡ HIV-positive Pedro Zamora, 22, stars on MTV's *The Real World*. He dies of AIDS on November 11, one day after the show's season finale.

➡ The Global Fund to Fight AIDS, Tuberculosis, and Malaria is first conceived at the G8 Summit. President Clinton reauthorizes the Ryan White Comprehensive AIDS Resources Emergency (CARE) Act, guaranteeing uninterrupted medical services for low-income, uninsured people living with HIV.

➡ Due to the introduction of new antiretroviral drugs known as protease inhibitors the year before, for the first time, the number of AIDS deaths in the United States declines.

➡ HIV is the leading cause of death worldwide for 15- to 59-year-olds. The Global Fund is formally launched at the International AIDS Conference in Barcelona.

➡ The FDA approves the use of an HIV test kit that provides results with over 99% accuracy in as little as 20 minutes.

➡ The Bill and Melinda Gates Foundation commits $287 million to AIDS vaccine research, the largest grant ever given to the field.

➡ HIV is the leading cause of death for Americans 25 to 44 year olds.

| 1995 | **1996** | 1997 | **1998** | 2000 | **2001** | 2002 | **2003** | 2004 | **2005** | 2006 | **2007** |

➡ Research finds that using AZT during pregnancy and at the time of delivery reduces mother-to-child HIV transmission. Eventually, the rate of passing the disease drops from 25–35% to less than 3% worldwide, when preventive measures are taken.

➡ At the urging of African-American leaders and the Congressional Black Caucus, and alarmed by the rising proportion of AIDS cases in black and Latino communities, President Clinton authorizes $156 million for prevention, care, and education campaigns that cater to those communities.

➡ Twelve-year-old South African AIDS activist Nkosi Johnson, born with HIV and a champion for the rights of others with HIV/AIDS, dies. At the time of his death, he was the longest-surviving South African child born with HIV.

➡ The President's Emergency Plan for AIDS Relief, a 5-year, $15 billion initiative to address HIV/AIDS, tuberculosis, and malaria is announced during the State of the Union address. More than 20 leading AIDS researchers and public health officials publish a paper in *Science* calling for "a more efficient and integrated HIV vaccine research enterprise" modeled on the Human Genome Project.

➡ After Nelson Mandela's oldest son, Makgatho Mandela, 54, dies of AIDS, the senior Mandela announces: "Let us give publicity to HIV/AIDS and not hide it, because [that is] the only way to make it appear like a normal illness."

➡ Improvements in drugs have largely turned AIDS from a death sentence into a manageable disease to those with access. Donors pledge up to $9.7 billion through 2008 to the Global Fund.

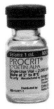

ROBIN SMALLEY

On Motherhood + HIV/AIDS

Robin Smalley

*Robin Smalley is co-founder and international director of **mothers2mothers**, an internationally recognized and award-winning organization that offers education and support for pregnant women and new mothers living with HIV/AIDS throughout sub-Saharan Africa.*

→ *m2m.org*

After twenty years in television as a producer/writer/director, I realized I needed to find a path that was more personally meaningful. Eventually, I became the director of the Media Project, a nonprofit that works with writers, producers, and network executives to incorporate information about reproductive and sexual health into television storylines. This was my first real immersion into the issues surrounding HIV/AIDS.

I was relatively content for seven years until tragedy changed my life forever. My best friend, Karen, went in for minor surgery but never came out of anesthesia. Her brother, Dr. Mitch Besser, flew in to sit bedside, as did I. Throughout the time we watched over her, he told me about an innovative idea called mothers2mothers. I was intrigued, but Africa was a million miles away and had little to do with me. However, when Karen died, my world fell apart. It had been a very bad year—I lost my mother, had battled breast cancer—and losing Karen was my tipping point. I went to Cape Town just to see the work he was doing. On my second day watching him work with the most incredibly heroic, joyous women I had ever in my life encountered, I knew I had to help. Eight weeks later, my husband and I relocated with our two teenage daughters.

Mothers2mothers is an innovative health-care facility–based education and support program for pregnant women and new mothers living with HIV. The program was developed in recognition of the special educational, emotional, and economic needs of women recently diagnosed with HIV. It is premised on three simple principles: first, that peer-based education and support constitutes an essential social intervention complementing medical services for HIV/AIDS; second, that mothers, as caregivers, comprise an affected community's greatest resource; and third, that mothers, employed as peer mentors, are integral members of the prevention of mother-to-child transmission of HIV (PMTCT) health-care team. It still blows me away when I see how many people don't realize that the transmission of the virus from mother to child is almost entirely preventable. People continue to think that if a woman is positive and pregnant, it is inevitable that her baby will be born that way as well. There is little recognition that all it takes is education and access to basic, inexpensive drugs to prevent this tragedy.

When I first arrived in Cape Town, the program was operating out of the back of Mitch's car. By the end of my year there, we had seventy-three sites throughout South Africa, with affiliated sites in Ethiopia and Botswana. Today three of us run the program together. We currently have over 200 sites in South Africa, Lesotho, Kenya, Swaziland, and Zambia, and are expanding into Rwanda and Malawi. We reach more than sixty thousand mothers every month and employ almost seven hundred HIV-positive mothers who would otherwise be considered unemployable. When I arrived in Cape Town, we were begging and borrowing, not knowing how we would meet expenses. This year our budget hovers around $11 million. We've been very, very blessed, but I still see the struggle as a real grassroots effort...one mother at a time spreading the lessons of education and empowerment in her village and township.

It isn't always easy or convenient to make a difference, but everyone has something they can give. Personally, I'd like to see parents talk to their children about HIV/AIDS so it isn't taboo. I'd like to see young people look at the world outside their own backyards, to recognize how lucky they are, and to fund-raise and to raise consciousness in their schools and communities. There isn't a reason in the world why there should be a single baby born with HIV anymore...this isn't a hopeless war...it's a battle that we can win, one mother at a time.

There isn't a reason in the world why there should be a single baby born with HIV anymore.

MOTHERS' CREATIONS

Mothers' Creations, an income-generation project of mothers2mothers, was started in 2002 to encourage the women participating to become economically independent. New mothers living with HIV, many of whom are the sole providers for their families, are trained in beading skills and design to produce high-quality beadwork. Mothers' Creations buys the beaded items from the women and then markets the items to vendors all over the world.

The program fosters independence and self-reliance by assisting the mothers in opening bank accounts and offering basic financial management training. Women who choose to bead fulltime can make as much as R500 ($70) a week, which helps pay for food, clothing, medicine, and shelter for their families. So far, more than 20 beaders have used their income to buy their own homes, and several others have started other business ventures.

TOBY TANSER

➡ On Promoting AIDS Awareness

Toby Tanser

*Marathon runner and coach Toby Tanser is the founder of **Shoe4Africa**, a volunteer organization that uses the popularity of sports to disseminate HIV/AIDS information and battle stigma in Kenya, Tanzania, and Morocco. The organization collects and distributes sporting equipment and uses its highly popular run/walk events as a platform for health educators and world-class athletes to speak about HIV/AIDS, reaching communities that have historically resisted traditional HIV/AIDS initiatives.*

➡ *shoe4africa.org*

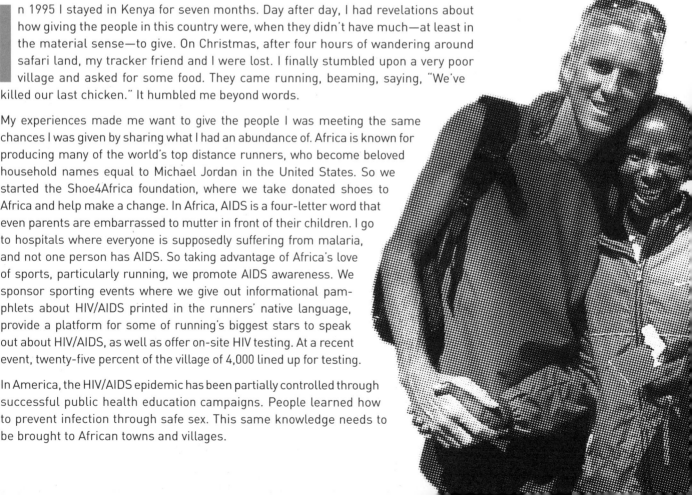

In 1995 I stayed in Kenya for seven months. Day after day, I had revelations about how giving the people in this country were, when they didn't have much—at least in the material sense—to give. On Christmas, after four hours of wandering around safari land, my tracker friend and I were lost. I finally stumbled upon a very poor village and asked for some food. They came running, beaming, saying, "We've killed our last chicken." It humbled me beyond words.

My experiences made me want to give the people I was meeting the same chances I was given by sharing what I had an abundance of. Africa is known for producing many of the world's top distance runners, who become beloved household names equal to Michael Jordan in the United States. So we started the Shoe4Africa foundation, where we take donated shoes to Africa and help make a change. In Africa, AIDS is a four-letter word that even parents are embarrassed to mutter in front of their children. I go to hospitals where everyone is supposedly suffering from malaria, and not one person has AIDS. So taking advantage of Africa's love of sports, particularly running, we promote AIDS awareness. We sponsor sporting events where we give out informational pamphlets about HIV/AIDS printed in the runners' native language, provide a platform for some of running's biggest stars to speak out about HIV/AIDS, as well as offer on-site HIV testing. At a recent event, twenty-five percent of the village of 4,000 lined up for testing.

In America, the HIV/AIDS epidemic has been partially controlled through successful public health education campaigns. People learned how to prevent infection through safe sex. This same knowledge needs to be brought to African towns and villages.

HOW TO... SOME TIPS ON HIV/AIDS

TIME

⏱ **Get tested** to know where you stand. It is not pointless. If you're positive, you can start to take care of your medical needs and protect your sexual partners. Knowing is the first step.

⏱ **Support research in ways that aren't obvious.** Researchers have given us answers, like how condoms effectively protect us from HIV. Now put them into practice. Go to credible sources of information, like governmental websites, to find out what's going on. Use this knowledge to start talking to others about HIV and to know what policies to support.

⏱ **Volunteer to participate in a clinical trial for an AIDS vaccine.** Even with enough funding, the discovery of a vaccine or cure for AIDS is not possible without scientific research and testing on people. Contact the AIDS Vaccine Clearinghouse (www.aidsvaccine clearinghouse.org) and ask about joining a trial in your local area.

⏱ **Help AIDS research using your computer.** Download a free software program from www.worldcommunitygrid.org that runs in the background on your computer. It captures otherwise wasted cycles of your computer and applies them to help model the evolution of drug resistance and to design drugs necessary to fight AIDS. When your computer has finished a FightAIDS@Home computation, the results are sent back to the Scripps Research Institute for analysis. **Visit fightaidsathome.scripps.edu.**

ITEMS

📦 **Give apparel and household items** to thrift stores that specifically benefit AIDS advocacy groups. Good alternatives are: Housing Works in New York City (www.housingworks.org), Boomerangs in the Boston area (www.aac.org/boomerangs), Community Thrift Store in San Francisco (www.sfcenter.org/commthrft. htm), Philadelphia AIDS Thrift (215-922-3186), and Out of the Closet in various California and Florida locations (www.outofthecloset.org).

📦 **Donate unused HIV medication.** AID FOR AIDS (www.aidforaids.org) accepts surplus HIV drug and medical supplies from any patient, doctor's office, pharmacy, or other supplier. They ship all unexpired antiretroviral and HIV prophylaxis medications in their original containers to more than 500 clients in 24 countries throughout four continents.

📦 **Promote AIDS awareness by sending e-cards from Art Action AIDS.** A project of the AIDS Taskforce of Greater Cleveland, or Visual AIDS (www.thebody.org/visualaids), one of the first national initiatives to record the impact of the AIDS pandemic on the arts community.

EXPERTISE

💼 **Become a sex educator.** Contact your local AIDS organization to find out how to get training and opportunities to volunteer. Spreading awareness will help stop the disease.

💼 **Chefs and nutritionists needed.** Help HIV/AIDS patients who have struggled with nutrition learn to stay healthy and strong. Pro chefs and nutritionists are invited to teach classes for low-income and HIV/AIDS sufferers through Share Our Strength's Operation Frontline (www.strength.org). In Florida, the Poverello Center needs people to help with its food bank for those with HIV/AIDS. Or cook meals or make deliveries as part of Project Open Hand (www.openhand.org) in San Francisco.

💼 **Using your touch to help.** Those sick with HIV/AIDS have a special need for healing touch, and research shows that socialization, support, and physical contact can boost the spirits and the immune system. Volunteers can sign up to provide massage, acupuncture, acupressure, and hair styling through Shanti programs (www.shanti.org) or the Housing Works' Women's Health Center (www.housingworks.org).

💼 **Document the lives of people living with HIV/AIDS.** It's important to know the individuals behind the disease. If you are a filmmaker visit a care or treatment center and ask patients to share their stories. Story Corps (www.storycorps.net) is a nonprofit project that records stories of everyday people and archives them in the Library of Congress.

DOLLARS

$ **Take a volunteer vacation to help people affected by HIV/AIDS.** There are many opportunities and programs available to people who are willing to pay for the experience and don't have medical expertise, such as coordinating recreational activities for children, supporting medical professionals, or assisting with in-home care and counseling. Go to Cross-Cultural Solutions at www.crossculturalsolutions.org for more information.

$ **Use a credit card.** Get an Elton John AIDS Foundation Visa card at www.ejaf.org. Every time you charge a purchase on the card, ten cents goes toward supporting groups like AIDS Action Committee, San Francisco AIDS Foundation, Whitman-Walker Clinic, and AIDS Project LA.

$ **Contribute money to purchase clean syringes for needle exchange programs.** These programs lower high-risk injection habits by up to 74 percent and help prevent the spread of HIV. Since Congress passed a ban on using federal funds for any needle exchange operations, organizations such as Prevention-Works! (www.preventionworksdc.org) and the San Francisco AIDS Foundation (www.sfaf.org) rely on private donations and/or local government funding, where legislated.

WHERE TO... SOME PLACES ON HIV/AIDS

→ **AARON DIAMOND AIDS RESEARCH CENTER**
www.adarc.org
The Aaron Diamond AIDS Research Center was established in 1991 to focus on the basic science of AIDS and HIV in a research environment conducive to the highest level of scientific creativity.

→ **ACT UP**
www.actup.org
One of the oldest HIV/AIDS activist organizations, ACT UP remains committed to direct action to end the AIDS crisis.

→ **AIDS ALLIANCE FOR CHILDREN, YOUTH, AND FAMILIES**
www.aids-alliance.org
AIDS Alliance for Children, Youth, and Families works to give a voice to the needs of people living and affected by HIV and AIDS through education and training.

→ **AIDSCARE INCORPORATED**
www.aidscarechicago.org
AIDSCare assists those living with advanced HIV/AIDS in the Chicago area to achieve a higher quality of life through housing, care, and supportive services.

→ **AIDS HEALTHCARE FOUNDATION**
www.aidshealth.org
The largest community-based HIV/AIDS medical provider in the nation, serving Los Angeles patients regardless of their ability to pay for medical care.

→ **AIDS RESEARCH ALLIANCE**
www.aidsresearch.org
A community-based, nonprofit medical research organization specializing in HIV/AIDS.

→ **AIDSMAP**
www.aidsmap.com
Aidsmap provides news, searchable databases of HIV treatment and care, worldwide HIV organization listings, and comprehensive patient information.

→ **AIDS WALK**
www.aidswalk.org
AIDS Walk provides a national database of AIDS walks.

→ **AMFAR, THE FOUNDATION FOR AIDS RESEARCH**
www.amfar.org
amfAR is an international organization that focuses on HIV/AIDS research, education, and public policy. Since 1985 amfAR has issued grants to more than 2,000 research teams and has invested $250 million from donations.

→ **AVERT AIDS EDUCATION AND RESEARCH TRUST**
www.avert.org
AVERT is an international HIV/AIDS charity that focuses on countries where there is a particularly high rate of infection or where there is a rapidly increasing rate of infection.

→ **THE BODY**
www.thebody.com
A comprehensive Web resource for HIV/AIDS that provides news, research, discussion boards, and general information for anyone affected by HIV/AIDS.

→ **CITY OF HOPE**
www.cityofhope.org
Innovative biomedical research, treatment, and education institution dedicated to the prevention and cure of HIV/AIDS and other life-threatening illnesses.

→ **CLINTON FOUNDATION HIV/AIDS INITIATIVE**
www.clintonfoundation.org
The Clinton Foundation HIV/AIDS Initiative's mission is to work with governments to increase the availability of high-quality AIDS care and treatment. The Initiative works with drug manufacturers and labs to lower the price of HIV/AIDS medicines, provides on-the-ground support for individual governments, and has launched programs specifically for children and rural populations.

→ **CROSS-CULTURAL SOLUTIONS**
www.crossculturalsolutions.org
Cross-Cultural Solutions operates international volunteer programs in 12 countries and places over 4,000 volunteers annually. Volunteers with CCS work on community-led initiatives in orphanages, child-care centers, schools, health clinics, hospitals, and various other organizations.

→ **DKT INTERNATIONAL**
www.dktinternational.org
DKT International promotes family planning and HIV/AIDS prevention through social marketing in the developing world. DKT sells more than a half-billion condoms every year.

→ **DOCTORS WITHOUT BORDERS**
www.doctorswithoutborders.org
Doctors Without Borders is an organization comprised of doctors and nurses who volunteer to provide urgent medical care to victims of war and disaster.

→ **ELIZABETH GLASER PEDIATRIC AIDS FOUNDATION**
www.pedaids.org
The Elizabeth Glaser Pediatric AIDS Foundation is dedicated to preventing and eradicating pediatric HIV infection through research, advocacy, and prevention. Their website provides information on pediatric HIV/AIDS and offers a variety of options for getting involved.

→ **ELIZABETH TAYLOR AIDS FOUNDATION**
www.elizabethtayloraids foundation.org
The Elizabeth Taylor AIDS Foundation provides funding to organizations providing critically needed support services for people with HIV/AIDS, prevention services, and education for populations most in need.

→ **ELTON JOHN AIDS FOUNDATION**
www.ejaf.org
One of the largest HIV/AIDS charities, the Elton John AIDS Foundation funds direct patient care services and AIDS prevention education.

→ **GLOBAL HEALTH COUNCIL**
www.globalheatlh.org
The Global Health Council is the seat of the Global AIDS Roundtable, a coalition of organizations working together to expand and improve HIV/AIDS programming.

→ **GLOBAL NETWORK OF PEOPLE LIVING WITH HIV/AIDS**
www.gnpplus.net
The Global Network of People Living with HIV/AIDS advocates for an improved quality of life for all people living

with HIV, focusing on human rights, empowerment, and sexual reproductive health.

→ **HEALING WELL**
www.healingwell.com
Healing Well provides in-depth information on HIV, including medical news, articles, community message forums and chat rooms, books and other resources.

→ **INTERNATIONAL AIDS VACCINE INITIATIVE**
www.iavi.org
Works to ensure the development of safe, effective, accessible, preventive HIV vaccines for use throughout the world through education, clinical trials, and policy.

→ **INTERNATIONAL COUNCIL OF AIDS SERVICE ORGANIZATIONS**
www.icaso.org
ICASO works to mobilize and support community organizations to build an effective global response to HIV/AIDS.

→ **KAISER FAMILY FOUNDATION**
www.kff.org
The Kaiser Family Foundation partners directly with major media companies to run large-scale HIV/AIDS information campaigns targeted to young people.

→ **KNOW HIV/AIDS**
www.knowhivaids.org
Know HIV/AIDS provides detailed information about HIV as well as a locator for HIV testing services.

→ **LOVE HEALS**
www.loveheals.org
Love Heals is dedicated to educating young people about HIV/AIDS through videos, lesson guides, speaker programs, and a girls' empowerment program. The organization places special emphasis on outreach to high-risk communities in New York City.

→ **MAGIC JOHNSON FOUNDATION**
www.magicjohnson.com
Develops programs and supports community-based organizations that address the education, health, and social needs of ethnically diverse, urban communities.

→ **MOTHERS2MOTHERS**
www.m2m.org
Mothers2mothers offers an effective, sustainable model of care that provides education and support for pregnant women and new mothers living with HIV/AIDS.

→ **NATIONAL MINORITY AIDS COUNCIL**
www.nmac.org
The National Minority AIDS Council is dedicated to developing leadership within communities of color to address the challenges of HIV/AIDS.

→ **PANGAEA GLOBAL AIDS FOUNDATION**
www.pgaf.org
Pangaea specializes in developing and executing HIV/AIDS treatment and prevention strategies focused on settings with insufficient health-care capacity and underserved HIV-positive populations.

→ **PRESIDENTIAL ADVISORY COUNCIL ON HIV/AIDS**
www.pacha.gov
The Presidential Advisory Council on HIV/AIDS provides policy recommendations on the U.S. government's response to the AIDS epidemic. It promotes prevention and advance research.

→ **PROJECT INFORM**
www.projectinform.org
Project Inform provides up-to-date treatment information, appropriate standard-of-care guidelines, and points to consider when choosing treatments for people living with HIV/AIDS.

→ **SAN FRANCISCO AIDS FOUNDATION**
www.sfaf.org
The San Francisco AIDS Foundation was founded in 1982 and is one of the largest AIDS service organizations in the U.S. Some of the services the organization provides include the client services department, financial benefits counselors, and a housing subsidy program.

→ **SHOE4AFRICA**
www.shoe4africa.org
Shoe4Africa distributes athletic shoes in Africa and sponsors training and events as well as HIV/AIDS educational campaigns.

→ **TREATMENT ACTION GROUP**
www.aidsinfonyc.org
TAG is an independent AIDS research and policy think tank fighting for better treatment, a vaccine, and a cure for AIDS.

→ **UNAIDS**
www.unaids.org
UNAIDS organizes and collects the resources of 10 UN system organizations to help the world prevent new HIV infections, care for people living with HIV, and mitigate the impact of the epidemic.

→ **UNTIL THERE'S A CURE**
www.utac.org
Until There's a Cure raises awareness and funds through high-profile public service advertising campaigns.

→ **WELL PROJECT**
www.thewellproject.org
The Well Project develops new resources to educate, nurture, and support the community of HIV-positive women, their caregivers, and their health-care providers.

→ **WOMEN, CHILDREN, AND HIV**
www.womenchildrenhiv.org
Provides information on the prevention and treatment of HIV infection in women and children, targeted at health workers and policy makers in resource-poor settings.

→ **YOUTH AIDS**
www.youthaids.org
YouthAIDS is an education and prevention program of Population Services International that uses media, pop culture, music, theater, and sports to help stop the spread of HIV/AIDS. YouthAIDS raises funding for more than 60 countries.

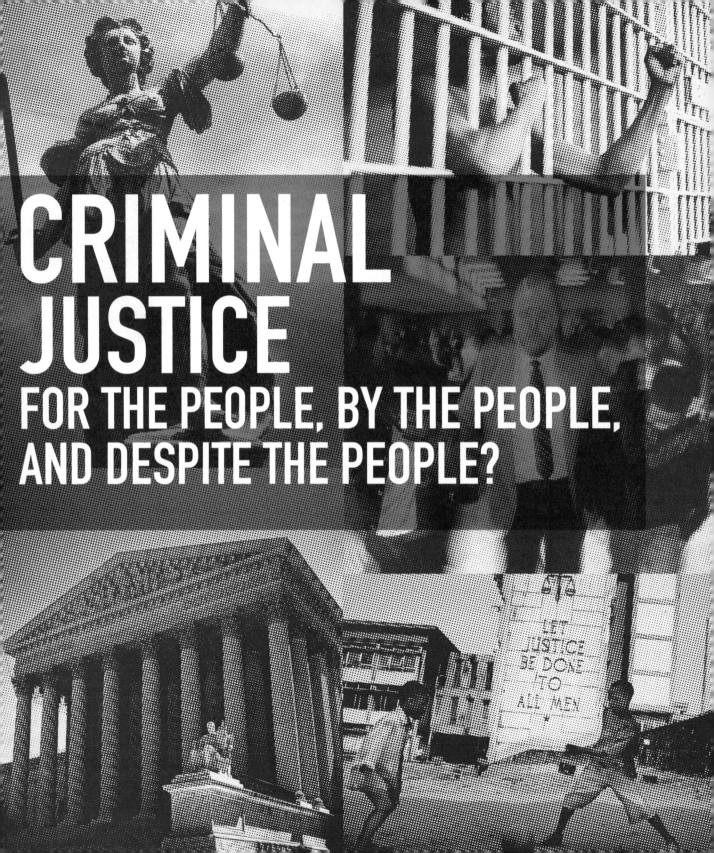

CRIMINAL JUSTICE
FOR THE PEOPLE, BY THE PEOPLE, AND DESPITE THE PEOPLE?

While speaking with several of the contributors for this chapter, I learned that, in this country, high school dropouts are eight times more likely to be incarcerated than their peers that graduate. That proves, beyond a reasonable doubt, that an education is a powerful weapon against jail time. Yet we continue to sink an inordinate amount of money into our ever-expanding jail system rather than our failing school system. The United States has less than five percent of the world's population, but almost a quarter of its prisoners. We have the highest rate of incarceration in the world, with one in every hundred Americans sitting behind bars. Interestingly, as Harry Belafonte points out in his essay within this chapter, less than ten percent of the individuals entering the federal prison system are incarcerated for violent crimes. Time after time, people first truly become a threat to humanity only after they've lived behind bars. Violence, poor mental and medical care, and the lack of rehabilitation or education opportunities exacerbate prior problems, and often create a whole new set. Upon release, ex-convicts lack what is necessary to assimilate back into normal society. Without job skills or an education, and saddled with a criminal record, most are virtually unemployable and the cycle of crime and incarceration continues. → **Could our blind quest for justice be doing society a greater collective injustice? — Kenneth Cole**

GOVERNOR MARIO CUOMO
BARRY SCHECK

→ **On Fighting the Death Penalty**

Governor Mario Cuomo

Known as an intellectual and challenging force for social responsibility and diversity, Governor Mario Cuomo has been called the nation's most gifted philosopher-politician. He served as the 52nd governor of New York from 1983 through 1994.

Barry Scheck

Barry Scheck is co-founder and co-director of the Innocence Project. He currently serves on the New York State Commission on Forensic Science.
➡ *innocenceproject.org*

BS: First I should say, and everybody should know this, Governor, that because you vetoed death penalty bills for, I guess, twelve years...

MC: Yes, twelve years.

BS: ...there are at least twelve innocent people in the state of New York who probably would've been on death row—perhaps executed—if not for your vetoes.

MC: I don't think there was anything extraordinary about my point of view. I was raised in South Jamaica, New York City, and had a great gift early in life. I happened to be a Shabbat goy—a gentile, usually male—who performs certain tasks for Jewish people on the weekend. And on Sunday mornings, I'd be an altar boy. I got to reading about their different codes and laws. One of the things you got to was the laws with respect to the death penalty. So I came at it with a religious view and concluded early on, if you can make mistakes—and all governments are terribly mistake-ridden—there's a chance you're going to kill somebody who's innocent. It just didn't make sense. Lock them up and make sure they don't hurt anybody else, but don't kill them because sometimes the proof will come many years later. And there are plenty of stories you can tell me about through your work with the Innocence Project.

> If you can make mistakes—and all governments are terribly mistake-ridden—there's a chance you're going to kill somebody who's innocent. —MC

BS: The basic mission of our project is, of course, to get as many innocent people out of prison as we can using DNA evidence. We began in 1992, after my colleague Peter Neufeld and I realized DNA testing had the power to both identify people who had committed crimes and demonstrate that individuals who had been incarcerated—and in some instances, sentenced to death—were actually innocent. It started with sexual assault cases, where one could do DNA testing on semen. Now, in murder cases, robbery cases, all kinds of cases, we

5 REASONS
FOR THE DEATH PENALTY

1 It is a deterrent and will stop others from committing crimes.

2 It prevents the criminal from killing others.

3 Modern science can fully prove a person's innocence or guilt.

4 It serves justice.

5 It gives closure to the victims' families.

TO ABOLISH THE DEATH PENALTY

1 It violates the basic human right to life.

2 It does not bring the victim back to life.

3 It's irreversible and there is a possibility that innocent people are being executed.

4 It discriminates against the poor, who are unable to afford good representation.

5 It is expensive, costing taxpayers several times more than the amount to keep someone in prison for life.

can take DNA—from clothing, from skin cells that are left in hinges of glasses, masks, even saliva that was found on a ligature—and use it to exonerate people. In addition to that, we now have data banks for certain DNA profiles to help law enforcement.

MC: In states that still have the death penalty, are there laws that require using DNA?

BS: The biggest problem we've had since 1992 is that we couldn't even get access to the evidence or get into court. We had to go across the country and establish it state by state. There were only six states in the country that had a clear right to go back into court without any time limits. We now have forty-three states that have post-conviction DNA statutes. But, in many jurisdictions, we're still fighting. You wouldn't believe some of the fights we have.

MC: How did they rationalize that? If you're operating with just common sense, it seems to me you could do it in baby talk. You know, "This is the best test."

BS: The argument is finality—that at some point litigation has to stop.

MC: Do some people use the availability of DNA and DNA tests as an argument for the death penalty? I can see someone arguing, "One of the reasons we shouldn't have a death penalty is that you kill an innocent person and it's too late to correct the mistake, obviously. But now that we have DNA working for us, there's less chance we're going to make a mistake."

BS: Just think of it—only ten percent of cases have biological evidence you can test that would be useful or definitive on the issue of identity. So what about all the other cases in the system that rely, perhaps, on false confessions, scientifically invalid, or even fraudulent forensic evidence? Cases where there's ineffective assistance by the defense counsel who don't have nearly enough money to defend their clients? We have to worry about the other ninety percent of the cases.

MC: What are the basic arguments against the death penalty and the basic arguments in favor of it today?

BS: Reasonable people can differ about the moral appropriateness of the death penalty itself. Obviously, many people believe that it undermines the moral fabric of society. It coarsens it and sets a terrible example of how we ought to build a civilized society. Then, there are problems of innocence. And it's very expensive. Every place in the country where you have capital punishment requires extra time and jury selection, more lawyers and experts. When you compare that with the average life span of a prisoner, the death penalty versus life without parole, the death penalty is more expensive. On the other hand, some feel it is a morally appropriate sanction for the most heinous of crimes. But even if you believe that, you cannot as a moral or practical matter abide what's happened in the United States with respect to the death penalty. It's simply not being administered fairly in terms of giving adequate resources in trials.

MC: Frankly, I feel more strongly about it now, because there's something that's happened in the world since that's become, in some ways, more brutal. You said it very neatly: The death penalty does affect the moral standards of the community. You get used to brutality, and we're too used to it. We love violence in this country. This country was born in violence—we took land away from people who occupied it in violence; we have sports that are violent. It's an embarrassment that this nation, given all the gifts of natural resources and the good lives most of us lead, is way behind much of the world. One of the arguments I used to make was, "Look, I'm a politician and I head up a political system, the government of the state of New York, and how many people in this room trust politicians?" Very few hands would go up. Then, "How many in this room think that politicians make a lot of mistakes?" And a lot of hands would go up. I said, "Okay, so the politicians really run the government," and a lot of people would nod. What makes you think that when you get into a courtroom, they're any less prone to make mistakes?

BS: George Will says that capital punishment is a government program, so skepticism is warranted.

MC: [Laughing] Of course, he's dead right.

BS: You see it in poll after poll: Sixty percent of people in this country, and internationally, say, "I'm for it." But if you ask them, "Are you for the death penalty, versus real mandatory life without parole, if you can make sure someone is not going to kill again?" then in many jurisdictions, fifty percent, if not more, are for mandatory parole. Those numbers move even further when you ask people whether the risk of executing an innocent person in worth keeping the death penalty. And that's one of the principal reasons that we are going to see the death penalty—I think in my lifetime, your lifetime—end in the United States.

MC: I think that's true. I hope we catch up to it soon.

> It's an embarrassment that this nation... is way behind much of the world. —MC

FACT

➡ Since the reinstatement of the death penalty in the United States in 1976, there have been more than 1,100 executions. It is currently legal in 36 states.

■ without death penalty
■ with death penalty

➡ The death penalty is still legal in 64 countries around the world. However, more than 90% of executions happen in only 6 countries: China, Iraq, Saudi Arabia, Pakistan, Iran, and the United States.

HARRY BELAFONTE

On Incarcerating Our Youth

Harry Belafonte

A longtime civil and social rights activist, Harry Belafonte has denounced the American justice system for its "prisons filled with victims of poverty." In response to the crisis of incarcerating young people, he created the Gathering for Justice to stop child incarceration. His many humanitarian efforts have also included serving as cultural adviser to the Peace Corps, UNICEF Goodwill Ambassador, amfAR board member, RFK Memorial for Peace and Social Justice, and founder of the Harry and Julie Belafonte UNICEF Fund for HIV/AIDS in Sub-Saharan Africa.

➡ *thegatheringforjustice.org*

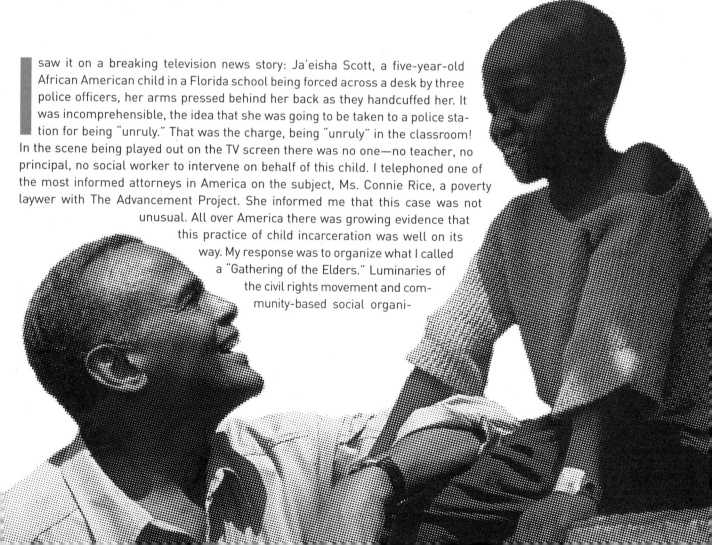

I saw it on a breaking television news story: Ja'eisha Scott, a five-year-old African American child in a Florida school being forced across a desk by three police officers, her arms pressed behind her back as they handcuffed her. It was incomprehensible, the idea that she was going to be taken to a police station for being "unruly." That was the charge, being "unruly" in the classroom! In the scene being played out on the TV screen there was no one—no teacher, no principal, no social worker to intervene on behalf of this child. I telephoned one of the most informed attorneys in America on the subject, Ms. Connie Rice, a poverty laywer with The Advancement Project. She informed me that this case was not unusual. All over America there was growing evidence that this practice of child incarceration was well on its way. My response was to organize what I called a "Gathering of the Elders." Luminaries of the civil rights movement and community-based social organi-

zations came together to exchange views on why, after all the work we have done, we had no engagement, no visible response to this tragic circumstance. How could this happen? We all searched for answers.

The United States of America has the largest prison population in the world. As a fact of public policy we build more prison cells than schoolrooms or health-care centers. We fill these prisons with a disproportionate number of young black and Hispanic men and women charged with nonviolent crimes. According to government statistics, of the more than two and a quarter million prisoners in our system, only seven percent have been incarcerated for violent crimes such as murder, rape, and armed robbery; the rest are typically involved in crimes related to property, drugs, immigration, and public-order issues. I believe that an infinitely larger number of prisoners should have been directed to social programs or service agencies and provided with opportunities for skills training and academic engagement. Unfortunately, the lack of parenting and proper counseling in their communities and in schools has forged a pipeline from the cradle to the penitentiary.

It became apparent that we could not come to workable solutions without the significant participation of the young people caught in this poverty and incarceration tragedy. I began reaching out to youth leaders from various backgrounds, including those who were once caught up in the criminal culture. The result of this undertaking created the Gathering for Justice, a movement engaging youth of all races, ethnicities, and religions to end child incarceration and violence. The purpose of the Gathering is to bring a moral voice to the table, as Dr. King, Gandhi, and Christ all did. They suggested a moral argument that was irrefutable, and beckoned societies to do the right thing. This, too, is our approach. Participants in the Gathering attend workshops studying nonviolence and its application to issues such as children being arrested, gang violence in our communities, gun control, education, and unemployment. So far, six thousand youth leaders from across the nation have come together, committing themselves to the aims of the Gathering.

What can you do to help? First, pull up www.thegatheringfor justice.org. Then go to our allies, the Children's Defense Fund, The Advancement Project, Barrios Unidos, or the United Nations; go to any source that talks about child incarceration. Take a look at what you're doing in your community. Ultimately, it is only through our common humanity that we can begin to heal our communities. As Dr. King has said, "Either we go up together, or we go down together. Let us develop that kind of dangerous unselfishness." With this understanding, let us look upon one another with new eyes. We belong to the human family and disowning one another is not an option. Ja'eisha Scott belongs to us all. The thousands of young people behind bars belong to us all. The soul of this nation belongs to us all. For each of us who dares heed the call to action in the face of indifference, we need only ask ourselves one question, "Am I not my brother's keeper?"

FACT

➡ A report from the Children's Defense Fund found that a black male born in 2001 has a 1 in 3 chance of going to prison in his lifetime; a Latino male a 1 in 6 chance; and a white male a 1 in 17 chance.

➡ A black female born in 2001 has a 1 in 17 chance of going to prison in her lifetime; a Latino female a 1 in 45 chance; and a white female a 1 in 111 chance.

African-American

Latino

Caucasian

America has the largest prison population in the world.

CHARLES GRODIN

On Fair Sentencing

Charles Grodin

Commentator, author, actor, and playwright Charles Grodin is a lifelong activist who has been recognized for his tireless efforts on behalf of fair sentencing and helping the homeless. He has served as a longtime board member of HELP USA.

➡ *helpusa.org; kidsincrisis-website.org*

In the mid-'90s, I had a cable show on CNBC where we often had panel discussions on various social, political, and criminal justice issues. At the time, there was also extensive coverage of the O.J. Simpson criminal trial, which opened my eyes and those of millions of others to how our criminal justice system sometimes works.

On one show, there was a discussion of New York's Rockefeller drug laws, which were considered among the harshest in the nation. Under these laws, if you were found to have four ounces of cocaine or heroin in your possession, or if you were caught selling two ounces of either drug, you could be sentenced to as much as twenty years to life in prison. On the panel that night were two men at opposite ends of the political spectrum: Randy Credico—the successor to William F. Kunstler, the famous liberal attorney who supported getting rid of the Rockefeller drug laws—and Senator Dale Volker, an upstate New York Republican who was a staunch supporter of the laws. Senator Volker allowed how there could be some people sentenced under the laws who should possibly get closer scrutiny.

Randy Credico called me after the program and gave me the names of four women serving fifteen or twenty years to life sentences. I took cameras to the maximum-security prison in Bedford, New York, and interviewed those four women. I then called Senator Volker, and he had me come to Albany, where I showed the video to the Republican senate leadership.

After showing the stories and the circumstances of these women's arrests, I asked that they all be given clemency. Senate leader Joe Bruno simply said, "I agree with you." He went to then Governor Pataki of New York, and three of the women were granted clemency that year and the fourth woman the following year. It was a classic example of both sides of the political spectrum coming together on an issue where the indisputable facts were put in front of them. It was also an example of using television in a way I feel it should be used in many situations. In 2004 New York state legislators voted to reform the antiquated Rockefeller drug laws. They are still considered too harsh by both political parties.

None of what I was able to do would have happened if I didn't have a cable show or name recognition from movies, which in no small part led to me being given a show in the first place. But that event provoked me to get involved with several other social and political situations, and the results of those involvements have led to the most gratifying events of my life.

FACT
Enacted in 1973 the Rockefeller drug laws require harsh mandatory minimum prison terms for the possession or sale of relatively small amounts of drugs. Under the laws, the penalty for selling two ounces or more of a drug is similar to that for second-degree murder, and the penalty is applied without regard to the circumstances of the offense or the individual's background or character. In 2004 New York state legislators voted to reduce the minimum sentences for first-time, non-violent drug offenders.

The results of those involvements have led to the most gratifying events of my life.

I've also seen that you don't need to be in movies or on television to be part of these efforts. Being a mentor to a kid is something most of us can do. It adds up to a few hours a month. I've been involved for years with Kids in Crisis in Connecticut. These are kids who have either been abandoned or abused. Most of the people who help Kids in Crisis are volunteers.

Every city and town in America has a version of a town hall that you can call and learn how you can be of service to others. Or to the overwhelming majority of you who are not technologically challenged as I am, go to the Internet. I urge you to be of help. It will be the best possible thing you can do—not only for others but yourself.

SCOTT BUDNICK

On Educating At-Risk Youth

Scott Budnick

*Film producer Scott Budnick has been actively involved in juvenile justice issues for ten years and has supported the appeal of four young men he believes received disproportionate sentences of life imprisonment. He is on the board of **InsideOUT Writers**, teaching creative writing to incarcerated and at-risk teens in order to discourage violence and help build a spirit of introspection and learning. He also serves on the board of the **Los Angeles Conservation Corps**.*

➡ *insideoutwriters.org*

I read an article in *Rolling Stone* magazine about Brandon Hein and his friends. As teens, they had been involved in a fistfight that escalated into someone dying, and they were sent to prison for life without parole. I found the sentences to be so grossly disproportionate, with enormous misconduct by the prosecutors and the judge. It shocked me in such a way that I immediately had to get involved. I've been helping their families get attention about this tragedy for more than a decade and have become friends with the young men involved.

I was introduced to InsideOUT Writers by another producer in the film business who knew about my interest in juvenile justice. I went in for the first time and sat with ten kids, ages fourteen to eighteen, all facing life in prison. I remember the topic was "forgiveness," and their writing really shook me up. I couldn't sleep for two nights, and knew I had to get involved in their lives.

Juveniles being tried as adults in Los Angeles County are seen as youth who can be thrown away and discarded without care or thought. InsideOUT

Writers shows them that they have a story, they have a voice, and they are better than their worst act. Unfortunately this perspective is not shared by the current corrections system. Education is nonexistent and not a priority. Mental health treatment is sorely lacking. Drug treatment is nowhere to be found. We currently have a ninety-one percent recidivism rate among juveniles in California. We fail nine out of ten times, and we don't care. The system is made to look tough on crime—bars, steel, handcuffs, razor wire—but it is not smart on crime. These kids' problems are not being fixed, and often the system is guilty of exacerbating them. We release these kids right back into the dysfunctional families and neighborhoods that produced the problems, with no services or treatment. Until the system works to treat the problem, taxpayers will continue to bear the burden of incarcerating these kids for many years, at a cost of $215,000 per youth per year.

Anyone can change. The kids who seem the most "lost" can have an epiphany at any time that allows them to completely commit to a better life. Never give up on a child, no matter what they have done, how much anger they possess, or how much pain they have experienced in their short lives. Have them believe in their goodness and it will shine.

I am currently working with the juvenile and adult prison system to create a pipeline for incarcerated youth to get into college programs, rather than the current system of throwing a teenager into an adult prison yard with adult inmates and no educational opportunities. I am designing a program with the California Department of Corrections and Rehabilitation to create "college dorms" where every inmate is either in community college or a four-year university. When they are released, these kids will not go back to their gangs and neighborhoods, but straight to a university to finish their education and get a degree. Watching a released kid follow his commitment to change his life and remain unrelenting in his passion to better himself is the most beautiful thing to see.

You can help by being a positive force in a young person's life. Remaining committed and most especially consistent is the greatest thing anyone can offer a young person struggling in a poor community. These kids have been starved for positive attention from a very young age. If we had enough role models, and especially more male role models, then gangs would be wiped out of our communities. You just need to make volunteering part of your weekly schedule and of the highest priority. Work within the corrections system to make courses accessible to all youth within the system. Demand the same for these kids as you would demand for your own son and daughter. They are children, and they need to know they can achieve their dreams with the right education and support.

WHAT KEEPS ME GOING

I currently have seven kids at an incredible boarding school in Colorado. They are about to become the first high-school graduates in their family. This keeps me going.

I have four kids from juvenile hall currently in college. This keeps me going.

I have kids working and going to school at the Los Angeles Conservation Corps. This keeps me going.

Seeing these kids achieve dreams that they never thought possible is all the satisfaction that I need.

JOHN WALSH

On Fighting for Victims' Rights

John Walsh

*Host of the crime-solving show **America's Most Wanted**, John Walsh and his wife Revé have been a driving force behind some of the most important pieces of child protection legislation in this country. In 2006, on the twenty-fifth anniversary of their son's abduction, the couple saw the **Adam Walsh Child Safety and Protection Act** signed into law. The Walshes are co-founders of the **National Center for Missing and Exploited Children.***

➡ *amw.com; missingkids.com; ncmec.org*

When Rupert Murdoch first approached me in 1987 to host *America's Most Wanted* (AMW), the first reality television program of his new Fox network, my first reaction was, "What is reality television and what the hell is Fox?" The show was modeled after a successful BBC program called *Crime Watch UK*, which used re-creations with the British police and Scotland Yard to catch criminals. For six months, I said no. I didn't have the time or interest in TV. Instead, I was busy testifying state-to-state to change legislation as it related to missing and exploited children, while trying to help build the Adam Walsh Center. Adam was my six-year-old son who had been abducted and murdered during the summer of 1981.

At the time of Adam's disappearance, I was working in hotel development. During the two-week investigation, I was shocked at how inexperienced the local police were with child abduction by strangers, and what little resources they had—that when your child goes missing, a jet full of federal agents doesn't take off from Washington D.C. and come to the rescue like they do in the movies. In reality, the FBI wouldn't even enter Adam as a missing child into the national crime information computer, which at the time held information on hundreds of thousands of stolen cars, boats, planes, guns, even a racehorse—but no unidentified missing or dead children. So, I mounted the search from a business standpoint. I camped out at the Hollywood, Florida, police station and had graphics and advertising guys from my company print and distribute posters. We tried to do everything innovative and different to get my son back alive. After Adam was found murdered, I was suffering from a broken heart; it seemed irrelevant to build hotels. We got tens of thousands of letters, and my wife Revé started reading them. People wrote that they, too, had missing children and asked how we mounted the search, the largest ever in Florida. So Revé started the first Adam Walsh Center in a donated old South Florida police station. The Adam Walsh Center eventually merged with the National Center for Missing and Exploited Children.

Twenty years later, we're still doing the show and have made over 1,000 captures, with sixteen from the Most Wanted list.

FACT

➡ Since 1994 stores across the country have been implementing the Code ADAM program, named in honor of Adam Walsh. Begun by Wal-Mart employees, workers are trained to go on alert, monitoring exits and initiating an immediate search once a child is reported missing. More than 70,000 sites are signed up.

➡ In 2003 the National Center for Missing and Exploited Children launched Team Adam. The program sends trained, retired law-enforcement professionals to aid in serious child abductions. Since its launch, Team Adam has deployed more than 27 times, searching in 43 states for a total of 313 children.

GET INVOLVED

AMW.com is the fourth most popular TV website in the world and has helped send tens of thousands of e-mails and letters to Congress. You don't have to donate money or march on Washington. We give you a sample letter for how to write your two U.S. senators and affect federal legislation. It's a simple system, and it works.

Meanwhile, the Fox producers showed me a pilot segment of AMW, which featured a profile of one of the FBI's Ten Most Wanted killers, David James Roberts. Roberts had been released from jail after being charged in a triple murder case (he had murdered three people, then burned their home down with them in it). During his release, he raped a woman and left her infant child on the side of the road to die in cold weather. After learning about this case, I talked it over with Revé, and we agreed that if the show could help catch this terrible, terrible guy, I should accept. So I went to Washington D.C. and shot the pilot. It aired in February 1988, and three days later, they caught Roberts, who had been hiding in plain sight, running a shelter for the homeless. That was our first capture. It was an amazing, mind-boggling experience. Now, 20 years later, we're still doing the show and have made over 1,000 captures, with 17 from the FBI's Ten Most Wanted list.

Since I first got involved, things have changed dramatically. We now have DNA databases, sex offender registries, a federal mandate to enter missing children into

GET INVOLVED

information clearinghouses for all fifty states, tougher penalties for people who prey upon women and children, hotlines, and a group called Team Adam that will fly in retired law enforcement professionals trained in locating missing children to assist small departments. But we still have cases that fall off the map, mistakes made, and more battles to win.

The Adam Walsh Child Protection and Safety Act, which became a law in 2006 after two years of intense lobbying, still hasn't been funded by Congress. Most people don't realize when legislation gets passed, it's not effective unless it has money and oversight attached to it. This bill would create a national sex offender registry to help states that have poor registries combat hardcore criminals that prey upon children. There are so many unsolved crimes that could be solved if everyone convicted of a felony had DNA put into the national database. It would also free hundreds of wrongfully convicted people.

At the end of each AMW episode I always say, "One person can make a difference." We've taken down some of the world's most dangerous fugitives, serial killers, rapists, child murderers, and drug dealers, and all those captures are because one person—a humble, average person—got out of their comfort zone and had the guts to pick up the phone. It's that personal choice, where an individual asks, "Am I going to do something to help somebody?" You can report a tip by calling 1-800-CRIME-TV, or by filling out an online form at www.amw.com.

> At the end of each AMW episode I always say, "One person can make a difference."

Revé and I will always be the parents of a murdered child. She always says it's like a horrible color that you can't explain to anybody, and you hope they never see it. But when I see other people do extraordinary things when they don't have that driving force, I'm always amazed. Their compassion and their humanity, their unwillingness to be complacent about the level of violence in America—that's what keeps me motivated.

One of the best defenses against crime is getting involved with your community. Neighborhood Watch groups all over the country have proven to be powerful weapons in the battle against crime, so check with your local law enforcement agency to find out if one exists in your area. If you don't have a crime watch group yet, you can talk to your neighbors about ways in which you can work together to clamp down on crime in your community. After you gather your collective, join Celebrate Safe Communities (www.ncpc.org/programs/celebrate-safe-communities), an initiative started by the National Sheriffs' Association (NSA), the National Crime Prevention Council (NCPC), and the Bureau of Justice Assistance (BJA) to help communities connect with other groups across the country and exchange ideas for neighborhood watch activities.

SARAH BRADY

On Gun Control

Sarah Brady

*Sarah Brady and her husband, Jim Brady, have lobbied extensively for stronger gun-control
laws and to reduce gun violence through education, research, and legal advocacy.*

➡ *bradycampaign.org; millionmommarch.org; protesteasyguns.org*

When President Ronald Reagan named my husband White House Press Secretary in 1981, it was a dream come true. We had a new baby, and all of a sudden, life was sort of perfect. Three months after Reagan had taken office, I was at home with our two-year-old son, Scott, watching a soap opera. The last thing you think when your husband goes off to work is that the day will end with him being involved in a presidential assassination attempt. Suddenly, I was being whisked to a hospital not knowing whether Jim was going to live or die from a gunshot wound. It was as if I'd become part of a soap opera myself. At one point, three networks read his obituary. They'd gotten it wrong. That even sounds like a soap opera.

In 1982, when he finally came home, the reality of how severe his injury was and how much care he needed set in. He had no use of his left arm or left leg. In 1983 I got a call from Handgun Control asking me if I'd get involved in a bill that was out in California. I'd become familiar with gun legislation in the early 1970s, working with a congressman on a bill to ban Saturday night specials, cheap guns often used for crime. I hesitated because I had so much on my plate between taking care of Jim and Scott. One day, on a visit to Jim's parents in Illinois, we got into a car to go swimming with friends. Scott, who was about four, jumped into the seat with me and found a little toy gun. I thought it was a good opportunity to talk about guns and told him to never point a gun at anyone. Then I realized it was a real gun—a Saturday night special—and it was loaded. I was livid. The man who owned it apologized, explaining that he needed it for self-protection. A few days later, I was watching the nightly news and I learned that the National Rifle Association had introduced a bill to do away with the 1968 Gun Control Act, which laid down guidelines saying nobody who is a fugitive, a felon, an illegal alien, or adjudicated mentally ill could own a gun. That was it. I went to the phone, called the NRA, and said, "My name is Sarah Brady, and I'm going to spend the rest of my life trying to put you out of business." The next day, I called Handgun Control (which was later renamed the Brady Campaign to Prevent Gun Violence) and said, "What can I do to help?"

We believed everyone needed a background check and waiting period in order to get a gun license. That was the beginning of the Brady Bill, which went on for seven years. We did not want to take away anybody's right to defend him or herself. We just wanted to keep guns out of the wrong hands and to educate people to the fact

**GUN LOBBY SPENDING:
DAVID VERSUS GOLIATH**

2007
Gun Control: $60,800
Gun Rights: $1,959,407

2006
Gun Control: $90,100
Gun Rights: $3,024,231

2005
Gun Control: $230,000
Gun Rights: $3,870,587

2004
Gun Control: $1,335,400
Gun Rights: $4,142,400

**The ratio of money spent
lobbying politicians by
gun rights groups to gun
control groups in 2006: 33:1.**

that gun ownership requires responsibility. During that time, we developed an amazing team of people and fought like David versus Goliath. We had very little money and couldn't run ads like the NRA did, but we had a wonderful press person to do press conferences and take advantage of free advertising. I started lobbying personally, making speeches all across the country, reaching out to all the police groups and getting their support. We knew we could not fight by ourselves. I worked in politics all my life and knew coalitions were the key. We got the support of almost every respectable organization you can imagine: the nurses, the teachers, the PTA, the National U.S. Conference of Mayors, and every major church in the country. Everywhere we'd go, we'd make sure we met with editorial boards of newspapers. Little by little, we grew. It was the most exhilarating work ever.

The Brady Law went into effect in 1994 and reduced gun violence tremendously, stopping the sale of more than 1.4 million guns around the country. The next year, we passed the Assault Weapons Ban. But that law expired in 2004. So, they're back on the market again. Are Jim and I motivated? Do we do as much as we can? Yes. My heart aches because I want to get out there more. Volunteerism is so important. You hear the stories of people whose lives have been totally shattered, how it can happen to anyone, anytime, anyplace. It's not just gangs or criminals. We're talking about being on a safe college campus or at a school. And there are so many things that can be done: You can join your local Million Mom March chapter to help build a coalition to educate the public and pass sensible gun laws. You can help organize a local "lie-in" to reinstate the Assault Weapons Ban on the April 16 anniversary of the Virginia Tech shootings. And you can create a short video for the Brady Campaign and the MMM at www.vidivoice.com—even just using your cell phone—to add your feelings and experiences with gun violence to a growing list of people who want change.

> **I went to the phone, called the NRA, and said, "My name is Sarah Brady, and I'm going to spend the rest of my life trying to put you out of business."**

MIMI SILBERT

On Giving Second Chances

Mimi Silbert

*As a national expert on criminal justice, Mimi Silbert's passionate drive helped turn the **Delancey Street Foundation** into a highly successful, self-sustaining rehabilitation program for ex-convicts and former homeless. It has five centers nationally.*

➡ *delanceystreetfoundation.org*

I grew up in the 1940s on Yiddish phrases and good Jewish cooking. Mine was an extended immigrant family for whom dinner table conversation revolved around how to make the world better. My parents had very traditional values: to love and support each other, to get educated, and to help others.

When my family moved from a small, working-class community to a more financially secure one, I watched as some of my friends from the old neighborhood struggled. My loyalty to those kids is probably the most immediate reason why I became interested in criminology—the inequity really irked me. I knew those kids who ended up in prison. I knew they had good hearts. They just got dealt a bad hand.

As a young psychologist working as a therapist in prisons, I decided that self-help was an answer to the problem of chronic criminals. I felt terrific because I was helping people. One day it struck me that everyone should feel that way. No one should be in the position of only receiving, because it would make you powerless, useless, and give you a victim's view of life.

In 1971 Delancey Street began with four residents, a thousand-dollar loan, and a dream to develop a model to turn around the lives of long-term substance abusers, the hardcore homeless, former felons, and others who had hit bottom by empowering them to become their own solution. We have taken in representatives of our society's most serious social problems as residents and, by a process of each one helping another, we have been solving the problems of poverty, illiteracy, lack of job skills, substance abuse, gangs, criminal behavior, homelessness, teen pregnancy, and every kind of abuse.

After an average of four years, our residents gain academic education, three marketable skills, accountability, responsibility, dignity, decency, and integrity. We have successfully graduated more than 15,000 people from America's underclass into society as successful, taxpaying citizens leading decent, legitimate, and productive lives. Our residents learn vocational skills through our training schools, which include a restaurant, a catering business, a moving and trucking school, furniture and woodwork production, and Christmas tree sales and decoration. They manage these income-producing enterprises so successfully that they earn sixty-five percent of the Foundation's entire working capital.

The entire Delancey Street organization is run completely by the former homeless and ex-convicts. We function as an extended family. Our daily operations are not funded, and we charge no fees. We pool all our resources. No one draws a salary, including me. There is no staff. The residents themselves run it, and we all live together. (I've raised my children at Delancey Street.) Everyone is both a giver and a receiver in an "each-one-teach-one" process. We believe that the best way to learn is to teach, and that helping others is an important way to earn self-reliance. Person A helps person B, and person A gets better. No one can undo the past, but we can balance the scales by doing good deeds and earning back our own self-respect, decency, and a legitimate place in mainstream society.

Despite the successes at Delancey Street, I have seen changes for the worse as well. There are more gangs on the street and in prisons; there is more fear and more anger among the citizenry; mobility is harder to achieve for those stuck on the bottom. While world poverty and hunger are certainly overwhelming, we must not forget that in our own backyard poverty, violence, hatred, and homelessness are growing.

One of the most important things that people can do is to hire those who have overcome homelessness, poverty, and past crimes. The residents at Delancey Street gain vocational, personal, interpersonal, and social skills necessary to make restitution to the society from which they have taken illegally, and often brutally, for most of their lives. In return, we ask from society access to the legitimate opportunities from which the majority of the underclass and ex-convicts have been blocked for most of their lives.

I ask that people not let fear lead them to exclude people from their lives. We need to include the underclass and people different from us. We need to connect with each other. If we need each other, we all feel better. We find strength. Problems turn into solutions. Fear and hatred turn to support and love.

HOW TO... SOME TIPS ON CRIMINAL JUSTICE

TIME

⏱ **Make an educated decision about where you stand on the death penalty.** Find a local group that works with prisoners and their families in your community. Use your voice to lobby, vote, and influence your legislators to help sway the country's position on capital punishment.

⏱ **Research the issues.** The gun debate is greatly influenced by opposing advocacy groups that can make it difficult to form a clear opinion. By understanding the laws and their consequences, you can vote to change legislation more effectively.

⏱ **Report a possible weapon threat** at school if you (or your children) have heard classmates talking about it. In three out of four campus shootings, the attackers told other students before they inflicted violence. Call the 1-866-SPEAK-UP hotline to make an anonymous, free report or visit www.speakup.com.

⏱ **Download a Missing Children screensaver or poster.** Help find missing children using the National Center for Missing & Exploited Children's database of photographs. By signing up at www.missingkids.com you can volunteer to expand the search by distributing posters or downloading a computer screensaver that updates automatically with the latest available information.

ITEMS

📖 **Donate books.** Many prisons lack basic dictionaries and encyclopedias. Send your old volumes to programs such as the Women's Prison Book Project, Midwest Pages to Prisoners, and UC Books to Prisoners to provide people in prison and prison libraries with additional educational resources and reading material.

📖 **Give away your used vehicle to a crime victims organization.** Check to see if the organization such as the National Center for Victims of Crime (www.ncvc.org) can handle the donation. It can be a good way of helping them raise funds for helplines and other necessary services and programs. Consult the Guide to Donating Your Car at Charity Navigator (www.charitynavigator. com) for more information.

📖 **Trade in toy weapons for non-violent playthings.** Organize an anti-violence event that lets children and parents in your community exchange toy guns for books or other non-violent items. Use it as a forum to start a discussion about what can be done to prevent violence at schools and in your neighborhood.

EXPERTISE

💼 **Research safety tips for firearms.** Forty percent of U.S. homes with children have firearms. If you or someone you know keeps a gun in the house, learn to store them safely, keep them unloaded, and locked separately from ammunition.

💼 **Train to be an auxiliary police volunteer.** Auxiliary police assist police departments by performing patrols, and providing additional support in event of disasters. As a volunteer you undergo intense training to observe and report conditions that require police services.

💼 **Mentor or tutor children with incarcerated parents.** With one or both parents in jail, these kids are one of the biggest populations of at-risk youth in our society. The Community Service Society (www.cssny.com), through its Retired and Senior Volunteer Program, mentors children with incarcerated parents, while programs such as the Words Travel Family Connection and the Storybook Project work with prisoners to provide their children the gift of a book and a recording of the parent reading the book aloud.

💼 **Become a crime victim advocate.** Provide crisis intervention, support, and advocacy to victims of crime and/or their families and friends by training to handle victim hotlines. Contact your local victims' centers to find out how you can help.

DOLLARS

$ **Fund a scholarship for children from disadvantaged families or foster care.** Education and expanded opportunities can help at-risk youth avoid a path that might eventually lead to violence, arrest, or incarceration.

$ **Make a donation to support programs for ex-offenders.** Delancey Street Foundation (www.delanceystreetfoundation. org) and the Doe Fund (www.doe.org) rehabilitation programs work to provide support, resources, and job training to the formerly incarcerated in order to empower them to become independent and self-reliant.

$ **Hire a formerly incarcerated youth or adult.** Keep an open mind. Evaluate each job applicant on their individual merits and don't make a blanket judgment based on a conviction. Job discrimination is one of the many barriers faced by those seeking to reenter society.

WHERE TO... SOME PLACES ON CRIMINAL JUSTICE

→ **AMERICA'S MOST WANTED**
www.amw.com
As a show and a website, *America's Most Wanted* enlists viewers' help in tracking down suspected criminals.

→ **AMERICAN ASSOCIATION FOR JUSTICE**
www.justice.org
Promotes fair and effective justice systems—and supports the work of attorneys in their efforts to ensure that any person who is injured by the misconduct or negligence of others can obtain justice.

→ **AMICUS USA**
www.amicususa.org
Amicus aims to improve public safety by helping inmates and ex-offenders through positive relationship-building, restorative justice practices, and individualized transition services.

→ **ANDREW GLOVER YOUTH PROGRAM**
www.agyp.org
Works to intervene and reclaim young people from lives of crime, and provides an overloaded court system with a reliable alternative to incarceration for youth.

→ **BOOKS THROUGH BARS**
www.booksthroughbars.org
Books Through Bars sends quality reading material to prisoners and encourages creative dialogue on the criminal justice system, thereby educating those living inside and outside prison walls.

→ **BRADY CAMPAIGN TO PREVENT GUN VIOLENCE**
www.bradycampaign.org
The Brady Campaign is the largest U.S. grassroots organization working to prevent gun violence by enacting and enforcing gun legislation.

→ **CENTER FOR COMMUNITY ALTERNATIVES**
www.communityalternatives.org
The Center for Community Alternatives is a leader in the field of community-based alternatives to incarceration through advocacy, services, and public policy development.

→ **CENTER FOR COURT INNOVATION**
www.courtinnovation.org
Nonprofit think tank that helps courts and criminal justice agencies aid victims, reduce crime, and improve public trust in justice. The Center combines action and reflection to spark problem-solving innovation locally and nationally.

→ **CENTER FOR EMPLOYMENT OPPORTUNITIES**
www.ceoworks.org
Provides comprehensive employment services to people newly released from New York State prisons and detention facilities.

→ **CENTER FOR HEALTH JUSTICE**
www.healthjustice.net
Center for Health Justice empowers people affected by HIV and incarceration to make healthier choices and advocates for the elimination of disparities between prisoner health and public health.

→ **COALITION TO STOP GUN VIOLENCE**
www.csgv.org
Comprised of 45 national organizations, the Coalition to Stop Gun Violence works to secure freedom from gun violence through research and strategic engagement.

→ **COMMUNITY RESOURCES FOR JUSTICE**
www.crjustice.org
Works with individuals in, or at risk of being in, the adult or juvenile justice systems through a mix of advocacy, research, and publications.

→ **CRIME AND JUSTICE INSTITUTE**
www.cjinstitute.org
The Crime and Justice Institute is a nonprofit agency that works to make criminal and juvenile justice systems more efficient and cost-effective and to promote accountability for achieving better outcomes.

→ **DELANCEY STREET FOUNDATION**
www.delanceystreet
foundation.org
Delancey Street Foundation is the country's leading residential self-help organization for substance abusers, homeless, and other marginalized people.

→ **DRUG POLICY ALLIANCE**
www.drugpolicy.org
Drug Policy Alliance is the nation's leading organization working to end the war on drugs to implement new drug policies based on science, compassion, health, and human rights.

→ **EQUAL JUSTICE WORKS**
www.equaljusticeworks.org
Equal Justice Works provides leadership to ensure a sustainable pipeline of talented and trained lawyers involved in public service.

→ **FAMILIES AGAINST MANDATORY MINIMUMS**
www.famm.org
FAMM works to change mandatory sentencing laws through the legislative process on the federal and state levels, participation in precedent-setting legal cases, and by educating the public.

→ **GATHERING FOR JUSTICE**
www.thegatheringforjustice.org
The Gathering for Justice is a movement that works to create a coordinated space to ending child incarceration.

→ **GREENHOPE SERVICES FOR WOMEN**
www.greenhope.org
Greenhope was established in 1975 in a convent that was transformed into a comprehensive residential treatment program for formerly incarcerated women, women on parole, and those referred by the courts as an alternative to incarceration.

→ **HOUR CHILDREN**
www.hourchildren.org
Hour Children is committed to the loving care of incarcerated mothers, ex-offenders, and their children, providing short- and long-term support services.

→ INNOCENCE PROJECT

www.innocenceproject.org
Innocence Project is a national litigation and public policy organization dedicated to exonerating wrongfully convicted people through DNA testing.

→ INSIDEOUT WRITERS

www.insideoutwriters.org
InsideOUT Writers provides positive and empowering experiences using creative writing as a means to foster socially responsible behavior among incarcerated and at-risk youth.

→ JUSTICE POLICY INSTITUTE

www.justicepolicy.org
The mission of the Justice Policy Institute is to promote effective solutions to social problems and to be dedicated to ending society's reliance on incarceration.

→ LAW ENFORCEMENT AGAINST PROHIBITION

www.leap.cc
LEAP is an organization of current and former members of the law enforcement and criminal justice communities dedicated to educating the public about the failures of the War on Drugs.

→ LEGAL COMMUNITY AGAINST VIOLENCE

www.firearmslawcenter.org
Legal Community Against Violence provides federal, state, and local firearms law summaries, Second Amendment federal case law summaries, and news updates.

→ LOS ANGELES CONSERVATION CORPS

www.lacorps.org
Provides at-risk young adults and school-aged youth with opportunities for success through job-skills training, education, and work experience with an emphasis on projects that benefit the community.

→ MAYORS AGAINST ILLEGAL GUNS

www.mayorsagainstillegalguns.org
Dedicated to making America's cities safer by stopping the flow of illegal guns into cities, the Mayors Against Illegal Guns Coalition is comprised of over 250 mayors from more than 50 states.

→ MILLION MOM MARCH

www.millionmommarch.org
Originally one of the largest marches on Washington, Million Mom March is a now a national network of 75 chapters around the country that work locally against gun violence.

→ NATIONAL CENTER FOR MISSING AND EXPLOITED CHILDREN

www.missingkids.com
Helps prevent child abduction and sexual exploitation; helps find missing children; and assists child abduction and sexual exploitation victims, their families, and the professionals who serve them.

→ OUR PLACE DC

www.ourplacedc.org
Supports women who are or have been in the criminal justice system by providing the resources they need to maintain connections with the community, resettle after incarceration, and reconcile with their families.

→ PRISON COMMUNITIES INTERNATIONAL, INC.

www.p-c-i.org
PCI offers several programs and services that work to change criminal justice from a punitive system to a rehabilitative system, including the Rehabilitation Through the Arts Program.

→ PRISON UNIVERSITY PROJECT

www.prisonuniversityproject.org
The Prison University Project provides excellent higher education programs to people incarcerated at San Quentin State Prison.

→ PROVIDENCE HOUSE, INC.

www.providencehouse.org
Emphasizing the dignity of every human being, Providence works to provide shelter and support to abused and formerly incarcerated women and their children.

→ PUBLIC DEFENDER SERVICE FOR THE DISTRICT OF COLUMBIA

www.pdsdc.org
Promotes quality legal representation to indigent adults.

→ SENTENCING PROJECT

www.sentencingproject.org
The Sentencing Project provides information about crime, courts, sentencing, criminal justice policy analysis, punishment, alternatives to incarceration, and reform.

→ VERA INSTITUTE OF JUSTICE

www.vera.org
The Vera Institute of Justice combines expertise in research, demonstration projects, and technical assistance to help leaders in government and civil society improve the systems people rely on for justice and safety.

→ WOMEN'S PRISON ASSOCIATION AND HOME, INC.

www.wpaonline.org
WPA is a service and advocacy organization committed to helping women with criminal justice histories realize new possibilities for themselves and their families.

ENVIRONMENT
IS IT US, OR IS IT WARM IN HERE?

Our offices sit on the West Side of Manhattan overlooking the Hudson River. The view is beautiful—but only a few years ago this was not the case. Thanks largely to the citizen-led environmental cleanup of the Hudson, the West Side waterfront is now a beautiful place to live, work, and play. The improved biodiversity in the river now also includes humans, as people canoe, fish, and even swim there. Adjacent parks and pathways make it easy to exercise and bike to work. Environmental concerns still lurk just below the waterline, including still-threatened fish populations and PCB contamination, but huge progress has been made. As with many issues addressed in this book, ordinary people rose to the occasion and found a solution, when our leaders chose not to. In this case, the Riverkeepers, a citizen's patrol and environmental watchdog group, led the charge in the Hudson's revival. These days, more and more everyday Americans, NGO's, and forward-thinking communities are taking environmental matters into their own hands. While the long-term results of the "green movement" are yet to be realized, the short-term results are often visible right outside our windows, proving we can, in places and at times, succeed in saving the planet from ourselves. ➜ **But do we have the collective will and desire to do everything needed to permanently change the tide? —Kenneth Cole**

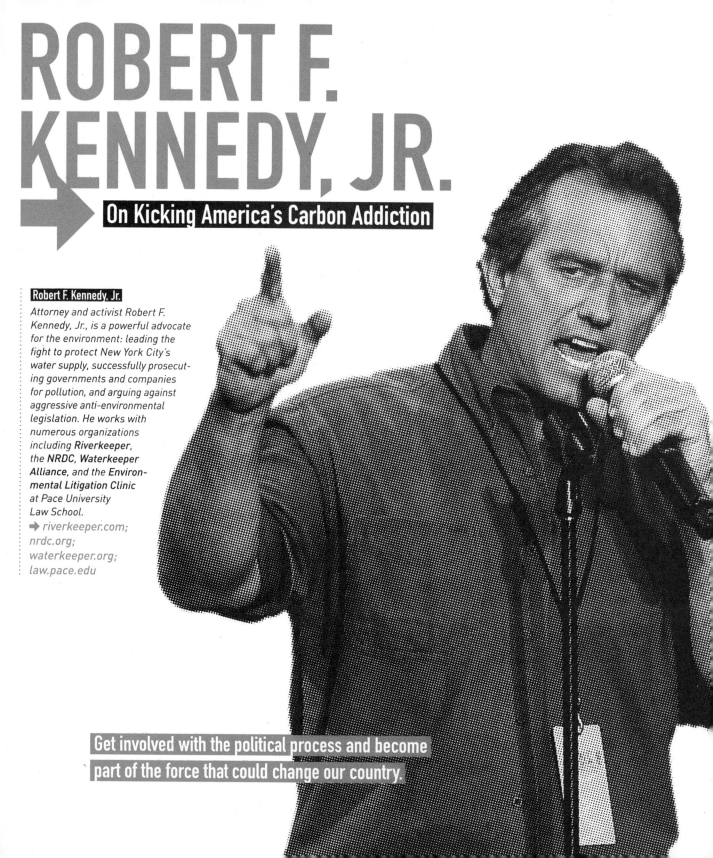

ROBERT F. KENNEDY, JR.

On Kicking America's Carbon Addiction

Robert F. Kennedy, Jr.

*Attorney and activist Robert F. Kennedy, Jr., is a powerful advocate for the environment: leading the fight to protect New York City's water supply, successfully prosecuting governments and companies for pollution, and arguing against aggressive anti-environmental legislation. He works with numerous organizations including **Riverkeeper**, the **NRDC**, **Waterkeeper Alliance**, and the **Environmental Litigation Clinic** at Pace University Law School.*

➡ *riverkeeper.com; nrdc.org; waterkeeper.org; law.pace.edu*

Get involved with the political process and become part of the force that could change our country.

Our addiction to carbon subverts everything we value as Americans. Fifty years ago, our country had half the wealth on the planet. Now, we're spending $1 billion per day borrowing money to import oil into this country, shifting that wealth to Middle Eastern governments who hate democracy, who are despised by their own people, and are funding terrorists who are attacking us. In addition, their oil and coal industries are the dominant energy suppliers to America, secured by over a trillion dollars in annual subsidies, effectively keeping much more efficient and cheaper renewable energy rivals out of the marketplace. It's not only destroying our economy, it's destroying the planet, through global warming.

If the U.S. were to de-carbonize our economy, as other nations have done, we would reduce our budget deficits by hundreds of billions of dollars a year. We would create tens of millions of jobs that can't be outsourced, make every American richer, and dramatically improve our trade deficits. Our children would have cleaner air and water, and we could avoid entanglements in $3 trillion Middle Eastern military ventures. The path to freedom from this addiction is free-market capitalism, not the phony free markets we have today that are rigged to protect the interests of oil, coal, and nuclear, the highest energy producers. A true free market will do what the marketplace is supposed to do, which is to reward efficiency and punish waste.

Nations that have de-carbonized have experienced immediate prosperity. In 1970, Iceland was the poorest country in Europe and 100 percent dependent on coal and oil. It was also one of the first nations to see, first hand, the devastating effects of global warming, which impacts higher latitudes disproportionately. Iceland made the moral decision to escape the carbon jones and today is 100 percent energy independent, with 90 percent of its electricity coming from geothermal sources. It is the fourth richest country by GDP on earth. Corporations from all over the world, which shunned it a decade ago, are fighting to get into Iceland to take advantage of its clean, safe, reliable energy supply.

In 1996 Sweden was also one of the poorest countries in Europe. Then they decided to de-carbonize their economy and escape the extensive dangers of nuclear energy. They closed two nuclear plants and placed a $150/ton tax on carbon. Entrepreneurs rushed into the space to create new energy sources out of everything from putrid garbage and woodchips to tidal, wind, solar, and geothermal power. Brazil—which was 100 percent energy dependent a few decades ago, and one of the poorest coun-

FACT

➡ 2007: U.S. Petroleum Consumption: 20,687,000 barrels per day

➡ 2007: U.S. Crude Oil Imports: 10,118,000 barrels per day

➡ 2007: Dependence on Net Petroleum Imports: 58%

Each represents 2,000,000 barrels of oil

⬛ (gray) Imported Oil
⬛ Domestic Oil

FACT

In fall of 1987, the Pace Environmental Litigation Clinic was established with Robert F. Kennedy, Jr., and Karl Coplan as directors. The clinic immerses Pace law students in environmental law while utilizing them to represent the Riverkeeper group in federal and state courts and administrative proceedings. Their efforts have led to precedent-setting decisions by federal courts under both th Clean Water Act and the Resource Conservation and Recovery Act. Other clinics have been established, modeled after the Pace program.

tries per capita in Latin America—is energy independent today. Forty percent of its fuel source is distilled from locally grown sugar cane, and the current economy has boomed into the richest in Latin America. And California, whose citizens use half the energy on average as other Americans, is by far our country's strongest economy.

Energy efficiency will make us more competitive and stronger economically. Japan spends seven percent of its GNP on energy. Germany spends eight percent of its GNP on energy. Our country spends fifteen percent, which means that every product we manufacture here costs seven or eight cents more than the identical product manufactured in Japan or Germany. Our addiction to carbon has embroiled us in a lethal and endless war that threatens to bankrupt our nation. It has destroyed our international prestige and credibility, it has poisoned our waters, it is destroying our beloved Appalachian Mountains. It has polluted most of America's rivers or streams with mercury, it's contaminated, it's destroyed the forests and lakes of Appalachia and the Adirondacks with acid rain. It causes millions of asthma attacks and deaths from respiratory failure every year, and it's stealing money from the pockets of every American at an astounding rate. In short, it's destroying everything that we value as a nation.

The pathway from addiction is much easier than the vested interests would have us believe. There are thousands of energy entrepreneurs waiting to flood the space and provide us with low-cost, clean, and efficient energy. But we must first level the playing field and give them a fair market in which to compete.

We can't solve this problem overnight, but people have to begin to realize it's a political problem. Get involved in the political process and support leaders who have the interest of our country at heart, rather than supporting indentured servants for the carbon cronies. You can get involved with the political process and become part of the force that could change our country and the future of humanity.

Our addiction to carbon has embroiled us in a lethal and endless war that threatens to bankrupt our nation.

TOP ENVIRONMENTAL CONCERNS

→ We are all connected. Everything—from the car you're driving and the plot of freshly mowed lawn you just drove by, to the plastic fork you tossed away—has a cause and effect. Our planet is a complicated living system and right now, our global system is suffering from a myriad of sicknesses.

Environmental Concern	What it is	Causes	Statistics
CLIMATE CHANGE AND GLOBAL WARMING 	The increased concentrations of greenhouse gases released into the atmosphere cause glacial melting, rise in sea level, ocean acidification, and severe weather patterns.	Humans burning fossil fuels for energy. Coal plants, cars, sea and air transportation.	A one-meter rise in sea level would flood 1% of Egypt, 2.5% of the U.S., and 17 % of Bangladesh.
PROTECTING BIODIVERSITY 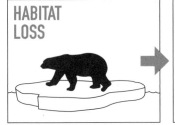	Biodiversity is the variety of life in an ecosystem that is necessary to sustain our existence. When biodiversity in our forests disappears, it means not only trees, but entire chains of animals and plant species.	Deforestation, climate change, deep-sea trawling, over-fishing, coastal pollution, pesticide use.	Nearly one-third of the world's animals are under the threat of extinction, including 30 percent of amphibians, 25 percent of mammals, 12.5 percent of birds, and 70 percent of plants.
HABITAT LOSS 	One fifth of our planet's ground surface has been transformed into urban-industrial areas, eliminating the natural eco-systems that house millions of species.	Urban development, forest fires, water and air pollution.	By 2032, over 70 percent of the planet's ground surface will be urbanized.
CLEAN WATER AND AIR 	Pollution kills wildlife, destroys habitats, and affects human health. Since marine systems are downhill of land, everything people use ends up in our waters.	Sewage and fertilizer run-off, coal plants, cars, shipping, and air transportation.	3 million people die prematurely from outdoor air pollution caused by vehicles and industrial emissions each year and 1.6 million die from indoor pollution.
INVASIVE SPECIES	Non-native plants or animals that out-compete the natural flora and fauna. Scientists have estimated that it has caused over 12 percent of plant species to become critically rare.	Global shipping, tourism, climate change.	Approximately 50,000 invasive species are brought into the U.S. each year, contributing to a 42% decline in endangered species.

BOB NIXON

→ **On Helping the Planet + At-Risk Youth**

Bob Nixon

Bob Nixon is a self-taught conservationist who left a successful movie-making career to found the **Earth Conservation Corps**, *a nonprofit program that recruits disadvantaged young people to help restore the environment while educating, inspiring, and opening doors for them. In exchange for their hours of community service, the program offers a stipend, health care, and an award toward education.*

➡ *ecc1.org*

In 1992, I arrived in Washington D.C. to launch the Earth Conservation Corps (ECC), a nonprofit aimed at empowering endangered youth through environmental action. I planned to stay for three months and then return to California to make more movies. There are two rivers in D.C., the Potomac on the west and the Anacostia on the east. When Lyndon Johnson decided to clean up the Potomac, he didn't pay any attention to the Anacostia because it was on the wrong side of the tracks. There are sixty-eight public housing communities, and all but two of them are within a mile of the Anacostia. It has no roads along its shores, and was for many years known as "the forgotten river." It is also one of the most polluted rivers in America, home to the largest sewage treatment plant in the world—not because Washington is that big, but because the local community has so little clout. Three billion gallons of raw sewage are pumped in every year within a thirty-mile radius. It's literally a dumping ground.

The first thing I did was recruit nine young men and women from Valley Green Public Housing Community, considered one of the most violent public housing communities in the country. I figured I'd match volunteers from the most forsaken place with the most polluted creek, get to work and see if something good might happen. I met about 100 kids on the first day. I think there are a percentage of people who really just love nature, and that was as true there as most anywhere. When I showed them pictures of the creek and asked, "Anybody want to volunteer to clean it up?" Nine said, "That's a disgrace. That's in our community? We're going to change that." Everybody else said, "Forget it." In the first three months, we pulled 5,000 tires out of the four-mile creek. Then, one of our core members, Monique Johnson, was murdered. Monique cared so much about the river that we had to keep going in her honor. Within the next year, two more of our kids were killed. Seeing up close and personal something that's very disturbingly wrong with America ruined my ability to go back to Malibu and filmmaking.

In the first three months, we pulled 5,000 tires out of the four-mile creek.

Washington is like a tale of two cities. I went from getting buzzed in at the White House to driving just a few blocks away where an entire community is living in extreme poverty. What continually amazes me is the level of talent and commitment that these

FACT

Waterkeeper Alliance is a grassroots advocacy organization with currently 177 local Waterkeeper programs focused on keeping our water resources (rivers, lakes, bays, coasts) clean. For more information on how to get involved, visit: www.waterkeeper.org.

young people have to fight against what's so clearly environmental racism. Of course, it's illegal and it goes on in every city, but nobody cares. Once we started to clean up and show people what was there—1,200 acres of beautiful National Park Service land, wild turkeys, bald eagles, a view of the Capitol—it started a civil rights battle. Since there is no congressional representation, we don't have a vote in Congress, which has since repeatedly tried to give away park land for various developments. They would never consider doing so in any park on the other side of the Anacostia. However, this has galvanized the community. We're fighting by trying to get public attention and showing people the wildlife they're losing. It will take years, but the river will get cleaned up, and it should be kept available to everyone. In this era where everyone is aware of global warming, paving over 100 acres of National Park with development, and walling off the local community would be egregious.

The most inspiring part has been how much our ECC members wanted to do something positive. They'd never been asked to be part of the solution to help their community. Rodney Stotts, who still works with us, said, "I'm America's nightmare. I want to do this because nobody has ever asked me to do something positive. And they don't think I can do it." All these years later, he's a program leader.

Look around, assess what's going on in your neighborhood, and just get involved. We're the Anacostia Riverkeepers and need people to adopt a section of river or creek, but you can also contact any of the 177 local Riverkeeper programs in the Water Keeper Alliance, a grassroots advocacy organization to protect our waters. Twenty dollars and/or a few hours can make a big difference.

We're fighting by trying to get public attention and showing people the wildlife they're losing.

HEATHER GRAHAM ➡

Heather Graham

Actress Heather Graham is an active supporter of several organizations including the **Natural Resources Defense Council** *and* **Global Cool**, *an international campaign to inspire one billion people to reduce their carbon footprint.*
➡ *nrdc.org; globalcool.org*

I remember watching *Hotel Rwanda*, a film about the Rwandan genocide, and thinking, "Jesus Christ, I feel so lucky." I'd gone to charity events for various issues, but wondered what kind of impact I was really having and felt like I wasn't doing enough. So I decided to try to find more active ways to give back, in order to make the world a better place. I'm still at a beginner's level, where I've mostly been giving money to charities. The thing is, there are so many issues I'm interested in—stopping genocide, women's empowerment, global health, the environment. Plus, I travel a lot and don't have a consistent schedule. So for the moment, the idea is to focus on working with just a couple of organizations I feel connected to.

My amazing business manager, Carrie, introduced me to the Charity Rating Guide & Watchdog Report published by the American Institute of Philanthropy, which informs you where charities spend your money. When I decide whom I want to support, we consult their book to pick the best ones to donate to. She also introduced me to Oxfam and how they help women through micro-financing. I sponsor a child for Children International, and support Students for a Free Tibet, Doctors Without Borders, and Amnesty International.

I don't want to talk myself up like I'm Bono. I'm still early on my path and I'm becoming more aware of different charities and which ones I want to be more involved in. The important things are to have fun with the steps you take, be accepting of the fact that you can't do everything, and to do what you can. I hope in my life I grow more and more powerfully involved, but at the moment, I'm going to continue to try to educate myself.

LAURIE DAVID

On Global Warming + Everyday Activism

Laurie David

*Global warming activist and trustee of the **National Resources Defense Council** Laurie David has spearheaded numerous public education and action campaigns, and raised millions of dollars for environmental concerns. She is a co-founder of the **Stop Global Warming Virtual March**, the award-winning producer of* An Inconvenient Truth, *and the author of* The Down-to-Earth Guide to Global Warming.

→ *nrdc.org*

"How do we make the movement to stop global warming the biggest movement the country has ever seen?" This was the question my friend Sheryl Crow, another avid environmentalist, and I asked ourselves a few years ago. For a long time, the issue of global warming sat on the shoulders of the environmental community—people we easily cast aside as tree huggers and Birkenstock wearers. But climate change can't be solved if it sits on the shoulders of a subgroup; it has to sit on all our shoulders. And since the rebirth of environmentalism, it's largely been the youth who are getting it loud and clear.

Knowing we couldn't achieve our goal without college students and campuses taking it on, we hit the road in a biodiesel bus on the Stop Global Warming College Tour. During stops at eleven universities across the southeastern United States, Sheryl put on free performances while I gave speeches on global warming and showed clips from *An Inconvenient Truth*. One of the most surprising things to us was how much was already happening on the campuses. Texas A&M had overwhelmingly voted to raise their student fees to buy renewable energy. Other schools had figured out how to

Biologists say we're sitting on the edge of mass extinction this generation because of global warming. We're all guilty; we're all contributing.

use vegetable oil from cafeterias to power their campus trucks. Over 500 campuses had signed a pledge to go carbon neutral. Yes, students are definitely getting it, but there's still such a long way to go.

Small actions by millions of people are critical: there are so many levels of activism. Activism is forwarding articles about global warming to your e-mail list. Screen a movie—there's a lot of films and *An Inconvenient Truth* is just one of them. Drive a hybrid. Google Alert your cause so every day you see all the headlines relating to the issue you care about. Stop idling your car. Weatherize your home. Carpool when you can. Buy green products. Stop buying things that are over-packaged. Tell storeowners to stop selling over-packaged items. Take shorter showers. Use cold water when you do laundry: hot water doesn't make it more clean. Be a meat reducer. Buy local foods. You don't have to have blueberries from Venezuela in the middle of winter. Use post-consumer paper products. We're much better off with trees in the ground then we are cutting them down to blow our noses. Don't over-dry your clothes—we over-everything everything. We don't need to live like that. The U.S. could reduce its energy usage by fifty percent in fifteen years just through energy efficiency in our houses and buildings.

In addition to the tour, I started the Stop Global Warming Virtual March to acknowledge that the globe is warming and humans are causing it. It only takes an e-mail address to become part of it. We send out news blasts and ask everyone to spread the movement by passing it on to three people. Ultimately, we want to make it a voting issue. I know if we get so big and loud that we can't be ignored, we can demand solutions from our government. The Virtual March now has over a million people signed on.

Biologists say we're sitting on the edge of mass extinction this generation because of global warming. We're all guilty; we're all contributing. So if you know that this beautiful world we're living in is facing catastrophic change, how do you get up in the morning and not work on this issue? How do you live with that knowledge, and not carry a canvas bag to get groceries or choose a hybrid car or stop idling or take shorter showers? Knowledge is a burden. Those who don't know are at peace, but those who do know are forced to take action.

COLLEGE ACTIVISM: A GREEN GROUNDSWELL

➡ Nearly 50 percent of colleges graded in the College Sustainability report have committed to fighting climate change through cutting carbon emissions. 59 percent of the schools are using high-performance green building standards in new construction, while 42 percent are using hybrid or electric vehicles. 37 percent of schools purchase renewable energy. 30 percent produce their own wind or solar energy. 70 percent buy food from local farms and 64 percent serve fair trade coffee.

➡ Representatives from almost 300 universities and colleges across the country have signed the American College and University Presidents Climate Commitment, a pledge to make their operations carbon neutral. They promised to eliminate or offset every iota of greenhouse gases resulting from light bulbs, flights and car trips by their faculty, and transportation of food to their dining hall.

➡ In December 2007, College of the Atlantic, with 300 students and only one major, human ecology, became the nation's first carbon-neutral campus.

AVERY HAIRSTON

 ## On Getting Youth Involved

Avery Hairston

*High school student Avery Hairston was inspired to think big in order to help the environment. With the help of fellow students, he founded **RelightNY**, a nonprofit program that uses donations from individual and corporate sponsors to supply energy efficient CFL bulbs for residents of low-income housing projects.*

➡ *relightny.com*

After I saw Al Gore's slideshow presentation on global warming, I understood the growing climate crisis but was unsure how a kid like me could make a difference. But I kept my eyes open and began to see that you don't need to drive a hybrid car or install solar panels to help the environment. I read about compact fluorescent light bulbs (CFLs) and how their energy efficiency is beneficial to our environment. The bulbs reduce the cost of electric bills, generate less heat, and last ten times as long as regular bulbs, reducing waste. Helping people switch to CFLs was one solution to the problem that I could focus on.

With help from my friends, I created RelightNY. My team and I have been very lucky to get support from many sources. We all wrote letters to families, friends, and corporations where we knew people. When adults hear about our plans, they are all very encouraging. JWT, a major advertising agency, agreed to take us on as a pro bono account. The Natural Resources Defense Council has given us advice on environmental issues and helped us get Open Space Institute to be our fiscal sponsor. We're working with HELP USA and the NYC Housing Authority to distribute bulbs. Big companies like HSBC, Citibank, and others have donated money. Our best resource, however, has been time. It is great to have a team of committed and passionate kids, like myself, to work with.

If I had one piece of advice for anyone else it would be this: find something you are passionate about. It is a lot easier to work on something you care about than something you don't. It is even better when you can work with your friends. Doing community service will be fulfilling no matter how much of it you do, so long as you have fun and care for what you are doing. I am hoping to achieve something greater than just CFL replacement. I want people to know that the small things might not make a difference separately, but together add up.

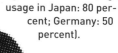

FACT

America is the biggest part of the global warming problem and the least likely to contribute to the solutions. For example, America is the largest contributor of green house gases (25 percent) but makes up less than 5 percent of the world population. And on the solution side, usage of CFL bulbs in America last year was only up to 6 percent, while other countries have begun using CFL bulbs in much greater numbers (e.g., usage in Japan: 80 percent; Germany: 50 percent).

NATE TYLER

On a Green Campaign

Nate Tyler

*Tireless campaigner Nate Tyler organized San Francisco residents to turn off all unnecessary lights for an hour. **Lights Out San Francisco**, a successful precursor to the nationwide Earth Hour, encourages people to think about energy waste and conservation.*

➡ *lightsoutsf.org*

When I was in college, I spent five weeks hiking Alaska's Brooks Range in the Gates of the Arctic National Park. Living in that wilderness for even that short period of time showed me just how delicate the earth is. Even striving to make no impact, our every action was immediately visible to us. The lesson stamped in my brain: Every individual can have an impact (positive or negative) and we must work to preserve these beautiful resources for future generations.

With Lights Out San Francisco, we set out to fight climate change by raising awareness about the simple and easy things people can do to save energy. For our event, we asked people to turn off all non-essential lights for one-hour and to install one compact fluorescent light bulb (CFL).

I called everyone I knew and asked them for help. The idea was so simple and compelling, almost everyone I contacted was excited and willing to get involved in some way. This includes my former colleagues at Google, my friends in the press, bloggers, software developers, designers, and volunteers.

As a result, the Golden Gate Bridge, the Bay Bridge, San Francisco City Hall, and all city monuments and countless businesses and residents turned off lights for an hour. With the help of our local utility PG&E and environmental groups we distributed 100,000 free CFLs. We managed to convince our friends at Google to turn the Google.com homepage black for the entire day of our event. I think this may have been a first of its kind promotion from Google. With their support, we reached millions of people with our message of energy conservation.

My advice to someone trying to start a grassroots movement is simply "Don't give up." Starting something yourself is hard but in the end, no matter how it turns out, it's worth the effort.

FACT

Earth Hour started in Sydney, Australia, in 2007. Over 2.2 million Sydney residents and over 2,100 businesses turned off their lights for one hour, which lead to a 10.2% energy reduction across the city.

The second annual Earth Hour took place on March 29, 2008. 24 global cities participated.

DANNY SEO

On Modern Eco-living

Danny Seo

On his twelfth birthday, Danny Seo founded the environmental organization **Earth 2000** with just a few friends and $23. By his eighteenth birthday, the eco-activist inspired more than 25,000 teenage crusaders across the country to join his campaign for change. Now a best-selling author, columnist, and television personality, he continues to encourage millions of people to live "Simply Green."

→ *dannyseo.typepad.com*

I remember picking up the newspaper on my twelfth birthday and reading stories about the ozone layer disappearing, the rainforests being cut down, and landfills overflowing with trash. My birthday is on Earth Day (April 22), so it was hard not to notice the climate crisis at a very young age. As my birthday wish, I decided to start an environmental group called Earth 2000, with the mission to save the planet by the year 2000. This was in 1989, and I figured I could save the world by the time I doubled my age.

Earth 2000 grew into one of the largest teenage nonprofit eco-groups in the U.S. But it wasn't until a reporter came to interview me at my house that the idea of sustainability and style came to light. She insisted that the way I lived my life back then—eco-friendly but with style—would one day be how everyone would want to live. So, by accident, I became a green lifestyle expert.

My own parents are one of my greatest success stories. I was a vegetarian, home-made-laundry-soap-making teenager. My mother was a Tide-detergent-loving fur wearer. Flash forward eighteen years: I'm talking to my parents about an upcoming television appearance where I was giving viewers simple ways to go green. My mother points out these panels she bought to insulate electrical outlets and save energy. I had never seen these before and thought, "Whoa. My mother is giving me a green tip." When I looked across the kitchen counter and saw a bottle of nontoxic, Method biodegradable hand soap sitting by the kitchen sink, it was almost too much!

Baby steps like these are a great way to start. Of course there are people I call the "dark green" group, who are truly living a sustainable lifestyle. They take one-minute showers, compost everything, maybe even grow their own vegetables, and have no problem dumpster diving for furniture. That's great and should be commended. But there are also people raising families who know they should do the right thing but aren't quite sure how to go green without sacrificing their entire lives. My work is about sharing ideas with these people so that they can turn from eco-dreamers into doers. I hope people realize as long as we all move in the right direction together, that is so much better than doing nothing at all.

It's never about how much money you have, but how much attention you can get for your cause.

My advice is to focus on the Big Picture. Does it really matter if you buy an eco-friendly knife or a regular one? Think about what really counts. A refrigerator operates 24/7, so it makes sense to choose one that's as energy efficient as possible. If you want to buy a hybrid car, why not look for a lightly used one? You can save money on gas and fuel, while saving money on the overall cost of the car. Bring your old rechargeable batteries and cell phones to be recycled as part of the nonprofit Call2Recycle program. Bring your old eyeglasses to LensCrafters to be repaired and donated to people who need them. If you want to take it one step further, collect old batteries, cell phones, and eyeglasses from your neighbors and colleagues and do one big drop-off to have the greatest impact.

It's never about how much money you have, but how much attention you can get for your cause. Use the Web to your advantage. Let's say you're a young person trying to get an elected official to vote for a bill you support or against one you do not want to see passed. You write letters. You send e-mails. You get others to do the same. Why not create a blog dedicated to your efforts? Most officials are probably savvy enough to have daily Google Alerts sent to their personal e-mail, and if you're constantly blogging about them, they will likely read what you have to say. This is just one way to think outside the box. Just one person can do it for almost no money.

DANNY SEO'S TIPS FOR LIVING GREENER

1 Most litter strewn on the streets isn't from litterbugs, but from overflowing trash cans. If your trash can doesn't have a lid, there's a good chance an animal can rip open the bag, or a gust of wind can pick trash up and scatter it. The solution is to make sure you have a tight-fitting lid on top.

2 When in doubt, don't recycle. Lots of people think it's better just to put everything into the recycling bin, even if they aren't sure if it's recyclable. They figure, "Well, they'll sort it all out. I don't want to add to the landfill." The reality is, if a load of recyclables gets contaminated with too many non-recyclable items, then the whole load of recyclables needs to be trashed. So, only recycle what is really recyclable and keep the questionable containers in the trash.

3 Make sure your gas cap is clicked tightly after filling up; a poorly fitted lid actually lets gas evaporate.

4 Use draft mode when printing out on an inkjet printer to extend the life of the cartridges.

5 Unplug TVs and electronics from the wall when not in use to avoid phantom charging (which wastes electricity).

6 Keep your freezer as full as possible to keep it as cold as possible; it uses way less energy that way.

7 Think hydrogen peroxide in lieu of bleach to keep your whites whiter on laundry day!

WOODY HARRELSON

On Living Sustainably

Woody Harrelson

*Actor Woody Harrelson is an outspoken advocate for environmental causes. A longtime proponent of preserving our forests and living in a sustainable way, he launched **VoiceYourself.com**, with his wife Laura. Together with a group of friends, they bicycled down the West Coast from Seattle to Santa Barbara to promote environmental awareness and conscious alternatives for our daily choices.*

➡ *voiceyourself.com*

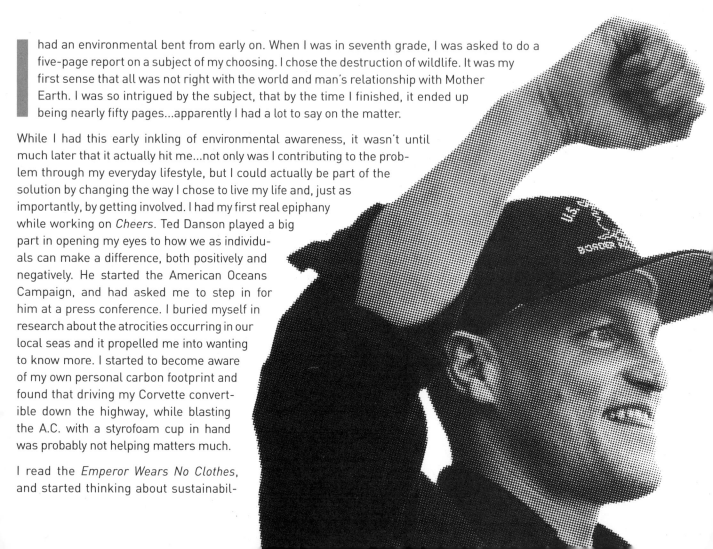

I had an environmental bent from early on. When I was in seventh grade, I was asked to do a five-page report on a subject of my choosing. I chose the destruction of wildlife. It was my first sense that all was not right with the world and man's relationship with Mother Earth. I was so intrigued by the subject, that by the time I finished, it ended up being nearly fifty pages...apparently I had a lot to say on the matter.

While I had this early inkling of environmental awareness, it wasn't until much later that it actually hit me...not only was I contributing to the problem through my everyday lifestyle, but I could actually be part of the solution by changing the way I chose to live my life and, just as importantly, by getting involved. I had my first real epiphany while working on *Cheers*. Ted Danson played a big part in opening my eyes to how we as individuals can make a difference, both positively and negatively. He started the American Oceans Campaign, and had asked me to step in for him at a press conference. I buried myself in research about the atrocities occurring in our local seas and it propelled me into wanting to know more. I started to become aware of my own personal carbon footprint and found that driving my Corvette convertible down the highway, while blasting the A.C. with a styrofoam cup in hand was probably not helping matters much.

I read the *Emperor Wears No Clothes*, and started thinking about sustainabil-

FACT

Living off the grid means disconnecting from commercial power and water utilities. *Home Power* magazine estimates 180,000 American homes are supplying their own power, with the number increasing by about a third each year.

ity for the first time. I began with small steps like seeking out hemp and organic cotton clothing, eco-friendly household cleansers, and recycled paper. The most important lesson I learned was awareness. Once you become aware of the problem, the easier it becomes to make changes that make a difference. I found I didn't have to deprive myself of anything, I just had to make better choices. And the beauty is that there are so many viable alternatives on the market these days. We can choose non-toxic cleansers and recycled goods for our homes, bio-diesel instead of petroleum fuels for our cars, and organic instead of commercial pesticide-ridden food for our families.

Nine years ago, my family and I moved into a small community in Hawaii that is completely off the grid. For me, living off the grid simply means not using power sources dependent on coal plants or extractive non-renewable resources that are raping Mother Earth while getting giant subsidies from our government. Most of the homes in our neighborhood run on solar energy, get their water from local streams and aquifers or use rain catchment, and most families grow at least a portion of their daily food needs. We have found that we don't need to sacrifice comfort and convenience for the good of the environment. If anything, we've improved our quality of life by returning to a lifestyle that is more in harmony with nature. Any place with a decent amount of daily sun can generate sufficient energy from solar panels. We are currently doing construction at our house and the workers are able to run all their tools and machinery, including the power saws, completely on solar energy. Initially, it didn't seem that clever financially, but in the long run the system pays for itself so we save money. In many places, electric companies are offering rebates and buying back excess energy produced so the industry could prove beneficial for many.

We grow most of our food following the biodynamic principles—tons of fruit trees, all our vegetables, and my personal favorite, coconuts. I still have to master climbing those damn trees to harvest the nuts, but I love the challenge. We still have to get to the store sometimes but when I hop in the car I'm burning biodiesel, and with gasoline prices headed towards the $5 per gallon mark on the island, I'm even more relieved that I can bypass those pumps. It feels good not to support the industries that are pushing Mother Earth towards the brink.

I started VoiceYourself.com to get all the people who care about the environment on the same (web)page. If we act in a unified and conscious way, we can change things. It starts with the everyday decisions. It's simple to say, "Instead of using Tide, Windex or Clorox, or any of the typical, petrol-chemical products that are so much more toxic than the things they purport to be cleaning, I'll use one of the many green products in the markets today." The most powerful tool we have is consumer choice. All the puppet masters, who control a lot of what goes on in society, can't control our choice as consumers. If we harness and unify our energies we've got a lot more sway than we realize. We might not have a revolution, but at least an evolution of some kind.

ALICE WATERS

On the Connection Between Earth + Plate

Alice Waters

*Renowned chef and owner of Chez Panisse, Alice Waters has been championing organic and seasonal food since 1971. As an advocate for sound sustainable agriculture, she believes that learning to make the right choices about food is the single most important key to environmental awareness. Her **Edible Schoolyard Garden** program and **School Lunch** initiatives transform the way schoolchildren in Berkeley relate to gardening and food, inspiring similar programs around the country.*

➡ *edibleschoolyard.org; schoollunchinitiative.org*

When I opened Chez Panisse, I knew I wanted to have a simple restaurant based on simple cooking. But I was also looking for flavor, like the tasty food I'd eaten when I lived and studied in France. Eventually, I ended up at the doorstep of the local organic farmers, and started serving food when it was in season, because that's when it had the best taste. It not only awakened me to food, but it awakened me to the cycle of life. I began to anticipate what was coming at certain times of the year, and to look forward to the farmers' market.

Slow food—local, seasonal, sustainable, organic food—is important because it brings people to ideas of biodiversity and sustainability through pleasure. We make decisions about what we're going to eat everyday, and depending on the food produced, there are health and environmental consequences, as well as cultural ones. As author Michael Pollan says, we're voting with our forks. We're voting to have a landscape or not have a landscape by what we choose to eat. Factory farming with its methane gases and use of oil, farm equipment, and pesticides contributes forty percent to the destruction of the ozone, not to mention the consequences of shipping food from around the world. Why are we buying garlic from China when California produces gigantic amounts of it? The planet depends on our choices.

There are a multitude of things you can do. Everywhere in this country there is a beautiful horticulture that wants to be rediscovered. When I travel to new places, I go immediately to the farmers' market and ask the farmers what they're growing and what they've grown in the past. Plant vegetable gardens in your backyards and rooftops, or community gardens in vacant lots. Salads and herbs can be grown in a greenhouse. Don't eat on the run, even if it only happens one day a week. In fact, cooking at home with your family and friends is something you can do every day. Learn how to make a little vinaigrette, how to sauté a piece of fish or chicken. Get some lettuce, tomatoes, and radishes from the farmers' market, slice them and pour your vinaigrette over it. How easy is it? You can make a dinner in ten minutes if you have the right ingredients. Read the labels when you go to the grocery store. Purchase apples from the state where you live, not from New Zealand. Ask your grocery store manager what day they get the local organic vegetables. I tell mine I'll bring my friends to shop because they want to sell you what you want to buy.

In addition, every student from kindergarten through high school, even college, should be educated about the consequences of the food choices that they make. The next generation needs to learn stewardship of the land and how to nourish themselves. We currently have two model programs, the Edible Schoolyard and the School Lunch Initiative, and are happy if others want to contact us to start similar programs in their local communities. The former is about engaging students in an interactive program in a garden and in a kitchen because when they grow and cook their own food, they want to eat it. The latter is a comprehensive strategy to change district-wide meal programs by integrating changes in the curriculum and transforming the quality of school food. It's important that we lobby the President of the United States to talk about food and agriculture, and to rebuild our public school system so we can feed every student local, wholesome, seasonal, sustainable food. Anything less than that is immoral. Every school on the planet should have programs like this, or else our kids and our planet are really going to suffer.

Once you understand where your food comes from, environmentalism becomes a part of you. It's not an abstract notion; it's a visceral connection. You want every landscape to be an edible landscape. You want to rip up every lawn and plant something tasty to eat. When we choose to connect this way, we come into a new relationship to food that teaches us a set of necessary values to share with this planet.

ALICE WATERS'S
...READING LIST

Alice Waters,
The Art of Simple Food

Carlo Petrini,
Slow Food Nation

Michael Pollan,
The Omnivore's Dilemma and
In Defense of Food

Eric Schlosser,
Fast Food Nation

John Peterson,
Farmer John's Cookbook: The Real Dirt on Vegetables

Books by Elizabeth David

Books by Randall Barry, a more poetic farmer

...FILM DOCUMENTARIES

Our Daily Bread (2005)

Darwin's Nightmare (2004)

Les Blank films, such as *All in This Tea* (2007) and *Garlic Is as Good as Ten Mothers* (1980)

...WEB SITES

The Edible Schoolyard,
www.edibleschoolyard.org

The School Lunch Initiative,
www.schoollunchinitiative.org

Slow Food International,
www.slowfood.org

Chez Panisse Foundation,
www.chezpanissefoundation.org

ALICIA SILVERSTONE

On Vegetarianism + the Environment

Alicia Silverstone

Actress Alicia Silverstone is a noted activist on behalf of the environment and animal welfare. She has been recognized for helping influence greater environmental awareness for children and has worked tirelessly to support numerous animal-related charities, from PETA to the Amanda Foundation.

➡ *peta.org; amandafoundation.org*

Ultimately, veganism opened my eyes. It's all connected: what we do to the planet, we do to ourselves.

When I was about twenty-one, I had a meeting with People for the Ethical Treatment of Animals (PETA), whom I'd already been working with. Vice President Dan Matthews and Senior Vice President of Communications Lisa Lange told me about pigs: how they were being treated on farms, how torturous their life was. All the words in the world cannot express the horror these animals go through.

It occurred to me that by eating animals, I was responsible for their suffering. I've always loved animals and was always trying to save whatever creature was in need of my help. I loved my dog, but I ate cows, pigs and chickens, and I realized that those animals are capable of feeling the same joy and suffering as my dog. If I wasn't willing to eat my dog, then how could I eat them?

My first two weeks of being vegan was a lot of me asking myself, "What can't I eat?" I ate a lot of unhealthy foods like French fries and potato chips. The funny thing is, I still looked and felt better just by eliminating meat and dairy. Initially, it was only about saving animals. Then, when my body and health changed, and I started to learn why I felt so good, I became sort of a health nerd.

Ultimately, veganism opened my eyes. It's all connected: what we do to the planet, we do to ourselves. The production of dairy and meat is taxing the earth. It's a very inefficient use of resources—the amount of water and grain used to create one pound of beef could feed a village. That is astounding. So if you care about the environment, your health, and animals, then go vegan. If you want to become vegetarian, but you're struggling, just do it as much as you can. Know that it's not all or nothing. Every choice we make matters for our health and the planet. Our choice of food can effect change on all levels and we do it three times a day!

But there are many other things you can do, too. Know that you are as powerful as any celebrity or government because of your choices on how you spend your money. You vote with your dollar. A few easy ways to make a difference is to buy organic and support your farmers' market; the food tastes better and they don't have to ship it from all over the globe. For your home, buy recycled toilet paper and paper towels, and make sure your soap is biodegradable. All it takes is looking at a label. Be mindful of all your purchases.

You can have everything you want. There is no need to sacrifice style and comfort. In fact, I had never felt more comfortable, healthy, connected, and empowered, not to mention spoiled with delicious tastes, until I went vegan. I believe in my heart that we can heal the world and ourselves.

THE WORST CARBON SINS

Eating meat. Livestock accounts for 18 percent of total carbon emissions.

Air travel. One six-hour flight accounts for one ton of carbon emissions.

Driving gas guzzlers. One gas-powered car emits an average of 9,760 pounds of carbon each year.

Energy use. Generating electricity is the one of the largest sources of CO2 emissions. If every family in the U.S. made the switch to compact fluorescent light bulbs, we would reduce carbon dioxide by more than 90 billion pounds.

Home heating and cooling. Turning your heat down by 2 degrees Fahrenheit in the winter and your air conditioner up by 2 degrees Fahrenheit in the summer can save more than 1/3 ton of carbon emissions per year.

LANCE BASS

On Getting the Word Out

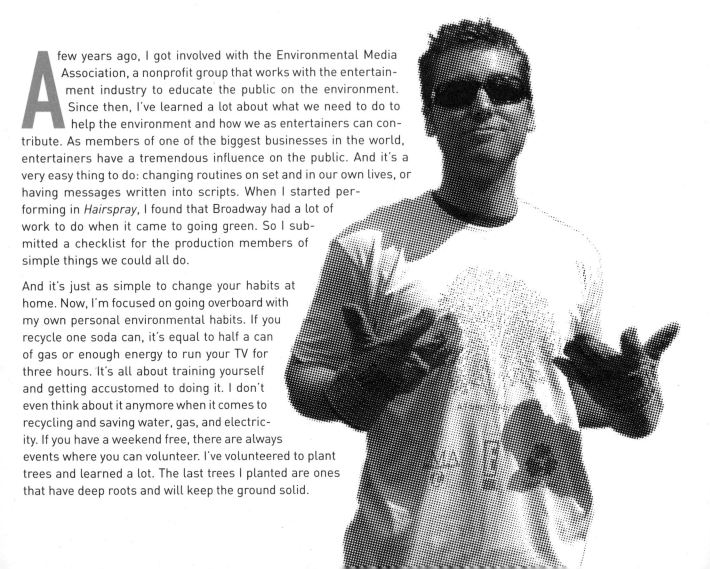

Lance Bass

*An enthusiastic environmentalist, Lance Bass is a board member of the **Environmental Media Association** and remains active in various charitable organizations, including The Lance Bass Foundation and the Entertainment Industry Advisory Board for the U.S. Secretary of Education.*

→ *ema-online.org*

A few years ago, I got involved with the Environmental Media Association, a nonprofit group that works with the entertainment industry to educate the public on the environment. Since then, I've learned a lot about what we need to do to help the environment and how we as entertainers can contribute. As members of one of the biggest businesses in the world, entertainers have a tremendous influence on the public. And it's a very easy thing to do: changing routines on set and in our own lives, or having messages written into scripts. When I started performing in *Hairspray*, I found that Broadway had a lot of work to do when it came to going green. So I submitted a checklist for the production members of simple things we could all do.

And it's just as simple to change your habits at home. Now, I'm focused on going overboard with my own personal environmental habits. If you recycle one soda can, it's equal to half a can of gas or enough energy to run your TV for three hours. It's all about training yourself and getting accustomed to doing it. I don't even think about it anymore when it comes to recycling and saving water, gas, and electricity. If you have a weekend free, there are always events where you can volunteer. I've volunteered to plant trees and learned a lot. The last trees I planted are ones that have deep roots and will keep the ground solid.

HOW TO... SOME TIPS ON ENVIRONMENT

TIME

Petition your local government. Help ban dumping of recyclable plastic containers and to expand bottle-deposit legislation. By mandating recycling over waste, we can reuse 45 billion plastic containers that would otherwise go to landfills.

Talk to the managers at your school or work cafeteria. Ask them to include more vegetarian options and consider buying organic food products. Reducing your meat intake will lessen the demand for high-density industrial farming, as will inspiring others to do the same.

Forget the trip to the tropics. Instead, take your time off to clean out your closets and cabinets, and recycle the clutter. You'll save airfare and hotel money, and about 1,950 pounds of CO2 for every 5,000 miles you fly.

Move closer to work. When you are in proximity to daily destinations, you can cut down on driving and fuel use by walking or biking. It's good for your health, your pocketbook, and cutting down on air pollution and carbon emissions.

Think green at home. Most of the 25 tons of CO2 emissions each American causes per year come from the home. Reduce this by using energy efficient appliances, planting trees around your home to cut down on air conditioning, and asking your energy company to switch to green energy.

ITEMS

BYOB (Bring your own bag). Worldwide, we use up to a trillion of the petroleum-based things each year. That's over 120 million bags an hour and less than 3 percent are recycled. They can take up to 1,000 years to disintegrate in landfills. Stop wasting plastic bags: carry a reusable cloth or canvas bag instead.

Become a Freecycler. The Freecycle Network is a grassroots organization that sets up a way for people to advertise things they want to get rid of for free to a local, online community. If your town doesn't have one yet, launch your own. The network can be started in any city, is open to anyone who wants to participate, and has accrued over 4,500 groups and 5,279,000 members around the world.

Build your own rainwater-catching system. Even though most rainwater is clean and chemical-free, most of us let it drain away. You can use rainwater to water your garden or your potted plants, to wash your car or your pets. Go to www.harvesth2O.com to learn more about rainwater harvesting.

EXPERTISE

Help produce a website. Grassroots groups need to get the word out about critical preservation efforts. Environmental crises often develop very quickly, making digital communications critical to organizing and responding to threats to local ecosystems.

Are you a good public speaker? Share your passion for the environment with others. Most state and national parks in the United States have programs that put volunteers in front of visitors to explain the natural features found there. Use your energy and enthusiasm to transform a staid walking tour or nature center talk into an exciting call to action for park visitors —especially kids! Search www.volunteermatch.org for volunteer opportunities in your region.

Start a community garden. Gardens benefit people in myriad ways: They improve the quality of life for their users, provide nutritious food, preserve green space, and reduce city heat. Consult the American Community Gardening Association at www.communitygarden.org for how to plan, develop, organize, and manage your garden.

DOLLARS

Buy local. Find out where and when your local farmers' markets or CSAs take place and go there to buy meat and dairy products. Small, organic animal farms generally raise their livestock more humanely and buying local saves energy and keeps farming (and money) in your community. Go the extra step and compile a list of vegetarian-option/organic-meat restaurants and food purveyors to distribute in your community via flyer or Web posting.

Save money and the planet. Join millions of other people during Earth Hour's global campaign to increase energy conservation awareness by turning off the lights on March 29.

Invest in saving the earth. Consider putting your money into socially-responsible mutual funds or buying stock in companies that are working to address environmental concerns. Start researching at www.socialfunds.com, www.socialinvest.org, or www.greenmoneyjournal.com.

Sponsor an endangered animal. You can support conservation worldwide by adopting an endangered species through organizations such as World Wildlife Fund (www.worldwildlife.org) or the Smithsonian National Zoological Park (nationalzoo.si.edu/Support/AdoptSpecies).

WHERE TO... SOME PLACES ON ENVIRONMENT

➜ AMERICAN COUNCIL ON RENEWABLE ENERGY
www.acore.org
With a focus on trade, finance and policy, ACORE promotes all renewable energy options for the production of electricity, hydrogen, fuels and end-use energy.

➜ AUDUBON SOCIETY
www.audubon.org
A national network of community-based nature centers and educational programs whose mission is to conserve and restore natural ecosystems, focusing on birds, other wildlife and their habitats.

➜ CENTER FOR BIOLOGICAL DIVERSITY
www.biologicaldiversity.org
Works through science, law, and creative media to secure a future for all species, great or small, hovering on the brink extinction.

➜ CLIMATE RIDE
www.climateride2008.org
The Brita Climate Ride is the first multi-day bicycle ride dedicated to raising money and awareness for meaningful climate change and renewable energy legislation.

➜ CLIMATE SOLUTIONS
www.climatesolutions.org
Climate Solutions offers practical solutions to global warming along with news items and in-depth articles on climate change and energy alternatives.

➜ CONSERVATION FUND
www.conservationfund.org
The Conservation Fund works to safeguard wildlife habitats, working farms and forests, community greenspace, and historic sites totaling more than 6 million acres nationwide.

➜ DAILY DANNY
www.dannyseo.typepad.com
Green living expert Danny Seo's eco-friendly and crafty ideas for everyday living.

➜ EARTH CONSERVATION CORPS
www.ecc1.org
Engages the strong minds and muscles of youth in the restoration of the Anacostia River. As corps members improve their own lives, they rebuild the environmental, social, and economic health of their communities.

➜ EARTH DAY NETWORK
www.earthday.net
Founded by the organizers of the first Earth Day in 1970, Earth Day Network promotes environmental citizenship and year-round progressive action worldwide.

➜ EARTH JUSTICE
www.earthjustice.org
Earth Justice is a nonprofit public interest law firm dedicated to protecting the environment.

➜ EARTH POLICY INSTITUTE
www.earth-policy.org
The Earth Policy Institute works on building an economy for the earth, and provides a wealth of information on green economics.

➜ EARTH RESOURCE
www.earthresource.org
Earth Resource provides resources to youth, communities, and business on making environmentally sustainable choices.

➜ EAT WELL GUIDE
www.eatwellguide.org
The Eat Well Guide is a comprehensive guide to finding wholesome, fresh, and sustainable food in the U.S. and Canada.

➜ ECO-CYCLE
www.ecocycle.org
Eco-Cycle is one of the largest nonprofit recyclers in the U.S. It provides award-winning educational programs to over 25,000 school children along with basic recycling services.

➜ THE EDIBLE SCHOOLYARD
www.edibleschoolyard.org
Develops eco-literacy in public school students by providing garden and kitchen activities with classroom lessons using ecological principles.

➜ ENVIRONMENTAL ACTION
www.environmental-action.org
Environmental Action has pursued environmental protection since the first Earth Day in 1970 and currently campaigns and lobbies for policy changes in regard to global warming, clean air, wilderness, energy independence, and the oceans. Environmental Action regularly sends out e-mail action alerts to members.

➜ ENVIRONMENTAL DEFENSE FUND
www.environmentaldefense.org
The Environmental Defense Fund links science, economics, and law to create innovative, equitable, and cost-effective solutions to environmental problems.

➜ ENVIRONMENTAL MEDIA ASSOCIATION
www.ema-online.org
Mobilizes the entertainment industry in an effort to educate people about environmental issues and inspire them into action.

➜ GLOBAL COOL
www.globalcool.org
Launched in 2007, Global Cool is a ten-year climate change campaign that aims to inspire one billion people to reduce their personal carbon dioxide emissions by one ton. The website offers practical suggestions for reducing carbon dioxide emissions.

➜ GREENPEACE
www.greenpeace.org
Greenpeace has offices in more than 30 countries and engages in direct action to enact environmental change. Its website offers numerous ways for users to get involved, including a green guide and a student network.

➜ INTERNATIONAL BICYCLE FUND
www.ibike.org
The primary purpose of the International Bicycle Fund is to promote bicycle transportation through education, advocacy, and demonstration projects.

➜ INTERNATIONAL SEED FEDERATION
www.worldseed.org
The ISF is a nonprofit and non-political organization whose members are mainly national seed associations and seed companies.

➡ LIGHTS OUT SAN FRANCISCO
www.lightsoutsf.org
A campaign that works to get people across the country to turn out all their lights for one hour to raise awareness about energy use.

➡ NATURAL RESOURCES DEFENSE COUNCIL
www.nrdc.org
The NRDC uses law, science, and membership support to protect wildlife and wild places, and to ensure a safe and healthy environment. The NRDC publishes reports on relevant issues and provides numerous outlets for people to get involved on various campaigns.

➡ THE NATURE CONSERVANCY
www.nature.org
The Nature Conservancy works with communities, businesses, governments, partner organizations, and indigenous groups to preserve important lands. Its website offers users the chance to make donations and volunteer.

➡ NEW GENERATION ENERGY
www.newgenerationenergy.org
New Generation Energy provides groundbreaking new investment options for consumers in the areas of renewable energy, conservation, and the environment.

➡ PETA
www.peta.org
People for the Ethical Treatment of Animals is a campaign based on the principle that animals are not ours to eat, wear, experiment on, or use for entertainment.

➡ RELIGHTNY
www.RelightNY.com
RelightNY supplies low-income housing units with CFL bulbs and works to encourage all New Yorkers to switch to CFL bulbs.

➡ RIVERKEEPER
www.riverkeeper.org
Safeguards the ecological integrity of the Hudson River, its tributaries, and the watershed of New York City by tracking down and stopping polluters.

➡ ROCKY MOUNTAIN INSTITUTE
www.rmi.org
Rocky Mountain Institute offers research and consulting services to businesses looking to green-up.

➡ SCIENCE AND INNOVATION FOR SUSTAINABLE DEVELOPMENT
www.sustainabilityscience.org
The Forum on Science and Innovation focuses on ways in which science and innovation can be applied to meet human needs, while preserving the life support systems of the planet.

➡ SIERRA CLUB
www.sierraclub.org
The Sierra Club is America's oldest grassroots environmental organization focused on the responsible use of the earth's ecosystems and resources. The Sierra Club offers opportunities for all levels of involvement, from letter writing campaigns to grassroots organizing.

➡ SLOW FOOD INTERNATIONAL
www.slowfood.com
An eco-gastronomic organization founded to counteract fast food and fast life, and the disappearance of local food traditions.

➡ STOP GLOBAL WARMING
www.stopglobalwarming.org
The Stop Global Warming Virtual March is an online grassroots movement to demand solutions to global warming.

➡ SUSTAINABLE TABLE
www.sustainabletable.org
Sustainable Table educates consumers on food-related issues and works to build communities through food. It provides tools for finding hormone-free milk and dairy products, recipes, cookbook reviews, and CSA and farmers' market locators.

➡ UNION OF CONCERNED SCIENTISTS
www.ucsusa.org
The Union of Concerned Scientists uses independent scientific research and citizen action to develop solutions for a healthy environment.

➡ UNITED STATES GOVERNMENT
www.usa.gov/Citizen/Facts/Facts_Environment.shtml
The U.S. government environmental website provides information and services for students, citizens, businesses, nonprofits, and government employees.

➡ US GREEN BUILDING COUNCIL
www.usgbc.org
The Green Building Council developed the LEED Green Building Rating System—the nationally accepted benchmark for the design, construction, and operation of high performance green buildings.

➡ VOICEYOURSELF.COM
www.voiceyourself.com
Promotes and inspires individual action to create global momentum toward simple organic living and to restore balance and harmony to our planet.

➡ WATERKEEPER ALLIANCE
www.waterkeeper.org
Works to provide a voice for waterways and their communities worldwide by providing public advocates for bodies of water.

➡ WORLD RESOURCES INSTITUTE
www.wri.org
An environmental think tank that provides information and proposals for policy and institutional change.

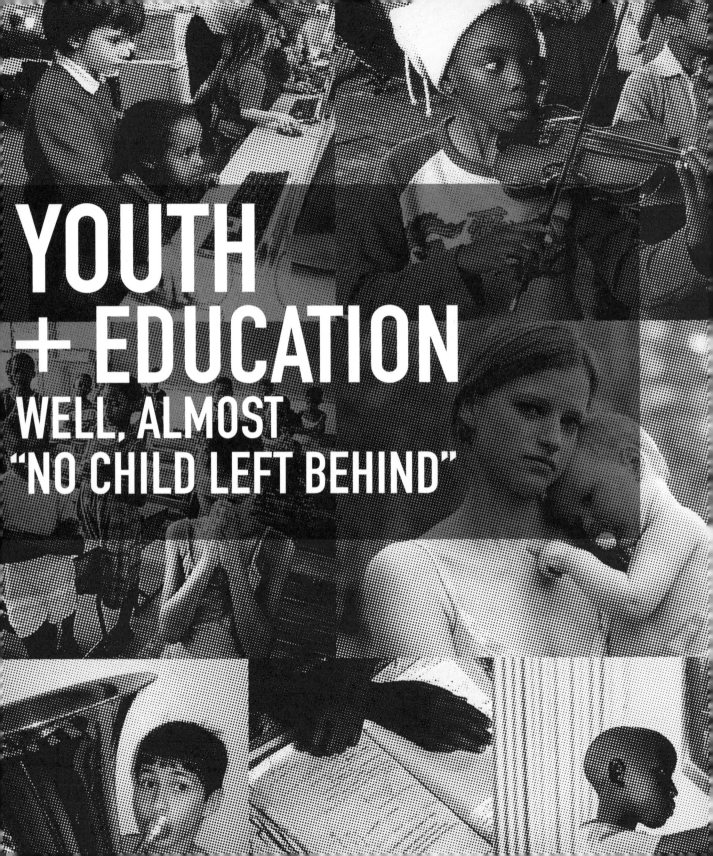

YOUTH
+ EDUCATION
WELL, ALMOST
"NO CHILD LEFT BEHIND"

recently heard a story that I thought made an interesting parallel for this chapter. We know that male canaries are born with the physiological ability to sing beautifully. However, if raised in isolation or without role models to teach them how to use their voice, they might live without ever singing a song. In other words, without a mentor to guide them, their potential will likely never be discovered, let alone realized. Not surprisingly, human beings that grow up without positive, moral influences or a fundamental education have only a few paths easily accessible to them. Often they become victims of untapped potential, with no one knowing what they could have accomplished if they had been given an equal chance. On the other hand, as the "child advocates" and role models within this chapter so clearly demonstrate, the people that work to empower children with confidence and knowledge ensure that those children have many paths to choose from. Much like the canary, a support system and positive role models provide our children with the ability to find their own voice and place in this world. It is up to all of us to provide those tools. ➜ **After all, if we don't see their potential who will? And if we don't realize it now, when will we? —Kenneth Cole**

JOHN SYKES
BARRY MANILOW

On Why Music Education Matters

Barry Manilow

Barry Manilow created his foundation, the Manilow Fund for Health and Hope,
to support grassroots organizations that focus on children's issues, music
education, cancer, AIDS, the homeless, and victims of abuse.
➡ *manilowfund.org*

John Sykes

John Sykes instituted the VH1 Save the Music program in 1997.
It has affected the lives of more than 500,000 children.
➡ *vh1.com/partners/save_the_music*

BM: Recently I had been learning about schools and music programs, something I never did before, and suddenly I get this call about talking to you about VH1's Save the Music—it's amazing that we're talking about this. I read that in 1996 you went to a school and found out they were out of instruments. Is that what happened?

JS: Pretty much so. I was participating in the annual New York City Principals for a Day program—they probably had a few hundred presidents and CEOs who went to school that day. And because I was in the music business, they invited me to a school's music program, oddly enough, to show it off.

BM: Were you still working for VH1 then?

JS: I was a couple years into the presidency of VH1 at the time. So I went to the school and I was shocked—they were

> **Music helps kids do better in math and science, and it's great for their artistic ability. —JS**

proud of their program, but I looked at the instruments and they were all broken. The drums were literally held together with gaffer's tape. The violins were, like, screwed together in someone's wood shop, and the school was struggling to keep this program going. I asked how much money it would cost to refurbish these instruments. They responded, "Oh, a lot of money. Five thousand dollars." I said, "I'll guarantee you, right now, we'll give you the five thousand. And let's see what it will cost to get a program going. " I was coming back over the bridge from P.S. 58 in Brooklyn, one of the great communities in this country, thinking, "I can't believe it. I knew the schools were bad, but I thought with all the money that comes from taxes, at least these schools should have the basics." And so I said, "We should do something for the schools in New York City and call it Save the Children or Save the Music or whatever." Oddly enough, three or four weeks later, I was appearing on *Good Morning America* to talk about something coming up in music. I'm in the green room watching the screen and there, being interviewed, were three neurobiologists from the University of California, Irvine, talking about a story that was about to break on the cover of *Newsweek*: what wires a child's brain, what helps them learn. And one of the big parts of this story was music. Music instruction actually makes kids smarter. Music helps kids do better in

FACT

In April 2008 Barry Manilow pledged roughly $250,000 worth of music supplies to the public middle and high schools in California's Coachella Valley.

math and science, and it's great for their artistic ability. So we started Save the Music in New York, and it really took off, then we added Newark, Westchester, and other parts of the New York area. Eventually I met President Clinton and Hillary and they completely embraced what we're doing and took it across the country.

BM: Well, who wouldn't? What's going on is really sad. Coming from Brooklyn, the music classes saved my life. I was this misfit for my entire high school years, until I got to the music class. Suddenly I was a human being, and I was respected. And then I left and went to the science class and had no idea what they were talking about, and then I went back to music classes and I was a human being again. I felt like I could actually converse with people, and I knew what I was talking about because I knew that world.

JS: There you go. One of ten million stories where music has changed a child's life and that's why we're staying with this program. More than making you a great musician, which it definitely did, it gave you self-confidence.

BM: Plus, the classes allow you to connect with other people, how the different sections play different pieces. Suddenly you're not fighting, you're collaborating. Certainly, I formed my own band and on I went, but if I hadn't had that music department, I really don't know what would have become of me. That was the key out of the slums of Brooklyn. And now I find out, these programs are not even there anymore. I got a phone call from somebody I knew to help donate a couple of instruments to a high school in Palm Springs where I live and I said, "Of course." I asked the music teacher to give me their wish list. I got this long list and sat there and said, "What? They need that many instruments?" So I gave them everything. My truck pulled up to the school and I put a card in there and said, "Happy holidays." Out came drums, tubas, everything they needed. They invited me to their concert and it was really a trip. Out of all the concerts that I've ever experienced, this was the one that moved me the most. This kid came over to me, he couldn't have been higher than my waist, and he said, "Thank you for my new tuba." It was probably bigger than he was!

JS: You changed their lives the way your life was changed. President Clinton said, much like you said earlier, "If I hadn't had music in my school, I wouldn't be president today." He was a kid from a broken family, and he didn't have his focus yet. And his music teacher, by giving him the discipline of learning the saxophone and playing the wind instrument, got him on a daily regime. It got him focused, and he became obsessed with it. And basically, everything else in his life picked up. It's your story.

BM: Music changes your life. It'll change these kids' lives. I was so crazed by what was happening with music education, I asked for the wish list of every school in the Coachella Valley down here in Palm Springs. It's a huge community and over the last months they've sent me their lists. Most of them need, what you said, people to fix their instruments. I'm going to donate everything they need. I didn't know that VH1—I mean, I knew you guys were doing it, but I only thought you were doing it for

FACT Save the Music donated more than $400,000 in special grants of new musical instruments to schools that were either directly impacted by Hurricanes Katrina and Rita or that took in a large number of evacuees.

the New York schools. And these schools down here, no one helps them.

JS: But here's the thing, we can. This program has grown organically, and we can help schools in your area. Our charter allows us to help public schools rebuild their music programs, allows us to donate instruments, and the only thing we ask is for them to hire a qualified music teacher. ·

BM: I just jumped. I just picked up the phone and said, "What do you need?"

JS: That's how it starts. It starts from the heart; it starts from your gut. That's what we did and now we've put out more than $40 million worth of instruments in schools. And while for a minute I feel good about that, at the same time, it's a drop in the bucket.

BM: I'm just learning about that too. It really is stunning. And of course, "No Child Left Behind" was the last straw for music education.

JS: Yes, because these teachers are so under the gun for math and science, they can no longer take a complete view of an education. What they don't realize is that a 360-degree education allows the children to grow.

BM: I'm a perfect example of somebody who was actually changed by music education, just like President Clinton. I know that it's bigger than me, it's bigger than writing a check, and it's bigger than having the truck delivery.

JS: Everyone can help. Whether you are Barry Manilow, or someone with just one-millionth of your success. Everyone who has a job can mobilize co-workers, can give a little bit of time or money, or pressure their local government to bring about change. It doesn't matter who you are, there are things you can do to take action to contribute to building a better future for these kids.

BM: I think that if people understood what we're talking about, that it's not just teaching kids to play music for fun, which it is, but it goes so much deeper, it's going to affect their entire lives in a positive way. That's the word you need to get out to the parents.

JS: I'd get tons of mail—teachers probably forced their kids to write letters, but after awhile, they started coming on their own. I had a parent in the Bronx writing, "My kid wouldn't go to school. He was completely unfocused, failing in school. Then he saw an instrument that was part of the VH1 Save the Music program, and he got hooked on it. Now he practices every day. He won't miss a day in school. His math scores are up. It's changed his life." How many times do we have to tell this story until our government understands it? The conservatives who think the arts are just a thrill, they should understand, from a selfish standpoint, that education is probably the greatest poverty fighter out there; if you educate kids, they won't need to fight.

BM: Absolutely. It's a wonderful opportunity to talk to you, John. Now I know who to send my people to.

MATILDA CUOMO

On the Importance of Mentoring

Matilda Cuomo

*Matilda Cuomo, former teacher and First Lady of New York State, established the first statewide school-based mentoring program, which in 1995 evolved into **Mentoring USA**, a national nonprofit organization that matches at-risk children with trained adult volunteer mentors.*
➡ *mentoringusa.org*

As First Lady, I was requested by my husband, Governor Cuomo, to bring together a bipartisan committee to develop a program to help children in New York public schools remain in school through senior year. At the time, the high school dropout rate was extremely high and work opportunities for teens were limited. In studying the family and academic experiences of students who had left high school, it was apparent that they lacked adequate personal attention and extra support during their academic years. In an effort to build consistent, supportive, personal relationships with students, to help guide them through lower, middle, and upper school years, I founded the New York State Mentoring Program.

Nationally it was the first statewide, school-based, one-to-one mentoring program targeted for at-risk children. By the time my husband's administration ended in 1994, more than 10,000 children enrolled in the program had graduated twelfth grade. In 1995 I was able to re-establish the NYS Mentoring model by founding Mentoring USA, a New York City–based nonprofit, providing one-to-one volunteer mentoring funded through the private sector. Volunteer mentors are required to complete training in anti-violence bias-related education, nutrition, literacy, wellness, and financial literacy. In addition, special training is provided for mentors of children living in the foster care system. Ours was the first organization in the country to mentor foster care youth in an effort to address their complex needs and support the foster parents.

There are three pillars of support for the child: the home, the school, and the community. When one of these pillars falters, the child suffers. As a former educator, I have great empathy for teachers currently working under difficult conditions such as large classroom sizes and rigorous standardized testing requirements. Unfortunately, there is not enough time in the school day to dedicate individual attention to every student. Mentors help fill this void by providing the one-to-one communication and sharing that every child needs.

FACT

According to a study by the Corporation for National and Community Service, 18% of all volunteers in America, approximately 11.5 million people, engage in youth mentoring activities each year.

Eighty-six percent of children who have good mentoring relationships go on to college.

Mentors meet with their mentees on a regular schedule in a group setting monitored by Mentoring USA's professional staff. During the school year, mentor and mentee pairs engage in activities and field trips in addition to one-to-one sessions focused on the mentee's academic progress. The majority of mentors continue to volunteer year after year because of the tremendous personal fulfillment they experience. The gift of personal time a mentor gives goes a long way: Eighty-six percent of children who have good mentoring relationships go on to college.

Mentors are doing something important and receive great satisfaction that they are helping their mentee develop socially, emotionally, and academically. Knowing that our mentors are making a real difference in the lives of children at risk and that these children have a greater chance of reaching their potential has made a real difference in my life.

APRIL DINWOODIE

➡ On Mentoring Foster Children

April Dinwoodie

*April Dinwoodie was adopted transracially when she was a baby. She is the founder of **AdoptMent** (Adoption Mentoring), a mentoring program for foster children, and the co-founder of **Changing the World One Child at a Time**.*
➡ *ctwocat.org*

Five years ago, I decided to search for my biological family. I have an amazing family, but the yearning to know more about where I came from was strong. As I searched, a whole new world opened up. I had never really known anyone else who was adopted—people just didn't talk openly about it. But when I came in contact with other adoptees, I realized how much we all had in common and how many of the same thoughts and experiences we shared.

At an adoption conference, I met a couple whose daughter was adopted transracially and was struggling with issues of identity. They asked if I would be a role model to her. My heart went out to this child who reminded me of myself at that age. Around the same time, I found my birth mother, but we did not have a reunion. She informed me via post that she had been raped and that is how I was conceived. As a result of this painful news and the realization that I may never reconnect with my birth family, I was inspired to create a specialized mentoring program where adopted adults mentored young people in foster care. I felt these kids truly needed the most support.

Mentoring is truly one of life's most meaningful gifts. I had always been a champion of mentoring through Mentoring USA, and one of my mentors, Matilda Cuomo, helped to bring AdoptMent (Adoption Mentoring) to life. I knew that MUSA would be the perfect place to incubate the program, and Mrs. Cuomo embraced the concept and helped launch our pilot program.

Once I got a closer look at the child welfare system, I realized that mentoring was not the only thing that young people in foster care needed. I had the good fortune to meet two individuals who became my partners in Changing the World One Child at a Time (CTWOCAT), which serves to bolster and support the child welfare system by training social workers, raising awareness of the needs of young people and the people who are working day in and day out with them and their families. With CTWOCAT, we can not only inspire young people via mentoring, we can also reinforce the system that cares for them. I am hoping we truly can change the world one child at a time.

GET INVOLVED

1 Be more aware of what is happening in child welfare—there is much more to the everyday lives of young people in foster care than what we read in the paper.

2 Pay attention to what your national and local lawmakers and politicians are doing (or not doing) to help the child welfare system.

3 Volunteer/donate/support grassroots and national charities that are helping families and young people.

TIFFANI THIESSEN

→ **On Being a Camp Counselor**

Tiffani Thiessen

*Tiffani Thiessen is a member of the National Advisory Council of **Make-a-Wish Foundation**. She also volunteers as a counselor at **Camp Rainbow Gold**, a free summer camp for children with cancer.*

→ *wish.org*

Camp Rainbow Gold is a one-week camp in Idaho, for kids who've been diagnosed with cancer. It's the ultimate kid's retreat, one that gives life-affirming experiences. I first became involved with the Make-a-Wish Foundation as a wish grantor when I just a teenager, and my eyes were opened to what strength and courage really meant. The challenges of cancer impact the entire family on every level—physically, financially, emotionally, and spiritually. I consider it a privilege to be included in the Camp Rainbow Gold experience. While the camp is designed to give these kids a week in which they can just be kids, it gives me even more.

Each summer, the kids meet in Boise, Idaho, where they are driven by bus to Sun Valley. As the buses make their way toward camp, motorcyclists (with teddy bears strapped to their bikes) from across Idaho, Washington, Oregon, and Wyoming, join the procession as escorts. Horns are blowing, people are cheering and coming out of their businesses to honor these kids. Upon arrival at camp, we are greeted by an incredibly beautiful location. It's a recipe for hope: eighty to ninety kids, aged six to seventeen, who have amazing strength and resilience. All you want is for them to smile and laugh. And to *hope*.

As a counselor, you're with these kids for twenty-four hours a day, seven days straight. You learn about their different cancers up close, as well as the treatments and the side effects of radiation and chemotherapy. And you become vested in the fight for their lives. Some of the campers have overcome their cancer but are still dealing with its effects. One kid, Chris, lost his arm as a young boy. Yet he learned to ride a bike and go rock climbing. You find such inspiration with kids like him. Everyone who partipates in Camp Rainbow Gold is touched by the exerience. It changes your life. And, while the camp is only a week long, it stays with you forever.

RACHAEL RAY ➡ On Kids + Nutrition

Rachael Ray

Television host and best-selling author Rachael Ray launched **Yum-o!** *in 2006. The nonprofit organization empowers kids and their families to develop healthy relationships with food and cooking by teaching families to cook, feeding hungry children, and funding cooking education and scholarships.*

➡ *yum-o.org*

FACT

According to the Alliance for a Healthier Generation, about 25 million kids (ages two to nineteen) in the U.S. are overweight or at risk of becoming overweight.

When I congratulated Oprah on her South African schools, she said, "You have to speak to people about what's important to you." Food has always kept me grounded. Nothing makes me feel better than a bowl of something I've made. So when I finally had the money to give back, that's where my brain went first: I created Yum-o!, an organization to help families get away from the powdered-packet food and arm them with affordable, yummy recipes for whole food living.

My grandfather grew all of his food and was a great chef. He worked fourteen-hour days as a stonemason before he'd come home and tend his garden at night. My mom was an immigrant kid, but to hear her tell stories about being a little girl, you'd think she was a princess in a castle somewhere instead of at a home with outdoor toilets. As I grew up, I didn't know what powdered mac and cheese, Doritos, or Pop Tarts looked like until I went to school and saw everybody else eating them. Everything I ate had anchovies, squid, and tons of garlic—the only added fat in our house was olive oil. We'd see what people were buying from the grocery store—you know, four for a dollar for this and that—and think, "Geez, you could buy one chicken for the same amount as any of these prepared or frozen foods, and make two or three great meals out of it."

It should be an embarrassment to every American that any child would go hungry in a country of plenty.

Yum-o!'s mission has three parts: cook, feed, and fund. Through our website, we educate kids and families about food and cooking. We are also partnering with the Alliance for a Healthier Generation, a joint venture of the William J. Clinton Foundation and the American Heart Association, to help fight childhood obesity and inspire students to make lifelong healthy

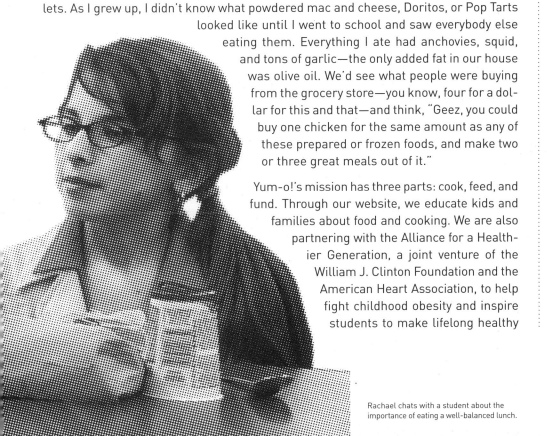

Rachael chats with a student about the importance of eating a well-balanced lunch.

eating decisions. There's something so empowering about taking a group of ingredients, and in just a short amount of time, turning it into something that appeals to all five of your senses. To help feed hungry kids, we take some of our money and give it to organizations such as Share Our Strength and grassroots organizations dedicated to feeding hungry children coast to coast. That's very important to me—to try to eliminate hunger among American children in my lifetime. It should be an embarrassment to every American that any one child would go hungry in a country of plenty. We also award scholarships to kids who want to go into cooking or some food-related field as a way to make a living. But most importantly, Yum-o! is an interactive community where people can connect with each other by sharing their favorite recipes and stories about their friends, families, and communities.

One of the greatest ways of getting kids to eat healthier is to involve them in the process of cooking.

One of the greatest ways of getting kids to eat healthier is to involve them in the process of cooking. The Yum-o! website is a great place to start: Kids and parents can find recipes for cooks of all ages, tips for getting started in the kitchen, and ideas for getting involved when it comes to food in their schools and communities—all in one place.

In the end, a movement like this really lives and dies with the kids. That's what keeps me motivated: seeing the number of children who get involved in cooking and what it in turn will do not only for their health issues, but their self-esteem as well. And knowing that good food really does change lives.

Rachael works with kids at Operation Frontline, a collaborative effort between Yum-o!, Food Network, City Harvest, and Share Our Strength.

MARJORIE STERN

Marjorie Stern

*Marjorie and Michael Stern's **Big Wood Foundation** has helped disadvantaged children for twenty years by providing scholarship funds. Their store, **A Time for Children**, donates 100 percent of its profits and provides job-training skills to underserved teenagers in New York City.*
→ *atimeforchildren.org*

I n the 1980s my husband and I had a store in New York City. I don't think we ever considered ourselves very giving. We were young, with two kids, and very occupied with our own lives. But after we sold the company, we felt very lucky and had a strong desire to give back. We became involved in children's issues in the city and over the years worked with the Children's Aid Society. Getting educated about the problems of an inner-city kid made a big difference in our lives. The more aware we were, the more interested we became.

At first I thought I could open a nonprofit retail store and give the proceeds to Children's Aid. Then I thought, "Why not get the kids involved, teach them about a retail environment, and help them get careers?" It's not just standing in the store and smiling. It's learning about display, how to merchandise, using a computer, and marketing. Kids from the first group have already gotten other jobs in the retail business. I keep pinching myself at how successful it's been.

Most people, given half a chance, would help. Once they hear the store is 100 percent nonprofit, they jump on the bandwagon. They see these sensational kids who are becoming wonderful sales associates and send me letters about what a great environment it is. People have even given me merchandise and said, "Just keep the profit." It's renewed my confidence in people and showed me that I can still make a difference even though I'm not young. I'm sixty-eight years old and I've learned that you don't have to stop at any point in your life. There's always something you can do.

FACT
100% of the proceeds from A Time for Children goes to the Children's Aid Society, a 155-year-old nonprofit that serves 150,000 disadvantaged children at more than 45 sites throughout New York City.

> Getting educated about the problems of an inner-city kid made a big difference in our lives. The more aware we were, the more interested we became.

CHRISTOPHER
"LUDACRIS" BRIDGES

On Empowering Urban Youth

Christopher "Ludacris" Bridges

*Hip-hop artist, actor, and entrepreneur Chris "Ludacris" Bridges has been honored for his commitment to the problem of runaway and at-risk youth. The **Ludacris Foundation** uses music and the arts to inspire and aid urban youth, supporting a variety of initiatives dedicated to underprivileged youth and families, children with disabilities, education, healthy lifestyles, and HIV/AIDS prevention.*

➡ *theludacrisfoundation.org*

FACT

During the holidays, the Ludacris Foundation focuses on underprivileged youth and families in housing communities around the country. Toys, food, and clothing are provided to children and their families.

When I worked for Radio One in Atlanta, I did a lot of volunteer work feeding the homeless and other things. I think that helped to fuel my desire to start the Ludacris Foundation. Plus, my manager, Chaka Zulu, and I have a love for making a difference. So for me, being involved with community work through the radio station was the foundation of what the Ludacris Foundation has become.

There are pros and cons to being a celebrity, but one of the most positive things we can do is use our name and status to create foundations that can help people—and for me, it is all about young people. The Ludacris Foundation was created to help young people achieve their dreams through the encouragement of the "Principles of Success": self-esteem, spirituality, communication, education, leadership, goal setting, physical activity, and community service. We aim to show the young people in America that they are the builders of their future. We primarily use music and the arts to connect with them by listening to their views, issues, and challenges. Our efforts reach youth at all age levels.

I became interested in the problem of teen runaways when I recorded "Runaway Love." It seemed a natural fit to partner with the National Runaway Switchboard to raise awareness about the runaway issue in this country. Between 1.6 and 2.8 million youths run away in a year, and the National Runaway Switchboard gets more than 100,000 calls a year from teens who are in trouble or looking for safety. Teen runaways are a major problem in this country and I think its one that's continually overlooked. This is not just a runaway problem; this is our problem. If I can use my voice to help a family find their child or encourage a young person to go home, that's what it's all about for me.

People can get involved in several ways: by taking time to listen to what our youths are saying to us (listen vs. talk); by becoming a mentor to one or more youths; by finding a cause or organization that supports youth and volunteering; and by contributing financially to youth causes. The young need to know that you really care—the way that you show them is by being consistent with your message and support. Offer encouragement and just listen to their problems. The most inspirational thing for me is that they have so much love to give. Young people just want to be loved and appreciated, and that's so important for all of us to see and understand.

ROSIE O'DONNELL

→ **On Aiding Disadvantaged Kids**

Rosie O'Donnell

*As a tireless crusader for children, Rosie O'Donnell has put her popularity to good use. The **Rosie's for All Kids Foundation** has awarded more than $27 million to benefit low-income families. **Rosie's Broadway Kids** is an arts education organization dedicated to enriching the lives of children through the arts. In 2008, Rosie's Broadway Kids opened the Maravel Arts Center, providing free performing arts instruction to public school children.*

➡ *forallkids.org; rosiesbroadwaykids.org*

W hen I was ten, my mom died of cancer. Afterward, I made a promise to God, in a musical-theater kind of way, that if I was given the ability to succeed in my life, I would take care of the kind of kid that I was. If any adult in the country feels disenfranchised, they can march on Washington. But as a child in trouble, the person you often need to drive you to these events is the abuser. So it's up to the people who were once those children to be their voice.

For me, it was Pat Maravel, a teacher from my junior high. I was a motherless kid and she was the first person who took the effort to hug me, and who made me feel I was loveable. She was my mom from the seventh grade on and she completely altered my life. When I became an adult myself, I would often go to abused children's homes or shelters and tell the kids, "I was once you and I just want you to know you can be anything you dream." Sometimes it would go right over their heads and they'd reply, "Do you know Ricky Martin?" But some did hear me.

The foster care system was set up in the early 1900s. Decades later, there are still half a million children in foster care, with only 141,000 placed in foster homes. That means there are nearly 350,000 children wandering around the country in state custody, essentially lost, a vast majority of which age out to homelessness or prison. How can you make a difference individually? It's not necessarily big, grandiose gestures by huge millionaires. It's one on one. It's eye contact and shared heartbeats. It's love at the end of the day.

Whatever your cause is, there's a way to help, even if you're short on time. You just have to say, "I've got two hours a week, what can I do to help?" If you're not sure where to go first, ask yourself what pulls you. Volunteer for whatever you have an affinity for.

FACT

Founded in 1997, Rosie's for All Kids Foundation has raised approximately $60 million, more than half of which has been contributed to providing real care and solutions for kids.

The first child abuse case was prosecuted under animal protection laws.

For me it's two groups: senior citizens and children. People between eighteen and seventy—I'm not that interested in. Then you just have to put it in a search engine. You could drive someone once a week to their doctor's office or deliver food to homebound people. If you're still stuck, go to your local public school, library, or women's shelter and ask to volunteer. If you like senior citizens, nursing homes are in constant need of human beings to look at and connect with.

There are millions of things available to every community. After September 11, 2001, I kept writing checks for millions of dollars thinking it would solve something. It solved nothing. I couldn't stand being so ineffective. As Dolly Levi says in the musical *Hello, Dolly*, "Money, pardon the expression, is like manure. It's not worth a thing unless it's spread around, encouraging young things to grow." I wanted a SWAT team that could come in and immediately help in a situation like that. So when Katrina hit, my foundation, Rosie's for All Kids, descended upon Baton Rouge, which is where a majority of the evacuees went. We had a grassroots effort, organizing a group of teachers, art therapists, and volunteers to set up a children's center in the biggest FEMA trailer park in Renaissance Village. The FEMA camp looked like prison. The children had no place to play, and the mental health stress on them was unbelievable. Later, there was talk in Washington about replicating it, but I'm not an evacuee-relocator expert. This was just my desire for the SWAT team. How did we do it? We went through the local churches. We had a troop of volunteers, sometimes simply going to Target, buying underwear for people. It's much more doable than you think.

If someone says, "I really want to serve humanity," I'd say, "Tell me what your dreams are. Tell me something in your childhood that you wished was different and go toward it."

Society will be judged not by actions of the bad, but silence of the good. It's night and you see a woman with a child broken down on the side of the road. You roll down your window and say, "Are you okay?" They say, "Yeah, we called for AAA." And you say, "All right" and drive off. But giving, really, is if you pull over and ask, "Would it be okay if I waited with you?" You have to take the extra step. How do you define the extra step? How do you find it in you to know to pull over and get out? If someone says, "I really want to serve humanity," I'd say, "Tell me what your dreams are. Tell me something in your childhood that you wished was different and go toward it."

JESSICA SIMPSON

→ On Giving a Little Love

Jessica Simpson

*An enthusiastic philanthropist, Jessica Simpson serves as **Operation Smile**'s International Youth Ambassador and helps to support **Casa Hogar Elim**, an orphanage in Nuevo Laredo, Mexico, she first visited at sixteen.*
→ *operationsmile.org; casahogarelimus.org*

Getting involved doesn't require you to give material things. It's a mind-set. It's about awareness and recognizing that there are others out there who are a lot worse off than you. My family and I have always believed in the importance of giving back. When I was growing up in Texas, my father was a preacher. He instilled in me the importance of helping others through the many missionary trips we went on every year. My family and I still sing some of the songs we learned for those trips!

I'll never forget my first time at Casa Hogar orphanage. Mama Lupita, the wonderful lady who runs it, takes care of all of these children, ranging in age from babies to teens. She teaches them to look after each other; the five-year-olds help with the babies while the teenagers supervise. It is inspiring to see how the orphanage gives these children unconditional love and the security of family. When I first started going there, they often would run out of electricity and on many days they did not have enough food to go around. When that happened, the older kids gave up meals for the younger ones.

God has blessed me with a way to help these kids and now, thankfully, they have enough food for everyone to get every meal and enough electricity to last them through every month. All I want to do for these children is bring love into their environment.

FACT
Mama Lupita began Casa Hogar Elim in her home in 1986 with four children she found abandoned. At the present time, she has more than 100 children ranging in age from infancy to 24 years old.

INVISIBLE ➡ CHILDREN

On Youth Helping Youth

Jason Russell, Bobby Bailey, and Laren Poole, co-founders

Young filmmakers Jason Russell, Bobby Bailey, and Laren Poole co-founded Invisible Children, a nonprofit dedicated to providing financial resources by documenting true, untold stories in a creative way. Their documentary film Invisible Children: Rough Cut *highlights the largely ignored crisis of child soldiers and night commuters, children who flee their homes every night to escape abduction by rebel armies, in northern Uganda. Invisible Children has inspired a grassroots movement of youth committed to making a difference.*

➡ *invisiblechildren.com*

n 2003 we went to east Africa with a desire to tell an honest story that would wake up America. Not knowing what we would find, we brought some janky cameras that we bought off eBay. Then the story sort of found us: Right in the middle of Gulu, Uganda, there were thousands of kids sleeping in the streets for fear of being abducted from their homes by a rebel army. We couldn't believe that this had been going on for two decades. Even worse, we couldn't believe we had never heard about it.

On a shoestring budget, we made a documentary called *Invisible Children: Rough Cut* with no expectations. But it connected to people and they asked what they could do to help. This spurred us to think that we could tackle this unseen war. Our mantra became: Ignite the unlikely. Meet them in their world and make it loud, new, and fun. Get the young people, like us, who would not otherwise care. We told the story of the kids in Uganda in a way that was real because we believe the more we relate with one another, the more it pushes us to realize that this isn't charity. It's faces with names.

In 2005 we created the nonprofit organization with a scholarship program and a bracelet campaign and launched them on the ground in Uganda to immediately help out (other nonprofits thought we were "too controversial" to partner with us). Since then, we've received over $15 million—in donations that average $20 or less. We're now providing scholarships for more than 800 secondary and university students, jobs to over 200 displaced men and women, and the renovation of eleven war-affected schools. Uganda is a different place, full of hope and peace.

And the people that are donating the money have changed too. We've held two major nationwide events in the U.S. to increase awareness about the situation in Uganda, each time in hopes that the war will finally end. In April 2006 the Global Night Commute brought more than 80,000 people out to sleep in the streets; within a few months, peace talks began and night commuting by children all but ceased. That was the first time we felt the force of this movement. A year later, we asked more than 70,000 Americans to displace themselves for one night. The Displace Me event was the catalyst for the U.S. State Department's appointment of a senior level diplomat to the peace talks. Now the war is almost over, and the youth of America have realized the power and potential of their collective voice.

Invisible Children is the rumble of the underground. We are a bunch of little people gathering together to achieve something big. If you learn anything from having met us, let it be this: It is up to you. Deliberately do life differently, even recklessly, because the world needs people to come alive. If you don't know where to begin, begin here: Watch the documentary, show some friends, and then pass it along. It may not be northern Uganda. It may not even be Africa. But allow "invisible children" to burst your bubble. We are kids, and we are making it happen.

THE BRACELET CAMPAIGN

The Invisible Children Bracelet Campaign trains and supplies the most vulnerable people in northern Uganda's refugee camps with everything they need to create bracelets made of reeds and recycled wire. The bracelet maker earns a generous salary from each bracelet they make. The bracelet is packaged with a short film that tells the story of a child affected by war and sold in the United States to raise funds for scholarships in northern Uganda.

If you learn anything from having met us, let it be this: It is up to you.

HARRY LEIBOWITZ

On Honoring Change-makers

Harry Leibowitz

World of Children was founded by Harry Leibowitz and Kay Isaacson-Leibowitz, both retired corporate executives. The organization has awarded more than $2 million in grants to change-makers for children in more than thirty-five countries.

➜ *worldofchildren.org*

Growing up in humble beginnings as the son of immigrant parents, I was sensitized at an early age to the hardships faced by children born into difficult circumstances. My father died suddenly when I was fourteen, and shortly thereafter the county sherriff came to repossess our furniture. This forced me to work fulltime all through high school and college. I learned firsthand how hard life can be for those in the underclasses of society. As an adult, I enjoyed a successful career that allowed me to live all across the U.S. and abroad. Through my travels, I continued to witness the suffering of children, and it left an indelible impression.

While recovering from cancer surgery in 1996, I had a vision for World of Children. While watching the Pulitzer Prize announcements, I realized there were no awards for those tirelessly serving children in need. I had an epiphany: I would dedicate my life to creating an award that honored and funded change-makers who are helping children around the world.

In order to qualify for a World of Children award, nominees must have been engaged in their work with children above and beyond their paid employment for a minimum of ten years. My biggest fear in the beginning was that I had set the bar so high that there would be very few people who could qualify. I was proven wrong. Over the past ten years I've had the honor of seeing how many incredibly dedicated people there are in the world—quietly putting their own lives on hold every day, and every year, to change children's lives for the better. It's been a real inspiration to get to know them and support their work. To date, we've awarded millions in cash grants to seventy change-makers, in more than thirty-five countries, on six continents. In turn, these individuals are spearheading nearly 100 organizations worldwide—in areas such as education, health care, career training, and fighting child prostitution—and collectively impacting millions of children through their work.

Conditions have worsened for children in some respects, and improved in others, since World of Children began ten years ago. Numerous events and developments have had devastating consequences for children: natural disasters like tsunamis, hurricanes, and earthquakes; political conflicts in developing countries; global health epidemics like HIV/AIDS and malaria; and extreme poverty and instability in regions that have made children more susceptible to predation by slave traders, warlords, and drug cartels. All these challenges powerfully underscore the need for everyone to be part of the solution in helping children worldwide. I've learned that ordinary people are extraordinary. One person can have a tremendous impact on the world. You don't have to risk your life or give up your day job—just make a commitment to help solve a problem that moves you.

WHAT ARE SOCIAL ENTREPRENEURS?

While some individuals make a difference in the world by contributing time or money—or both—to existing organizations or causes, a social entrepreneur takes a different approach to creating change.

A social entrepreneur is like a business entrepreneur in that he or she sees "white space"—a gap—in the world and builds an entrepreneurial venture to address that unmet need and effect social change in new, strategic, and innovative ways.

Inderjit Khurana, founder of the Ruchika School Social Service Organization (RSSO) and Train Platform Schools and one of World of Children's 2007 honorees, is an inspiring example of how a social entrepreneur capitalizes on opportunities to solve problems and create social value through inventive measures. As a schoolteacher in Orissa, India, Inderjit used to take the train to work. Each day she encountered dozens of street children begging for money instead of attending school. When she learned that millions of India's children lived on the streets, without any hope of enrolling in a traditional school, Inderjit vowed that if the child could not come to the school, then the school must come to the child.

She founded "train platform schools"— pop-up schools created right on the railway platforms—to equip children with the basic levels of education necessary to allow them to enjoy productive lives and make positive contributions to their communities. Her inexpensive and cost-effective idea has since grown from a single train platform school to a thriving program that reaches more than 4,000 underprivileged children in India's Bhubaneswar region. It is well on its way to becoming a model for effectively changing the lives of the poorest children throughout India and the world.

JANE FONDA

On Preventing Early Teen Pregnancy

Jane Fonda

*Jane Fonda has been an outspoken and passionate political activist and feminist since the 1960s. Her dedicated support of women and children led to her establishing the **Georgia Campaign for Adolescent Pregnancy Prevention**, the **Jane Fonda Center for Adolescent Reproductive Health at Emory University**, and the **Grady Health System for the Teen Service Program and Clinic**.*
➔ *gcapp.org; janefondacenter.emory.edu*

The concept for the Georgia Campaign for Adolescent Pregnancy Prevention (G-CAPP) began fourteen years ago after I attended the UN Conference on Population and Development in Cairo, Egypt, as the Goodwill Ambassador to the United Nations' Population Fund. At that time, Georgia had the highest rate of adolescent pregnancy in the U.S. At that conference I learned that to successfully address the problems of adolescent childbearing, one needed to look beyond the traditional family planning agenda to understand all the complex social, economic, and gender dynamics that shape the behavior of young people.

Back home, I vividly remember looking into the eyes of a fourteen-year-old girl in the hospital, in labor with her second child. I was told she lived in a shack that lacked running water and electricity. Her expressionless eyes stared right up at me, as though challenging me to judge her. I wish I had kissed her. She needed someone

> The problem with the "just say no" message isn't the "no," it's the "just." This is not a simple issue.

to take her in his or her arms and not let go for about twenty years. I wondered if anyone ever had—except for during sex. I knew it was likely that she had been sexually abused. I knew intuitively that unless one could change the conditions of her life, there would probably be more children to come. Even assuming there was a family planning clinic accessible and affordable to her, what would motivate this child to avail herself of the services? What future could she see for herself that would be compromised by having children so soon?

Research confirmed what I had learned at the Cairo conference: Girls who grow up in poverty and without hope of bettering their situation will tend to be teen mothers. All together, more than eighty percent of teenage mothers grow up in poor neighborhoods. Their lives and the lives of the boys who impregnate them are often scarred by violence and disorder. Chances are their mothers were themselves teenagers when they had them and lacked the skills

FACT

G-CAPP was founded in 1995. At the time more than 29,000 teens were becoming pregnant annually in Georgia and about 7 of every 100 girls were becoming mothers.

The organization launched a statewide 15 by 15 goal to achieve a 15% reduction in the adolescent pregnancy rate for girls ages 15 to 19 in Georgia by year 2015.

to prepare their children for life. Studies show that sixty percent or more of mothers fifteen years and younger have been sexually abused! Sexual abuse robs a girl of a sense of identity, of ownership of her body. For these girls, the idea of negotiating contraceptive use with a partner would be anathema. Middle-class girls and boys are more motivated to postpone sex or use contraception because they see a future for themselves. Disadvantaged girls see nothing to lose by early parenthood. Hope, I was discovering, is the best contraceptive.

Gender role stereotypes also directly affect a girl's sexual behavior. Our culture portrays girls who carry condoms as "loose" or "cheap," whereas boys with condoms are considered responsible. Our culture teaches girls to try to be popular by having boyfriends and to be malleable, to please. Public policy, to the extent it exists at all in relation to adolescents, tends to assume that girls have autonomy over their lives in general and their sex lives in particular. Another misconception is that male and female adolescents form a homogenous group with common needs and interests. These misconceptions arise from a failure to fully appreciate that adolescence is a time of heightened vulnerability for girls, a time of silence, passivity, and devaluation, while for boys it is a time of increased power and social validity.

G-CAPP seeks to broaden the traditional adolescent pregnancy prevention agenda to address the social antecedents that lie beneath the problem behavior. These include poverty, unemployment, violence, drugs, lack of good parenting, school failure and dropout, child abuse, alienation from mainstream society, racism, and gender bias. This approach necessitates working not only with girls but also with boys, not only with their mothers but also with their fathers, with their communities, and with society at large. We have community-based programs for boys and girls from middle through high school, as well as programs to help young mothers finish school and become good parents. Educating voters on this issue is a large part of our work. So is training the adults— parents, teachers, social workers, physicians, youth ministers—to better understand adolescent development and how to turn around the effects of poverty, abuse, and racism. Keeping our issue on the front burner in the legislature is critical to countering the efforts of those who think the "just say no" message is effective for all adolescents. The problem with the "just say no" message isn't the "no," it's the "just." This is not a simple issue. Since we began in 1995, adolescent pregnancy rates in Georgia have dropped eight percent. I am very proud of our work.

The best thing all of us can do is pay attention to our teens, try to understand and to love each of them as our own. As always, love is the answer and any way we can express this directly through volunteerism will make a difference.

HOW TO... SOME TIPS ON YOUTH + EDUCATION

TIME

⏱ **Ask your district superintendent** or your community's school principals to create district/school health teams that focus on creating programs and curriculum to highlight physical fitness and nutrition. For example, a Pennsylvania school started a "Walking Wednesday" project where students and adults, led by "special guests," walk to school once a week.

⏱ **Contact your local legislators.** Ask them to support federal health care and programs like the State Children's Healthcare Insurance Plan, which could cover 10 million children and ensure that poor children get the medical care they need.

⏱ **Spend a day beautifying a school.** NY Cares Day (www.nycares.org) is an annual event that mobilizes volunteers to paint murals, organize libraries, and clean up classrooms. Contact your local schools to find similar opportunities or suggest that you organize a clean-up day for them.

⏱ **Become a foster parent, or if possible, adopt.** There are roughly 500,000 U.S. foster care children—victims of neglect or abuse who need temporary placement in a safe, stable environment. Meanwhile, 115,000 children are waiting to be adopted.

ITEMS

📦 **Make wishes come true.** Make-a-Wish Foundation uses donations of goods such as frequent flier miles, hotel loyalty points, computer equipment, and building materials to help them fulfill the dreams of sick or dying kids. More than 40% of wish items come from donations. Visit www.wish.org.

📦 **Get socially responsible gifts for children.** Instead of the usual toys and games, explore options such as the "XO" One Laptop Per Child program, which provides a school-aged child in the developing world with a free computer when you purchase one for your own personal reasons.

📦 **Donate school supplies.** Teachers spend about $500 out-of-pocket on school supplies a year. Help out by donating art supplies, computers, musical instruments, or fulfilling teacher wish lists through sites such as www.iloveschools.com, www.adoptaclassroom.com, www.donorschoose.org, or www.theteacherswishlist.com.

📦 **Make a Lifebook for a child in foster care.** Children trapped in a tumultuous foster care environment often need a sense of stability. Lifebooks contain personal information about the child—photos, names of foster families, memories, friends, significant dates and feelings from and about their time in the system. Learn more about creating them from Foster Club, a national network for youth in foster care (www.fosterclub.org).

EXPERTISE

💼 **Mentor, coach, or tutor a child.** Mentoring is a great way to give children a positive role model and help them succeed, while enriching your own life. Big Brothers Big Sisters (www.bbbs.org), the Boys & Girls Clubs (www.bgca.org), and Mentoring USA (www.mentoringusa.org) are good places to start.

💼 **Advocate for abused and neglected children.** Train to be a CASA, a court-appointed special advocate for children. Appointed by judges, CASA volunteers typically commit to handling one case at a time, staying on until the child is placed in a safe home. Learn more at National CASA (www.nationalcasa.org).

💼 **Support youth leadership opportunities.** Consider inviting young people to participate in youth councils, boards of directors, and community councils. Junior Achievement (www.ja.org) welcomes volunteers with real business experience to help guide students.

💼 **Teach at-risk youth a job skill.** Adults can help provide invaluable job training to at-risk youth through organizations like Bikes Not Bombs (www.bikesnotbombs.org), and Homeboy Industries (www.homeboy-industries.org).

DOLLARS

$ **Integrate a fund-raising aspect** into your next company event or birthday party. There are many worthy children's organizations that rely upon your support.

$ **Make a will and include a charitable bequest to your favorite alma mater.** The biggest philanthropists of the 20th century all gave generously to schools, teachers, and libraries. A planned gift to any institution will help continue a legacy of support.

$ **Instead of buying your friends material presents, sponsor a child on their behalf.** Through organizations such as Save the Children (www.savethechildren.org), you can provide educational and medical resources that benefit a child from around the world. Sponsorships are ongoing and last as long as you choose.

$ **Fund a school field trip.** It doesn't matter whether it is to a musical or theatrical performance, a museum, an aquarium, or a national park. Contact your local school principal to find out specific details on how to make it happen.

$ **Help build a playground.** Kids need exercise and fresh air but too many playground structures are old or not accessible to children with disabilities. A donation to organizations such as Boundless Playgrounds (www.boundlessplaygrounds.org) or Imagination Playground (www.imaginationplayground.org) will help give kids a new and improved place to play.

WHERE TO... SOME PLACES ON YOUTH + EDUCATION

➡ 826 NATIONAL
www.826national.org
826 National is a network of nonprofit writing centers offering one-on-one tutoring and workshops for students to encourage an appreciation of the literary arts.

➡ ADVOCATES FOR YOUTH
www.advocatesforyouth.org
Dedicated to creating programs and promoting policies, Advocates for Youth helps young people make informed decisions about their sexual and reproductive health.

➡ AUTISM SOCIETY OF AMERICA
www.autism-society.org
ASA is the largest grassroots autism organization in the world. ASA is dedicated to increasing public awareness about autism.

➡ BEST KIDS, INC.
www.bestkids.org
Best Kids trains and supports mentors who provide positive, consistent, and caring adult relationships that will guide and inspire youth who live in group and foster homes.

➡ BRIDGE OVER TROUBLED WATERS, INC.
www.bridgeotw.org
Bridge Over Trouble Waters enables at-risk and homeless youth to achieve a healthy and productive adulthood through prevention, intervention, and education services.

➡ BUILDING EDUCATED LEADERS FOR LIFE
www.bellnational.org
BELL exists to increase the academic achievements, self-esteem, and life opportunities of children in low-income, urban communities.

➡ THE CANDIES FOUNDATION
www.thecandiesfoundation.org
The Candies Foundation is dedicated to educating youth about the consequences of teen pregnancy.

➡ CHANGING THE WORLD ONE CHILD AT A TIME
www.ctwocat.org
CTWOCAT is a family-focused organization dedicated to promoting positive change in the child welfare systems to improve the lives of children.

➡ CHILD WELFARE LEAGUE OF AMERICA
www.cwla.org
This association of nearly 800 public and private nonprofit agencies assists more than 3.5 million abused and neglected children and their families.

➡ CHILDREN'S DEFENSE FUND
www.childrensdefense.org
The Children's Defense Fund fights for children's rights and social well-being, especially the needs of poor and minority children.

➡ CHILDREN'S HUNGER ALLIANCE
www.childrenshungeralliance.org
The Children's Hunger Alliance works to break the cycle of childhood hunger through education, leadership, advocacy, and service.

➡ CITIZEN SCHOOLS
www.citizenschools.org
Citizen Schools is a leading national education program that mobilizes adult volunteers to help improve student achievement by running after-school skill-building apprenticeships.

➡ CITY YEAR
www.cityyear.org
City Year unites young people of all backgrounds for a year of full-time service, giving them the skills and opportunities to change the world.

➡ COLLEGE TRACK, INC.
www.collegetrack.org
College Track exists to help students who have the desire, but lack the resources and support, to attain higher education and fulfill their own best promise.

➡ COMMONWEAL FOUNDATION
www.commonweal-foundation.org
Commonweal Foundation supports education programs and projects assisting disadvantaged youth.

➡ GEORGIA CAMPAIGN FOR ADOLESCENT PREGNANCY PREVENTION
www.gcapp.org
G-CAPP helps ensure teens have the opportunities, skills, and support services they need to avoid adolescent pregnancy.

➡ IMENTOR
www.imentor.org
iMentor matches high school–aged youth one-to-one with volunteer adult mentors based on shared career and personal interests.

➡ INNER CITY–INNER CHILD
www.innercity-innerchild.org
Inner City-Inner Child is an award-winning program that encompasses an early learning through the arts program and a professional development program.

➡ INVISIBLE CHILDREN
www.invisiblechildren.com
Invisible Children is a movement and film working to improve the quality of life for war-affected children by providing access to education and innovative economic opportunities for the community.

➡ JANE FONDA CENTER
www.janefondacenter.emory.edu
The mission of the Jane Fonda Center is to advance scientific knowledge about adolescence with an emphasis on adolescent reproductive health.

➡ KIDS IN CRISIS
www.kidsincrisis-website.org
Kids in Crisis offers free, temporary shelter, counseling, medical care, and educational support for children struggling with issues such as abuse and neglect.

➡ THE LEAGUE
www.leagueworldwide.org
The League is a cooperative, international "league" of schools and community organizations where young people learn to give.

➡ LUDACRIS FOUNDATION
www.theludacrisfoundation.org
The Ludacris Foundation helps young people achieve their dreams, uplifts families,

and fosters economic development in communities.

➡ MAKE-A-WISH FOUNDATION
www.wish.org
Make-a-Wish grants wishes to children with life-threatening medical conditions.

➡ MANILOW FUND FOR HEALTH & HOPE
www.manilowfund.org
The foundation was created by Barry Manilow to support local grassroots organizations focused on cancer, AIDS, children's issues, and music education.

➡ MENTORING U.S.A.
www.mentoringusa.org
MUSA provides structured, one-to-one mentoring to young people in New York City and Los Angeles.

➡ NATIONAL FOSTER PARENT ASSOCIATION
www.nfpainc.org
This national organization supports foster parents.

➡ NATIONAL INITIATIVE FOR CHILDREN'S HEALTHCARE QUALITY
www.nichq.org
The National Initiative for Children's Healthcare Quality works to improve the quality of health care provided to children.

➡ OPERATION SMILE
www.operationsmile.org
Operation Smile is a volunteer medical services organization that provides reconstructive facial surgery to indigent children and young adults.

➡ PAGE AHEAD CHILDREN'S LITERACY PROGRAM
www.pageahead.org
Guided by the fact that literacy is essential to lifelong success, Page Ahead provides new books and develops reading activities that empower at-risk children.

➡ PLAN USA
www.planusa.org
Plan USA helps address the causes of poverty and its consequences for children's rights and their lives.

➡ PLAY 4 LIFE, INC.
www.play4lifeonline.org
Play 4 Life, Inc., is a national nonprofit organization committed to transforming the lifestyles of America's youth through health and fitness awareness.

➡ PREVENT CHILD ABUSE AMERICA
www.preventchildabuse.org
Prevent Child Abuse America has chapters in 43 states.

➡ ROSIE'S BROADWAY KIDS
www.rosiesbroadwaykids.org
Rosie's Broadway Kids enriches the lives of children through arts education with professional dance, music, and drama instruction.

➡ ROSIE'S FOR ALL KIDS FOUNDATION
www.forallkids.org
The foundation serves economically disadvantaged and at-risk children.

➡ SAVE THE CHILDREN
www.savethechildren.org
Save the Children works to ensure the well-being of

children in need in the United States and around the world.

➡ SESAME WORKSHOP
www.sesameworkshop.org
The Sesame Workshop creates innovative and engaging content to help all children reach their highest potential.

➡ STARLIGHT STARBRIGHT CHILDREN'S FOUNDATION
www.starlight.org
Starlight Starbright improves the quality of life for seriously ill children and their families by providing entertainment, education, and family activities designed to help them cope with pain, fear, and isolation.

➡ TEACH FOR AMERICA
www.teachforamerica.org
Teach for America is a teacher corps of recent college graduates who commit two years to teach and to effect change in under-resourced urban and rural public schools.

➡ TEEN LINE
www.teenline.org
Teen Line provides a teen-to-teen hotline and associated community outreach services.

➡ A TIME FOR CHILDREN
www.atimeforchildren.net
This children's store gives 100 percent of its profits to Children's Aid and provides training to inner-city teens.

➡ TRANSFORMED TEENS
www.transformedteens.com
Transformed Teens works with at-risk African-American teens.

➡ UNICEF, THE UNITED NATIONS CHILDREN'S FUND
www.unicef.org
UNICEF is a non-partisan organization working in 191 countries to advocate the protection of children's rights globally and to combat childhood poverty, violence, disease, and discrimination.

➡ US COALITION FOR CHILD SURVIVAL
www.child-survival.org
Organizations and individuals dedicated to improving the survival and healthy development of the world's children.

➡ VH-1 SAVE THE MUSIC
www.vh1.com/partners/save_the_music
VH-1 Save the Music is dedicated to restoring instrumental music education in America's public schools.

➡ WORLD OF CHILDREN
www.worldofchildren.org
World of Children recognizes and supports individuals who are devoting their lives to helping children.

➡ WORLDTEACH
www.worldteach.org
Worldteach provides opportunities for individuals to live and work as volunteers in underserved areas overseas.

➡ YUM-O!
www.yum-o.org
Yum-o! works to empower children and their families to develop healthy relationships with food.

VOLUNTEERISM:
THERE'S MORE THAN ONE WAY TO OUTFIT CHANGE

As demonstrated in the many inspiring stories preceding this chapter, as well as the various "how to help" and "where to go" guides, there are countless reasons and ways to get involved. Some dominant themes include: utilizing your unique skills, getting involved in something that is personal to you, and becoming a part of a collective group. We leave you with a handful of examples of such modes of service, and a few lasting essays that should inspire you to find your own unique path of service.

UNUSUAL WAYS TO MAKE A DIFFERENCE

With today's hectic schedules, we can all relate to feeling like we are too busy to volunteer. But the key to changing the world isn't setting aside special days just to give back. It's making volunteering part of your life in ways that actually make sense for you—no matter how much time you have to give or how unusual your interests. Here are some unique ways you can make a difference:

➡ Become a PR powerhouse

Green Media Toolshed's Media Volunteer program asks volunteers to make 10 15-minute calls to update a press contacts database it makes available for activists.

➡ Shop for good causes

Heading to Target for some family shopping? Call up your local schools and ask if they need anything, or get involved by shopping for elderly neighbors. There are hundreds of shopping opportunities you can find just by doing a quick search.

➡ Pick up a golf club

Need a new excuse to play your favorite game? The Salvation Army (www.salvation armyusa.org) has summer day camps to introduce youth to golf. Volunteer caddies help the kids practice and navigate around the course for them.

➡ Go on vacation

There are many programs all over the world that would welcome your time and interest. Whether you want to help conserve the Amazon or are looking to aid children in South Africa, there are a plethora of short-term volunteer-friendly vacations that you can sign up for.

➡ Be creative and have it count

VolunteerMatch's "virtual" volunteering category (volunteermatch.org) has dozens of opportunities you can do from anywhere. There are listings for cartoonists, playwrights, musicians, poster designers, illustrators, and even poets.

FACT

➡ Approximately 61 million Americans, 26% of the adult population, volunteer for an organization.

➡ Volunteers spent an average of 52 hours a year on volunteer activities.

➡ 35% of all volunteers help religious organizations; 26.2% help education and youth service organizations; and 13% of volunteers help social or community service organizations.

➡ Volunteerism is at a 30-year high, but 70% of Americans are still watching from the sidelines while two-thirds of nonprofits struggle to find the volunteers they need.

KEVIN BACON

On a New Fund-raising Model

Kevin Bacon

Kevin Bacon is the founder of *SixDegrees.org*, a charitable social networking website that serves as a place to learn about and fund-raise for the favorite charities of its members.

➡ sixdegrees.org

first heard about the Six Degrees of Kevin Bacon game about fifteen years ago. I thought it was a funny idea that wouldn't last, but it stayed in the collective consciousness. So I started to think about the essence of it—which is the connectivity of all the people living on this planet. When we do things of a positive nature, it's going to affect people not just down the block, but everywhere. I'm just like everyone else who picks up the newspaper and feels frustrated by everything going wrong in the world, the suffering, the injustices. There is a strong sense of powerlessness. Sure, I've played benefit shows with my band, donated money, gone to plenty of rubber-chicken dinners, but I wanted to do something with a more conceptual value, as well as a dollars-and-sense value.

With the help of a friend, I obtained the website sixdegrees.org. Once I had it, I didn't know exactly what do with it—only that I wanted it to be of a charitable nature. I started talking to friends and family. I would reach out to people who were already in the world of philanthropy and ask, "What do you think about this idea?" I didn't know anything about starting something like this. Through discussions, the idea evolved to a place where people could go that would be a fun, celebrity-based site. But instead of finding out what handbags or restaurants celebrities like, they would find out about the causes that are important to them and, with a couple of clicks on customized celebrity fund-raising "badges," be able to donate money. As that idea continued to morph, I was introduced to the Network for Good. I realized that they were already doing my idea, minus the celebrity component. They do a huge amount of donations on their site, so instead of competing against them, I had them become the engine that drives Six Degrees.

While the celebrity component is fun, what's really driving the site are regular people starting their own badges and reaching out to their friends, families, and people in their communities in order to raise money in a more grassroots way. The Warren Buffetts and Bill and Melinda Gateses of the world, with their ability to donate millions, sometimes billions, of dollars, are incredibly inspirational. But what I'm interested in is a million people with $10. It's about the concept of spreading goodwill and volunteerism, and remaining socially conscious—social networking with social consciousness.

We've now had a few contests on the site, including one where the goal was not necessarily to raise the most money, but to accrue the most individual donors. I was very inspired to learn that the winners were all people who had something they cared deeply about and felt empowered by getting a chance to reach out to people for help. One woman, a triathlete mother of two, had multiple sclerosis. The day she got diagnosed, a friend of hers saw me talking about Six Degrees on a talk show. After the friend told her about it, she took all that frustration and anger she had with her diagnosis and channeled it into trying to win this contest. In the end, she was one of the top winners and kicked off a life of activism vis-à-vis MS research. Those kinds of stories are the most exciting for me. I go back to this idea of feeling powerless. It's amazing how a ten- or twenty-dollar donation to something can turn your day around. And that's what we're hoping will happen.

FACT

➡ Americans gave a record $306 billion to charitable causes in 2007, a significant increase from previous years.

➡ 83% of this amount was donated by individuals, not corporations or foundations.

➡ 450,000 donors have contributed more than $175 million using the Network for Good giving system.

Kevin Bacon volunteers at the 2007 City Harvest Pre-Thanksgiving Mobile Market in New York City.

VOLUNTEERING AS A GROUP

As corporations have long recognized, great results can come from bringing together people with shared passions. When groups collaborate on like-minded goals such as helping others, it allows relationships to be born, friendships to deepen, and leadership skills to blossom. Volunteering is also a great opportunity for families to spend time together. You can bond with your loved ones while also giving back to the community. Here are some tips to help make your group volunteering work:

➡ Look for organizations with a history of hosting group volunteers.
Start at VolunteerMatch (www.volunteermatch.org), where you can search a database of opportunities marked "Great for Groups." Find opportunities that can accomodate the skills, interests, and maturity of all the members of the group, especially if younger children are participating.

➡ Don't assume everyone is on the same page.
Choose an activity together. Discuss the goals with the group beforehand to ensure everyone is excited about the activity. While one person may be content to just spend the day outdoors, another may want to be as productive as possible.

➡ Take advantage of free tools to organize your group.
Post schedules, provide directions, etc., to keep everyone on track. Google and Yahoo! both offer free group tools, and social networking sites like Facebook and MySpace can be efficient, private forums for members to communicate.

➡ Consider breaking up into smaller groups.
This not only helps the organization match you with its projects, it also fosters friendly competition.

➡ Plan a post-volunteer social activity so you can debrief and relax as a group.
Conversation over dinner or drinks is a great way to share experiences and insight while keeping the momentum going.

FACT
States with a high volunteer rate have lower rates of mortality and incidence of heart disease. Health problems are more prevalent in states where volunteer rates are lowest.

TOP STATE VOLUNTEER RATES
1. Utah - 46%
2. Nebraska - 42%
3. Minnesota - 40%
4. Alaska - 39%
5. Kansas - 38%

"Never doubt that a small group of thoughtful, committed citizens can change the world. Indeed, it is the only thing that ever has." —Margaret Mead

LEARNING TO BE OF SERVICE

Each year, millions of students take advantage of service-learning programs to escape the narrow halls of academia and make real change—and the fact that they're getting credit for their work helps too. Service-learning is a form of "experiential education," which extends classroom lessons to the world of community service and volunteering. Most programs combine meaningful service with instruction and reflection. The goal is to enrich the learning experience, teach civic responsibility, and strengthen communities. There are numerous potential service-learning projects that can enliven a student's studies. Just think how much more interesting your last semester would have been with the following syllabus:

➡ Sociology

Help a soup kitchen design and conduct a survey of its aid recipients.

➡ Environmental sciences

Salvage recyclable materials from the local landfill and then report on how the community could improve its conservation efforts.

➡ Immigration studies

Use your spring break to travel and work with nongovernmental organizations assisting migrant laborers and factory workers in Mexico.

➡ Accounting

Work with neighborhood leadership/advisory boards to put on workshops for residents of low-income areas on household finances and budgeting.

➡ History

Study the history of homelessness in your community to help grant writers and program staff at local social service centers better serve and understand the homeless.

➡ Political Science

Volunteer at a community mediation center where you can get trained to help resolve family, workplace, and neighborhood disputes.

The best service-learning projects pair students with volunteer opportunities related to their course of studies. And it makes sense—nonprofit organizations can often plug students directly into social, political, economic, and cultural issues as they are unfolding. For more information and materials, visit Learn and Serve America (www.servicelearning.org) or the National Service-Learning Partnership (www.service-learningpartnership.org).

FACT

➡ An estimated 10.6 million students nationwide have participated in community service as part of a school activity or requirement.

➡ Students contribute more than 1.3 billion hours of community service each year.

ALAN DERSHOWITZ

On Mandatory Pro Bono Work

Alan M. Dershowitz

One of America's foremost legal scholars, distinguished Harvard law professor Alan Dershowitz is a well-known commentator and advocate on a variety of issues, including national security, torture, civil liberties, and the Middle East peace process. His many books include **Chutzpah, Preemption** *and* **The Case for Peace**. *Professor Dershowitz has received the William O. Douglas First Amendment Award from the* **Anti-Defamation League of B'nai B'rith** *for his advocacy work.*

I get thousands of requests from around the world to represent people in legal trouble. Most of them are poor and can't afford to go to the established law firms. Although I take half my cases on a pro bono basis, I can help only a handful of people each year, unfortunately. The letters and e-mails I read daily make it clear that the problem is only getting worse. Every professional needs to pitch in if we are going to solve it.

The sad reality is that those people in the world who most need medical, legal, and other essential types of help are the ones least likely to be able to afford them, and that these professional resources are most readily available to those who need them least, namely the extremely wealthy and enfranchised elite. This is truer in free-market, capitalist societies than in those where resources are more equitably distributed, but it is true to some degree everywhere.

Professionals are generally accorded by the state monopolies to provide, and charge for providing, services such as medical care, legal advice, etc. These monopolies are extraordinarily beneficial to those who receive them, both financially and in terms of their status in society. In many parts of the world, those who are granted monopolies by the state need do nothing in return except to perform their duties without violating the norms of their professions. There is no obligation to provide needed resources to those who cannot afford them. This is not as it should be. Anyone holding monopoly status should be obliged to provide free services—within reason, and consistent with other professional and personal demands—to those most in need of those services and least likely to be able to afford them.

In practice, this would mean mandatory pro bono requirements for all professionals. Every licensed doctor would be obligated to spend, say, ten percent of his or her time providing free medical resources in clinics and poor neighborhoods. Lawyers and accountants would similarly be required to donate ten percent of their time to causes ranging from representation of the poor to support of human rights around the world. The definition of public service should be broad and nonpartisan. For some, assisting at an abortion clinic would constitute public service consistent with their ideology. For others, counseling poor women against abortion and in favor of alternatives to it might constitute public service that would not conflict with their religious preferences.

The point is not to make public service for professionals an act of charity but rather an obligation growing out of the monopoly status they have been accorded by the state. The Hebrew word for charity (*tzedakah*) derives from the word for justice (*tzedek*). This should be a universal concept. Justice demands that professionals who have a monopoly on providing an essential service do their part to ensure that this service reaches those most in need of it, regardless of their ability to afford it. Some will argue that compulsory pro bono work will be resented and not provide the satisfaction that comes with pure charitable giving. I disagree. The point of charity is not to make the giver feel good, but rather to serve the interests of those most in need. Moreover, any professional would be free to go beyond the mandatory minimum pro bono hours and provide charitable contributions of time or other resources. I believe this would create a win-win situation for those receiving the services and those providing them. The benefits to the former should be obvious. Although it is not the goal of this proposal to help sharpen and broaden the professional skills of those providing the services, that would be a predictable consequence of expanding their scope. But there would be other benefits to the providers as well. I know from personal experience how gratifying human rights work can be. My travels to the Soviet Union during the 1970s on behalf of Soviet dissidents and refuseniks were among the highlights of my career and gave me insight that I use to this day. My work on behalf of death-row inmates in the United States provided similar benefits.

Fairness demands some reallocation of professional resources away from the most privileged and wealthy and toward those most in need. There are many organizations in every part of the country that need professional volunteers to assist in their work. Seek them out. You can help repair the world.

GET INVOLVED

Doctors Without Borders / Médecins Sans Frontières
Provides emergency medical care to millions of people in nearly 60 countries around the world. On any given day, close to 27,000 doctors, nurses, logisticians, and other qualified professionals can be found providing care around the world.

International Senior Lawyers Project
Volunteer lawyers who offer pro bono service to international projects and human rights around the world.

Engineers Without Borders
Has more than 200 developing and established chapters working on over 170 projects in 41 countries.

MBAs Without Borders
Matches experienced business volunteers with local businesses and NGOs.

The point of charity is not to make the giver feel good, but rather to serve the interests of those most in need.

DR. ROBERT COLES

On the Call to Service

Dr. Robert Coles

*Longtime Harvard professor, prolific author, and child psychiatrist Dr. Robert Coles is known for his pioneering work with children and his commitment to civic engagement. His 1993 book, **The Call of Service: A Witness to Idealism,** explored the many ways people have experienced the transformative effects of volunteerism, and how by serving others we are also serving ourselves. Among his honors, Dr. Coles has received the Pulitzer Prize, a MacArthur Fellowship, and the Presidential Medal of Freedom.*

We learn by doing, being, and connecting. "Only connect," said E.M. Forster. Community service and volunteer work are forms of human connection in which people not only reach out to help one another, but learn from one another. It's a mutuality that truly matters. As we respond to others, we need to put some part of ourselves on the table—not wantonly or exploitatively, but simply with a willingness to make some human connection that drives the encounter to perk along. Sometimes, the people in trouble offer us a certain kind of soulfulness, and, in their own way, become our teachers. We find out what we don't know and perhaps might need to know. Ultimately, the call of service is a learning experience, not an intellectual exercise so much as a kind of moral inwardness that is also enlightening.

My college had its own campus, called the Yard. It was also a public space that people could use as a shortcut to the subway station. During those years, I volunteered as a tutor in a community center. One of my students, an eighth grader who lived only a few blocks away from that Yard, said that he and his brother were afraid to walk in the Yard, as convenient as it was. I was stunned, and told him that anyone could walk there. And he said, "Oh, no. I'm not 'anyone.' That place is next door, but for me it's across the ocean." I tried to point out that as citizens, we all have certain rights that are equal. But he wasn't having of my platitudes. He said, "The world is basically yours. For me, the world is something I have to watch out for all the time." It was quite a lesson for me. At that point, I started moving beyond my assigned role. I brought him a book by Chekhov, and suggested he read one or two of the stories. And he got turned on by Chekhov, and his teacher wanted to know how he'd come in contact with that author. Now my young friend (the student) was excited—and studied more and more, harder and harder. Eventually, he went to college. He once asked me what had prompted me to do tutoring. I said, "I don't like to call it tutoring. I like to call it getting to know other people and becoming friends with them." That exchange did a lot for both of us—getting us away from language that can distance people from one another.

At the same time, I know that we can get a bit proud of ourselves from our service work, and I'm not condemning that. But, unfortunately, the danger for us is that we may become patronizing, insensitive in our efforts to reach out to others. We underestimate what others can offer us. In his *Let Us Now Praise Famous Men*, James Agee includes a section about what it meant for him to work with sharecroppers in Alabama in the 1930s. What he ultimately learned there is a recognition of who he was—and, too, some of the dangers of the kind of smugness and self-importance that can come upon a person who sees himself as reaching out to others. How do you avoid that outcome? For starters, you try to avoid all such moral and psychological hazards by a little bit of introspection— inquire into yourself, even as you try to learn about and be of help to others.

What advice would I offer someone who wants to do service? Read some of William Carlos Williams's "doctor stories," in which he describes what he's learning from his needy patients. Read Tolstoy's "Are the Peasant Children to Learn from Us, Or Are We to Learn from the Peasant Children?" It is a beautiful essay that summarizes the mutuality of human connectedness in which the person who goes out to be of assistance is also the person who learns and, yes, is assisted. We share with people at different stages in our life, and with different aspects of our own good fortune. I would encourage all of us who are teachers, physicians, lawyers, or business people to hand along our own volunteerism to others—setting an example which may well encourage the young to follow us. I continue to volunteer, sometimes with youth, and other times with people like me who are old and struggling with the illnesses of the elderly, including Alzheimer's disease. Such folks can remind someone like me that I may be old, but I'm spared certain aspects of age that others haven't been spared. We reach out and share with others in the hope that when and if we come to a position of neediness, others will reach out to us. We're glad that we're doing the volunteer work we're doing, but we ought to see it as a shared effort and sometimes an effort for us to grow as we work to connect with others. I repeat: Serving others means oneself being challenged to think and see things a bit differently, and consequently, being challenged and prompted to become more aware of the world—its wide range of people (all sorts and conditions of human life).

FACT

➡ People who volunteer live longer: Studies have found that people who volunteer have lower mortality rates, even when taking into account factors such as physical health, age, socioeconomic status, and gender.

➡ Engaging in regular volunteer work leads to better physical and mental health in older adults. Volunteering older adults develop social networks that act as a buffer against stress and illness.

➡ According to research findings published in the journal *Science*, giving money to other people promotes happiness. People needn't be wealthy and donate millions to charity to experiece these benefits; small amounts, even $5, can make a difference.

CORPORATE RESPONSIBILTY

Corporate social responsibility has picked up since the 1970s and has progressed well beyond traditional activities such as grant-giving. Now, many corporations are embracing a more holistic approach to philanthropy that can include employee volunteering, corporate giving matches, product donations, and pro bono services. Heightened expectations and pressure from employees, business partners, and customers can convince companies to take a more active role in philanthropic efforts. And many firms are discovering that giving back can be good business. Experts say corporations with active employee volunteer programs have better recruiting, less staff turn-over, and a more positive corporate reputation.

While many companies provide extra paid time off for volunteering, some have found other creative ways to inspire staff to get involved. One company prints information on its product labels, showing the number of volunteer hours accrued by employees on its environmental initiatives. Another company showcases its employees who volunteer on the NYSE ticker in Times Square.

There's just one caveat: Despite the fact that some innovative businesses have a wide open policy where employees may volunteer, some have restrictions. That said, many of today's most successful employee volunteer programs came from the cubicles and not the corner office.

Some ideas for getting your company's support:

➡ Align with your company wellness program. Studies show that people are healthier and live longer when they volunteer.

➡ Start an online discussion group on your company's intranet site to gather interest.

➡ Work with your communications or marketing team to gather inspiring employee volunteer stories and promote them in company newsletters.

➡ Suggest a fund-raiser for a local nonprofit (perhaps employees vote on the organization) with activities like "dunk the CEO" or intramural sports competitions.

➡ Start a volunteer buddy system. Ask your colleagues to partner up and help motivate each other to participate in regular volunteer activities.

➡ At a team or staff retreat, suggest that one activity be a volunteer project for team-building.

FACT

➡ A recent study found that despite a weakening economy, corporate giving grew by 5.6 percent in 2007.

➡ 8 out of 10 Americans say that corporate support of causes wins their trust, and their business.

For the past 25 years, volunteerism and community service has been a fundamental part of the culture at Kenneth Cole Productions. Following are some ways the company and its associates have given their time, skills, items, and money to help make a difference and effect positive social change.

> ❝ To be aware
> is more important
> than what you
> wear. ❞ —KENNETH COLE

TIME

⏱ Hundreds of company associates, vendors, friends, and family fund-raise and participate in AIDS Walks in 11 cities annually. In New York, the country's largest AIDS Walk, the Kenneth Cole team consistently ranks among the top 20 in both fund-raising and number of walkers.

⏱ Kenneth Cole employees work with Mentoring USA to serve as mentors to inner city kids, in particular the New York City public school PS111. As mentors they spend time with the kids, building their confidence and self-esteem through a series of educational projects, often mentoring the same students from 3rd grade through 6th, when they move to another school.

⏱ Since 1998, Kenneth Cole associates have fund-raised and participated in the Hyannis Port Challenge, a 100-mile bike ride in support of Best Buddies' mission to enhance the lives of people with intellectual disabilities.

EXPERTISE

💼 The most visible of Kenneth Cole Productions' efforts has been its use of marketing and advertising as a vehicle to bring socially relevant issues to the forefront. Over the years, topics such as HIV/AIDS, homelessness, free speech, gay rights, women's rights, racial equality, cultural acceptance, gun safety legislation, and capital punishment have been the focus of provocative ad campaigns in an attempt to create awareness and inspire intelligent conversation. Milestones in such advertising initiatives include the first AIDS awareness campaign in 1985, bi-annual advertising campaigns for Kenneth Cole New York, annual pro-bono advertising and marketing campaigns created and funded by Kenneth Cole Productions on behalf of amfAR, and the largest public service AIDS awareness initiative, "We All Have AIDS," discussed in detail in the HIV/AIDS chapter.

ITEMS

📦 Through its retail stores, Kenneth Cole Productions has sponsored a shoe drive each February for the past 16 years. Customers are encouraged to donate a pair of lightly worn shoes for someone who needs them in return for a discount on a new pair. As of 2006, this initiative has collected over 1 million pairs of shoes, which are distributed by HELP USA, America's largest service provider for the homeless.

▣ The company donates wardrobes to individuals recently released from death row after DNA testing proves them innocent of that which they were convicted.

▣ The company hosted the launch of the NYC Condom Campaign, of which Kenneth Cole was a co-chair, and continues to distribute free NYC condoms in each of its New York stores.

DOLLARS

$ Through its retail venues, the company has donated a portion of its sales to amfAR every World AIDS Day for the past 20 years.

$ The company used the high-profile launch of two initiatives with fellow advocate Jon Bon Jovi—the new fragrance, RSVP, and a limited edition leather jacket collection—to donate proceeds to HELP USA and the Philadelphia Soul Charitable Foundation.

$ In support of the Awearness Campaign, Kenneth Cole Productions created an ongoing T-shirt program of which $10 from every T-shirt sold is contributed to the Awearness Fund.

FACT

In recognition of the company's social initiatives, Kenneth Cole has received many prestigious awards, including the 2008 Empire State Pride Agenda Equality at Work Award and the 1996 CFDA Dom Perignon Award for Humanitarian Leadership.

ACKNOWLEDGMENTS

KENNETH COLE WISHES TO THANK:

➡ *AWEARNESS* was created by, and in honor of, the numerous crusaders who act as the agents of change so crucial to our communities. You have filled this book with your stories and the world with hope. Thank you all for demonstrating the power of volunteerism.

To my mother Gladys and late father, Charlie, who taught me the importance of doing well by doing good. Without their unwavering support I would not be where I am today. To my brothers Evan and Neil, Neil's wife Lizzy, my sister Abbie and her partner Glenn, and all my nieces and nephews, who have offered their unconditional support and devotion throughout our journey.

There is no greater example of the power of giving back than my wife's family, all of whom do so much, led by three-term governor of New York Mario Cuomo and his wife Matilda, who have committed most of their adult lives to public service. Andrew Cuomo's vision and talent founded HELP USA which Maria has since stewarded to become the national model it is today.

To all my associates who always give it their all, even on some nights and weekends. Thank you for sharing the vision and your commitment and loyalty. Naming everyone would require another chapter but without you Kenneth Cole Productions would just be a name.

My gratitude also goes to those who helped turn this vision into a book. Leslie Kolk and Chris Yoham who put in an enormous amount of time, creative energy, and most importantly talent in guiding this project from the beginning to the "Kenneth you are going to miss the deadline" end, thank you. Alex Paris, for helping me to do the "write" thing and Ly Nguyen for making it look good. My colleagues Meredith Paley, Samantha Cohen, Ibby Clifford, Angela Niles, Wendy Smith, Cindi Berger, and Christina Stejskal who helped turn an idea into a cohesive book. To Donna Peda, for her organizational skills, help in overall coordination of this project, and most importantly dedication. To all the assistants, publicists, and gatekeepers who granted us access to the stories. And last but far from least, Betty Wong and Charlie Melcher of Melcher Media for their knowledge, support, and guidance.

This book demonstrates that ordinary people, extraordinarily inspired, regardless of resources, can make the world a better place.

MELCHER MEDIA WISHES TO THANK:

➡ David E. Brown, Francis Coy, Max Dickstein, Liam Flanagan, Patty Gloeckler, Zachary Greenwald, Christopher Hampton, Claudine Ko, Ricky Marson, Kate McGovern, Evie McKenna, Lauren Nathan, Amy Pastan, Andy Pressman, Lia Ronnen, Holly Rothman, Jessi Rymill, Lindsey Stanberry, Anke Stohlmann, Alexandra Tart, Anna Thorngate, Scott Wald, Rebecca Wiener, Megan Worman.

CREDITS